WITHDRAWN

HARVARD LIBRARY

WITHDRAWN

Of Time, Light and Hell

New Babylon

Studies in the Social Sciences

19

MOUTON · THE HAGUE · PARIS

Of Time, Light and Hell
Essays in Interpretation of the Christian Message

by

BOHDAN CHUDOBA

MOUTON · THE HAGUE · PARIS

Library of Congress Catalog Card Number: 73-92 332
© 1974, Mouton & Co
Jacket design by Gerard Zuidwijk
Printed in Hungary

*Tu sei colei, che l'umana natura
nobilitasti si, che il sio Fattore
non disdegno di farsi sua fattora.*

You are she who has so ennobled
human nature that its Worker
did not disdain to become its work.

                      Dante, "Paradiso"

Acknowledgements

The author should like to express his gratitude to Mr and Mrs Antonio and Stephanie Di Nunzio for their friendly and generous support, to the professor Bernhard W. Anderson of Princeton University, to the Chanoine Émile Berrar, archpriest of the cathedral of Nôtre-Dame of Paris, to the professors Juan José López Ibor of the University of Madrid, Jean Meyendorff of St Vladimir's Orthodox Theological Seminary in Scarsdale, and Jacques Waardenburg of the University of Utrecht, who have read all or parts of the text, for their critical interest, as well as to Mr Harry James Price and Miss Jill Jarrell for their assistance in preparing the final version of this book.

Contents

Acknowledgements / VII
Preface / XI
1. The Old and the New Myths / 1
2. Time as History's Background / 31
3. Time and the Unity of the Person / 51
4. Of Hope and Anguish / 71
5. Man in the Exploding Time / 99
6. The Death of History? / 139
7. Of Light and Hell / 165
Notes / 189
Index / 229

Preface

> We never are, we continuously become...
> Julien Green, *Diary*

> Whatever troubles man, troubles him
> in his feeling of time. Time is the
> cave.
> Simone Weil, *Cahiers*

> To a moment I should like to say: Stay
> with me, you are so beautiful; perhaps
> not all the days of my earthly existence
> are meant to disappear in eternal recur-
> rences...
> J. W. Goethe, *Faust*

If one were to select the one idea or the one concept that has become the most popular in the New Age, it would have to be the concept of the "beginning".

The very name of the New Age – contrasted with that of the Ancient Age and the Middle Ages – points to the paramount concern with the beginning, which has increasingly characterized the life of man during the last two or three hundred years. Anyone who has devoted some time to the study of recent history must be impressed by the impatient presence of this concept, a presence pervading all the fields of man's activities. We find it in practically every creative and cultural manifestation. To begin anew, to start, to break a current custom, to liberate someone or something from something else, to witness a new undertaking or to come forward with an astonishing idea – frequently more astonishing than truthful. Has there been anything else which would have fascinated the modern and post-modern man to a greater extent? Has there been, above all, a more widely accepted idea in the philosophy of our days than that of "to be there", in which the "there" is symbolized by a finger always pointing into the "future" and always predicting some change?

Many centuries of the human past obviously lacked this feverish preoccupation. The ancient and even the medieval man enjoyed living in the present. Occasionally, he remembered what was known as "primordial time" – the time when things had been better because man was closer to his Creator. But while engaged in creative work man worked mainly for the present. Besides, his time was spread around him, as if in a circle. The sun came and went, and so did the seasons and the years. Time returned to him in many ways—as in the liturgical festivities. Most important of all, in the back of his mind, the primeval myth concerning the finite nature of time was always present.

Since the days of the "Enlightenment" in the eighteenth century, however, much has changed in this respect. An "Enlightened" scholar started a new life the day he conceived his own "Enlightenment". According to such a scholar there had been no enlightenment in the past, but there would be much more of it in the future. There would be "progress", there would be an exodus from the dark past, perhaps an accelerated exodus and an escape into the bright future.

It is obvious that the modern and post-modern preoccupations with the future have not been brought about by any material circumstances. The "Enlightened" doctrine of the "automatic progress" preceeded, by half a century, the industrialization of production and, actually, by almost two centuries its automation. But, above all, in what seems to be one of the most characteristic aspects of the new climate, one became much more concerned with bringing about a change than with its results... least of all, durable results. It is the hurried beginning of an accomplishment, not the accomplishment itself – and even less its durability – which seems to fascinate the new man.

"In my end is my beginning", asserted an old proverb. It meant that by fulfilling his earthly task man enters the true life. In the thinking of the last two hundred years, this proverb has been reversed: "In my beginning is my end". Man's goal, the entire meaning of his life, seems to dissolve in his capacity to begin something, to break away from all that is stable and durable. The great anxiety which envelops our times can be obviously interpreted as basically an aversion to the inherited, an impatience with repetition. The far-reaching charm, almost bewitchment, which Henri Bergson exercised over the generation immediately preceeding the First World War, and even over some younger readers, was rooted in his proclamation of a necessary "change" which he called *élan vital*. Surpassing intelligence itself and leaving it trailing in its wake, Bergson's change became the supreme law of man's existence.

While the generation which called itself "modern" was so pleased with Bergson, post-modern man did not manifest as much enthusiasm for the relativist identification of time and space – although this, too, fitted his needs. Technology proved closer to his heart than science. He had already grasped the enthralling illusion of rapid transportation. The sumptuous railroad terminals of the nineteenth century had replaced the cathedrals and partially even the theatres as architectural centers of cities. Next, the gigantic airfields and the superhighways were to come into vogue. If man could no longer begin something new, let him move fast from place to place; this, too, seemed to mean a new beginning.

The contrast between this modern and post-modern behavior and the ways of life which used to characterize Antiquity as well as the Medieval and even the Baroque phase of European civilization seems only partially explainable as a manifestation of man's creative nature. Throughout the greater part of history, the human creative capacity strove for stable and durable values, themselves directed against passing time, whose illusory character had always been suspected. Old kings were after durable peace, while post-modern presidents are frequently after "new frontiers".

There must be some significant change of mind hidden behind these striking transformations of human behavior. Has our attitude to history changed? Or is it perhaps something even deeper, some very basic change in our concept of time and of its significance?

Far from thinking of time as of an unending line, ancient man had conceived it as a closed circle. The four seasons of the year and the daily path of the sun were to him the most usual symbols of this concept. Occasionally he multiplied the circular character of time by speaking of "great years" and of "returning historical situations". But he was constantly aware of the entire reality being anchored in "a beginning which is also an end", in a fountainhead of time of which the passing time of our daily experiences is only a peripheral reflection. Thus he labored, wrought, built and composed with his mind fixed on the fountainhead of all time. He wanted his accomplishments to be *classical*–something which would forever preserve the beauty of a passing moment.

In all the civilizations of the past every work of art, for instance, used to be an independent, autonomous value. As late as the sixteenth century, when Giorgio Vasari was describing, with admiration, the accomplishments of several generations of artists, the thought never entered his mind to group them into "schools" or "trends" or to regard some of them as "predecessors" or "epigons" of others. Above all, he never thought of treating them as links in a chain or as segments of a development.

The unusual nature of the concepts which arrived later – the concepts of "development", "evolution" and "progress" – is not that they denote a strife toward better values, but rather that they denote a deprecative, despising attitude toward values already established. They also seem to speak of a growing anxiety. As to modern and post-modern man's anxiety to begin for the sake of beginning and to avoid any continuation or repetition, has it perhaps resulted from a deep premonition of an impending, extremely decisive moment?

When there is no threat, nor fearful expectation hidden in the situation in which we live, we usually do not think too much about the future. We rather accept experiences as they come. When, however, an event is approaching about which we feel insecure, we try to do things hastily or even console ourselves, almost subconsciously, by talking about future plans. Much of this peculiar atmosphere seems to dominate the history of recent generations.

Works of historians reflect it. Bulky volumes are published daily in large quantities, multiplying the "patterns of development". They talk not only about the "rise of man" and the "march of man", but also about "global approaches", "expansions" and "repercussions", about "bipolarisms" and "monopolarisms", "challenges" and "solutions". These and many other paraphernalia invented by modern historiography seem to be here to cover up the increasing emptiness of the historian's trade. At the end of such volumes there is usually some talk about the "current awakening of peoples". One does not seem at all tired of such phrases–although this "current awakening" has now been current for almost two centuries. The resulting impression among the young people is that of an increasing impatience with history itself. A long road has been travelled – but hurrying where?

Granted that the historical experience is here to enrich and to expand the personal experience of each of us, contemporary historiography can only make us more restless than we already are. In the olden days, man stood surrounded by the circular or cyclical idea of time, between one solstice and another, between sowing and reaping, between the beginning and the end of liturgical festivals. He accepted the historical experience and converted it into foundations and buttresses of his own truly present work. The great invasion of ideas concerning the future, however, has changed his way of life considerably.

But while we can describe this change as a basic estrangement from the archetypal traditions, we may also see in it one of the integral parts of the drama of history. Is it too much to imagine that a particular act of the historical drama can stand under the sign of the future and of expectations while another act of the same drama, its initial act, had stood under the sign of "primordial time" and of remembering? No matter how strange it may seem to a scientist who usually insists on following a linear projection of "ascending time", some aspects of the historical experience seem to support a "juxtaposition of epochs".

There seems to be, above all, an almost direct opposition between the proto-historical epoch, in which man was surrounded by innumerable opportunities for creative work – so much so that practically every step he took resulted in the creation of a new value – and the epoch of mass-production in which only a lucky few can truly express themselves creatively, while the great majority of men are constrained to pushing of buttons and to acting according to prescribed patterns. Primeval man stood in the midst of vast, open spaces. He was a novice loaded only with mythical, *i.e.*, ever valid experiences. The post-modern man stands in a crowd, hardly able to lift his elbows and constrained to move only where the multitude moves. And yet his tired heart is loaded with desperate and mostly illusory expectations.

This contrast between epochs looks like the contrast between the beginning and the end of an individual life, between surprise and anxiety, between two preoccupations: With learning and with uncertainty. The stability of the intermediate situations was perhaps the stability of a balance between the past and the future. As long as man maintained a balanced position between the past and the future, the future did not particularly disturb him. But once he concentrated his entire attention on the future, this future appeared to him threateningly dark and unknown. The spectator was seized with anxiety. He began to run and tried to accelerate his activities. He became addicted to change and speed – and to try desperately to become what he is not.

José Ortega y Gasset used to say that man was not a thing, but a drama. This is even more true of history. The events of a drama are usually accelerated as the drama approaches its end. The essence of such an acceleration may well be hidden in the dreams followed to exhaustion by the protagonists. But the larger such visions loom above the horizon, the more they may resemble a mere illusion.

Since time immemorial, historiography has primarily meant biography. The very ancient myths spoke of heroes. Modern man, true enough, often describes myths as "narrations without historical or scientific basis". But the myth was certainly a very personal experience. To the primeval man, it was the experience of the Creator and the created man. To the later ancient man, it was the hero's own experience and fate. To the medieval man, it was the experience of Christ and that of the good, noble knight. Only relatively recently did historiography come to regard as its primary object the experience of mankind, a collective entity facing the mystery of passing time. This mystery itself, however, has gradually changed into a false myth. It has become an oppressive, bothersome, foggy substance which slumps the tired shoulders of the historian and weighs heavily on the memory and the intelligence of the student.

We may speak, as has been observed, of this nightmare as of "development", "evolution", "progress" or the "march of man". But no matter which name we use, it leads us away from the substance of history, away from the life of the hero. Thomas Carlyle knew something about this degeneration of historiography. But many other nineteenth century historians were, in their aping of the scientific method, more willing to listen to Arthur Schopenhauer's preaching about the blind, struggling will as the essence of history; to Nietzsche's "eternal recurrence of all things"; and to Henry Bergson's vision concerning the *élan vital*.

Under the impact of such thoughts, history books began to overflow with "trends", "generations", "schools" – under all of which the human person, even the exceptionally creative person, was gradually submerged. Not only political and social history, but also the history of the other various branches of man's intellectual activity suffers under this rule of collective terms and categorization.

Few have had the courage of Henry Adams to point out where the way was leading: Toward acceptance of false myths, toward a sheer struggle for power, toward the reign of the managed, remote-control civilization. And yet it would seem that it is only under the sharp focus of a prominent person's life that the problems of a century or of a generation really come to a forefront; by being confronted with such a person's life – not just a bare lexicographical item – the student of history would realize better than ever the ways in which past experiences enrich his own intellect.

After all, is it really true that history began with a "very slow process", described sometimes as "the emergence of homo sapiens from the prehuman populations"? Do we not know that creative acts – and how otherwise could history be described but as a series of creative acts? – have extremely little in common with "processes of emergence"? Should we not also be aware that "prehuman populations", with all their tool-producing or food-collecting instincts, are material for zoologists, not for historians? Are critical students of man's past really willing to regard history as a story of "societies free of cosmic theories"? Do they not realize that every creative act is based on a "theory" and that every "theory" is cosmic in its very essence? Every theory is essentially cosmic, even if man sometimes tries to cope with various situations using himself as the center of the cosmos. Writing to A. R. Wallace on 22nd December 1857, Charles Darwin stated: "I am a firm believer that without speculation there is no good and original observation."

The historian has to tell the truth. He can walk no other path. If a psychologist decides to "descend to the elements" and forget about the whole, he only changes his métier: He becomes a zoologist or a specialist in the study of the human nervous system. If a historian assumes a similar attitude, he loses his *raison d'être*. The scientist's conclusions are based on generalizations. The business of the historian is to deal with what is unique and cannot be subject to generalization. But then the historian's goal should also be to help man understand himself and things as they are.

In an epoch which takes its pleasure in analysis it may not be very popular to speak of the *phýsis* – in the ancient Greek sense of the word – of an entire thing. Among scholars whose hearts are set on "demythologization" it may not be an agreeable experience to have to point constantly to the fact that every human theory is still primarily a *theoria*, a vision – and that every vision is either truly or falsely mythical. In the midst of scientists who adore the allegedly continuous stream of time it may not be fashionable to point out that a sun-flower has a meaning different from that of a sun-flower seed. We seem surrounded by scholars who often cure their anxiety and restlessness either by marching with the lonely crowd or by ending in an intellectual suicide. Among such men, it may be very difficult to insist that not the crowd, but a person – a person conceived rather as an intellect centered on a cosmic vision than as a "constructed and manageable apparatus" – is the concept which makes sense in the study of history.

But if such is the historian's duty, his only "magisterium", does he still have, in the circumstances which dominate the world, the possibility to exercise this duty? Will he be granted the opportunity to speak by the society which surrounds him – a society of an increasingly managerial nature?

Such questions loomed constantly before me when I decided to start a research which eventually led to the present book. Perhaps I had imagined, at the very first, that it would only be a study in the changing concepts of history. It appeared very soon, however, that a much longer journey was in store for me.

What I am now about to place before the reader is, in fact, a discourse in which the problems of historiography have been relegated to a secondary place. The great mystery of time itself and, to a greater extent the way in which time is envisaged by the Christian message have occupied the stage.

I admit willingly that one of my original motives was the disgust with the untruthful slogans and false myths which so many modern and post-modern historiographers have accepted as their guiding principles. In a way, my attention would hardly have been turned to the archaic and ancient myths, had it not been first exposed to the false myths of our own days. If we cannot live without myths, I had to ask, then what kind of myths should we choose to live with?

From a general contemplation of myths my attention was attracted to the concept of "passing time" and to time's general significance. As this subject is not only of historical, but also of religious nature, it appeared to me necessary to study the Christian message in its entirety – with particular emphasis on the Christian vision of time and history. It became equally necessary to learn what some other traditions of religious character had or still have to say on the subject.

All in all, the experience of preparing this book has been of a tantalizing kind. And yet, while any essay written on the subject of time must necessarily assume an eschatological character, the tenor of this work is rooted in the present moment of decision. Anyone scanning through its pages might perhaps be occasionally deterred by what may seem a crowded display of merely philological lore. But this book has not been written only to complete and register the final results of a long labor of research. Its real, foremost mission s to bring as much solace to the reader as our time will accept.

The Old and the New Myths

> Meaningful existence has the same relationship
> toward becoming which truth has toward faith.
> Plato, *Timaeus*

> Only such man possesses truths who
> possesses them in parables.
> An Arab proverb

> It remains to be seen whether civilization
> can base its values for long on something
> other than a religion.
> André Malraux, *Anti-mémoires*

"At the present time..." "Right now..." "At this very moment"...

How often do we use expressions such as these. They form an essential part of our vocabulary. We would find them in the oldest extant written monuments or again in the talk of some primitives. They came down to us from the earliest narrations. They belong to the archetypal myths. They seem to interrupt a flowing stream.

It would be possible, perhaps even easier, to start the discussion of our topic by asking how many different types of time are there. How does one measure time? What hope do we have of surviving long periods of "terrestrial" time while travelling from one planet to another? But all these questions would lead us again to the main quest: What do we mean by the expression "At the present time"?

Attempting to answer this question we usually proceed to trace back our recollections. We may still realize the meaning, for instance, of the word "chipmunk" by remembering the small animal we saw, years ago, at the edge of a wood. Could we realize what time means by returning to the experiences of our childhood? "Wait, until I finish this", someone in our home used to say, "then I shall have the time..." We have encountered the word in colloquial phrases such as this. Perhaps in those days it did not seem mysterious to us at all. We probably understood it as an obstacle – hearing often the harsh "this is not the time" – or as a command, whenever we were told that "it was really high time that..." When we learned a little more about it, suddenly the truth described by Augustine as well as by Henri Amiel was revealed to us. Strange thing, time: Extant, whenever mentioned; non-existent the moment we forget about it. Since Augustine's days it has remained a mystery – no matter with how many mathematical equations or volumes of forgotten lore one might have surrounded it.

Had we asked our parents, we would have heard about similar experiences. And soon we would have been left travelling over centuries and milleniums into the most unaccessible recesses of the past. It would have become clear to us that the concept of time first entered history as a mythical concept. Having realized that much, we would have probably been tempted to turn away from the topic. A myth? A half-truth? A fairy tale to be enjoyed and forgotten?

The issue, however, has not proved that simple. It has also refused to leave us. We are unable to forget time just because it seems to have reached us from the realm of myths. We cannot dismiss myths as "mere myths", either.

Perhaps it is not without significance that the opinion describing a myth as "an unsuitable mode of expression that tends to conceal its purpose" came originally from the disciples of the German philosopher Martin Heidegger. The totalitarian climate of the Nazi and similar empires – to which Heidegger's work belonged – and the efforts to destroy the true image of history have indeed very much in common. Above all, they are essentially connected by the fact that they both create false myths.

When, for instance, the apostles of "demythologization" describe the tradition about Christ's victory over death and evil as "absurd in the present-day culture which believes neither in Satan nor in his hosts", they are only creating a new myth, and a very false myth – the myth of an imaginary, non-existent world, in which there exist allegedly only imperfections of mechanizms and arrangements, but no evil. Such a world, of course, does not exist. No one who has seen the bombed cities of our century can accept without denying his own heart the falsity of the conception of a world without evil.

Again, if a contemporary thinker claims that he is not interested in Jesus as "a phenomenon of the past", but still calls himself an "existentialist Christian", he becomes guilty of producing a false myth concerning a crucified and risen Christ who has never lived and is "not an established fact of history", but a mere existential experience "addressing me and you in preaching". In this way, not the historical Christ *(der jüdische Christus)*, but the abstrusely false Christ of the Modernists *(der Stifter Christus)* has become the Christ of Martin Buber.

Totalitarian leaders, such as Heidegger's divinized Hitler, have done their best to abolish the truly mythical tradition, according to which it was possible to distinguish between right and wrong in relationship to a living God. At the same time, however, they kept producing false myths, in which the same moral distinction was connected with a non-existent "race" or "people's cause". In a similar way, again, the pseudoscientific scholars, branding as rationally impossible the tradition about Christ the Saviour, have only produced an irrational belief in Progress the Saviour or *Point Omega* the Saviour.

But perhaps the most widely publicized and false myth is that which speaks of man alone as victor over death and evil.

Our age has possibly reached here a stage which the major civilizations of Antiquity had not had the opportunity to reach. The Buddha's intellectual suicide as well as Socrates' decision to drink the cup of venom or K'ung Fu-tsu's wish to hide behind a barrier of ceremonies were all attempts to escape sorrowful experiences. To those ancient men the sorrowful experiences made little sense. Today, some thinkers – following Peter's odd misunderstanding mentioned in *Matthew*, 16:13, where he asks Jesus not even to think of death – again do not see much sense in suffering. Only their thought appears to be something more than a mere will to escape the incomprehensible. There is more in their mind than there was in the Buddha's decision to forget about any kind of volition. Post-modern men decided to achieve their divinity through an act of self-assertion. In contrast to the ways suggested by the Buddha, K'ung Fu-tsu and Socrates, which were escapist in character, one has to qualify the new wisdom as predominantly self-assertive.

Each civilization represents a set of religious, artistic, social, scientific and technical values, established, inherited and shared. Such values grow from a cultural activity – which, as an essential aspect of man's intellectual character, also forms the core of history. Cultural, creative activity distinguishes man's life from the merely vegetative existence of the different units of the physical world – each of which fulfills a purposeful, often complicated, but statistically describable course. Because of man's creative activity, the rapidly and perhaps increasingly often changing drama of history differs essentially from the constantly repeated ways of animal behavior as well as from the statistically discernible regularities of the surrounding universe.

Man's creative activity has, since its very first appearance in this world, stemmed from a number of archetypal concepts and myths. These have formed the framework of every culture. Expressing man's basic experiences they have always provided his mind with categories of a practically inescapable power. They are to man's mind what the laws of perspective are to his sight – a truly essential aspect. Even the most "rationalist" philosophers had to reintroduce myth into their thought under the guise of "analogy."

Myths are not arbitrary pieces of imagination. Nor can they be explained away as "flowers of poetic creativeness". The basic experience from which they grew had other aspects beside the poetical one. Some scholars speak of these other aspects as "cults". Occasionally, man's basic experience seems to have been hidden by overgrown imagination or again almost silenced and pushed into the background by a dream or a willful vision. But it could not be destroyed. History indeed moves "from myth to act"; only the act never gets rid of the myth; without it, it would remain meaningless.[1]

The primeval civilization as well as all the subsequent civilizations of the ancient epoch began with some awareness of the Cosmic God and of the Act of Creation. There is, in fact, no concept of man which would not be strictly dependent on this awareness. The earliest testimonies to the creative activity of man presuppose that, recognizing the "names" of the different objects around him, he was aware of the One Intellect, the source of all the particular meanings. There might have appeared "atheists" who spent their lives denying the validity of this or that symbol of God. But they were hardly able to forget him: indeed they seem perpetually chained to the task of denying him. Myths concerning the Cosmic God and Creation were later connected with the concept of Cosmic Order – the intellectually accessible order on which the cosmos is based. The mythical traditions of the Bantu-Ruanda, for instance, do not seem to contain any "story of creation". Nevertheless, their very conservative language disposes of at least nine different names for the One from whom everything comes, the Source, the Unifier of all meanings. God, however, remained the "Wholly Other". He might have created and maintained the Cosmic Order, yet he was not identical with it. Even the Absolute Self, about which the philosophers of Ancient India spoke, is timeless, while the Cosmic Order remains identical with escaping time. As the Cosmic Order provoked astonishment, awe and the sense of beauty, art appeared. As it also provoked curiosity and a will toward power based on systematic description, science came into being.

Man's own situation was always regarded as exceptional. From the very first, two concepts stood in the very center of man's moral thought: the concept of good (what leads toward God, into freedom) and the concept of evil (what conduces to slavery, isolation and mere submission to the cosmic processes). These two concepts can in no way be "deduced" from the instinctive behavior of animals. They frequently ignore whatever the instincts prescribe. Eventually, through the combination of scientific knowledge with instinctive inclinations, technology appeared. The horizon of culture was complete. Such were the basic features of Antiquity.

With the rise of our own, world-wide civilization a new but basically similar story began. One of its roots was in the life and teaching of Jesus – the man who, fulfilling the archetypal myth concerning the Hidden Face of God and his promised new Revelation (Epiphany), came and stood in the center of the drama of history. But Jesus was a truly ancient man. The Christian tradition never denied or contradicted the basic primeval and ancient traditions. The Cosmic God continued to act as the Creator and the Lord of the universe. Indeed, through Jesus he had entered the very center of history. Moreover, Jesus came forward with an answer to the problem which had plagued the wise men of Antiquity: The meaning of man's sorrowful experiences. He revealed the significance of suffering as an opportunity for creative love. In the realm of art he opened wide the gate of reality, even of the seemingly disharmonious reality – such as that of God who came to die as man. In the realm of social thought, he offered mankind a moral doctrine based on the principle of creative love and willingness to sacrifice; but he expressly attached it not to any change, revolutionary or evolutionary, of the extant social order, but rather to our attitude toward the "everyman on the street" *(plēsion)*.

When, around 1500 AD, the Christian tradition began to spread into the most distant regions of the world, it looked as if it would saturate those regions with its own values. Actually, while the Christian faith spread, very thinly, over the world, its original center had already begun shedding the Christian concepts. It also attempted to get rid of the archetypal myths. But as these proved unforgettable, they were only transformed, falsified. Today, in our world-wide "remote-control" civilization, only a few essentially Christian values remain. The commonly accepted belief that everyone is entitled to all the education he can grasp is a Hebrew-Christian tradition; but even the concept of education is being quickly replaced by that of "instruction". The concept of world history is of Christian provenience; the Ancients knew only of regional or tribal historiography. The public hospitals as well as some other charitable institutions are of Christian origin. But even these few remnants gradually recede into the background. The entire scene has suffered an essential change. When Daniel Halévy spoke of the "acceleration of history", he was describing an important aspect of this change.[2]

It is well known that ancient teachers of wisdom remained very creative as long as they were willing to move in the direction which had been pointed to them by the archetypal ideas. It is also known that Jesus spoke in parables bearing a close resemblance to the primeval myths. He said he had arrived to confirm and corroborate the tradition and not to abolish it. The New Age, on the other side, is characterized by a falsifying tendency, extending from the sphere of religion through that of art and of social relations into the realm of science. So far, for instance, it has manifested a notable preference for meaningless words such as "chance"—a "missionless element which accomplishes purposeful missions." Few scholars have had the courage of the mathematician Hilbert whose *Foundations of Geometry* admitted that concepts such as "point" or "straight" have no meaning outside the postulates in which they are used.

A true myth, it should be underlined once more, is an imaginative description of a real experience. We can hardly escape it, for, as C. S. Lewis once said, "it has struck roots far below the surface of the mind". Even if a modern lexicographer feels inclined to define it as "a story the origin of which has been forgotten", the story still reflects a very real experience. In contrast to this, in a false myth the real experience is replaced by a wishful thought, a dream, a pretentious ambition. Thus, for instance, in a true myth, the appearance of the first spring blossom can be described as a gentle action of the southern wind which touches the buds. Although of little accuracy and truthfulness – because it ignores many essential factors participating in the appearance of the blossom – such a description is, nevertheless, a true myth. The tepid wind is one of the real aspects of the spring. However, the moment someone were to assert that it suffices to flourish a twig with buds to attract the southern wind, a pretentious lie would invade the myth: real experience has been substituted by a dream centered around the dreamer's own alleged power or influence. The flourishing of a twig is certainly not an experience gained from the coming of the southern wind.

Both the old and the new mythologies begin with the myth of creation, a myth concerned with the bringing forth of purposeful, alive things. But the old here differs essentially from the new. An ancient Hebrew narrator spoke of two trees planted in the garden of Eden: The tree of life and the tree of good and bad – the second of them bearing the fruit of assent and negation, love and selfishness. A post-modern scientist, discussing the possibility of manipulating and "turning of" the defective genes in the inherited genetic material, speaks directly of "creation" and even of "playing God" and adds: "Once you take the first step, you are down on the road toward deciding what we would like for man to be." The old myth spoke of a Creator who gave man the possibility to say "yes" or "no". The new myth tells of a creator who is about to determine tyranically and perhaps irrevocably what man must be. The pretentious will to power replaces love and the myth about the creation of man becomes a false myth.

Both narrations, nevertheless, are operational. The new man is just as obliged to use operational myths as was his primeval predecessor. A contemporary historian, for instance, has to operate with mythical concepts such as "the Renaissance" or "the Romantic generation", because he has no other way of correlating the time in one human life with the time in another. A contemporary physicist has to speak of electricity as of something "running" or "streaming", of neurons as "obeying" the "orders" conveyed to them from the brain by chemical "messengers", or again of corpuscles "animated" by great velocities–coining thus, undoubtedly, beautiful mythical parables. "This writing desk", says a contemporary physicist, "is solid..." Then he quickly corrects himself: "Actually, in the light of our knowledge, it is not solid..." But even having corrected himself, he is still well within the region of myths: If the expression "solid", derived from the falsely mythical concept of "continuity", has only a mythical meaning, the expression "not solid" can hardly possess any other quality. "The word," states López Ibor, "acquires a kind of charisma; while the revealed truth is being rejected, one accepts as revelation the truth derived from a certain state of mind".[3] For some time the disciples of the "Enlightened" school of thought – Voltaire's generation could have hardly found a more mythical adjective than that of "Enlightened", derived from the most archaic symbolism of light – lived under the illusion that replacing parables by abstract words – such as "analogy" – they were escaping mythology. But Molière's laughter about the *virtus dormitiva* of opium has never stopped resounding around them.

Throughout centuries, not only in the ancient civilizations but also in our own, "remote-control" civilization, the various scientific theories which man has invented, corrected, thrown away and reinvented, were all theories in the ancient Greek sense of *theoría*, meaning a "spectacle." They were all projected interpretations. They all assumed that there is an order in the cosmos and that summary descriptions of natural processes ("empirical laws") can be drafted to facilitate the comprehension of the entire *theoría*, of the entire cosmic vision.

Some post-modern teachers of logic have expressed doubts about the significance of the concept of the "theory" as well as about that of words such as "true" or "false" and of the very verb "to explain". While expressing these doubts, they also manifested an aversion to the creative nature of every "theory" or "explanation". In contrast to Blaise Pascal who did not hesitate to regard even a geometrical proposition as a *sentiment*, they seem to prefer the opinion that a "theory" is nothing but "a factor unifying all available perceptions". But what else are expressions such as "factor" or "unification" than mere mythical concepts? They certainly are not provided for us by our perceptions.

"Complete understanding of the phenomena of radiation", to quote, by way of example, a wiser logician, "demands the interpretation of facts even where observation is frustrated by the nature of the facts themselves; it is the function of theory to explain observed facts; observation is not, by itself, explanation. Similarly, though we may all be familiar with changing and persistent objects, it does not follow that we understand what is presupposed in dating and relating them, in temporal continuity and succession, in distinguishing the permanent from the changing".[4]

"Explanation", indeed, stems from the fact that human words not only indicate things, but are also meant to represent their purpose (in ancient Greek: *phýsis*). A little child indulges in language-play even when there is no one to listen to him; he seems already to know that he can ask only as much as his words will carry. Thus his words are created more by being directed toward ideas than by reflecting perceptions. Lyov S. Vygotskij, the Russian scientist who during the somber Stalinist days ventured to evaluate critically the superficial affinity between the cries of the animals and the human speech, pointed also to how both the intellect and the language reflect the reality in a way essentially different from that in which mere perception and the resulting merely animal cries reflect it. While Vygotskij's famous predecessor, Ivan P. Pavlov, had described, in his "second signal system", the means whereby man reacts to physical stimuli in terms of his own, intellectual and symbolic conception of reality, Vygotskij himself has shown that it is in "word-meaning" that thought and speech achieve their union and that these "word-meanings" are dynamic formations; sense can change words and ideas often change names; thought must pass first through meanings and only than through words.[5]

It is interesting to notice how the force of the archetypal, mythical notions continues to dominate the thinking even of men who would be the last to admit it. Bertrand Russell, for instance, advises his scientific disciples to substitute logical constructions, wherever possible, for inferred entities. But logical constructions are only exercises in the employment of archetypal notions-categories. The same scholar does not hesitate to describe "the matter of a given thing" as "the limit of its appearances". Such a description – actually it can be found already in one or two fragments of the ancient Greek Philolaos – would have delighted any primeval *mythopoios*.

One of the most curious attitudes to mythical concepts may be found in philosophies which proclaim "agnosticism". In their moral teaching they most frequently come forward with the "golden rule of behavior" or some other form of "idealistic selfishness". And yet the "agnostics", while denying even the operational value of the concept of God, readily embrace other mystical concepts, such as *élan vital*. They restrict their vision of the cosmos in one direction while setting their imagination loose in other directions. They are capable of reaching, sometimes, as far as the concept of the "antimatter". In their final conclusions, however, they seem mostly inconsistent. The "golden rule of behavior" (do not do to others what you would not like the others to do to you) is not presented by them as it is in the *Gospels* – in strict dependence on the fatherly love of the Creator – but rather as a selfsufficient principle. As such it indeed seems to have the quality of a real principle for a man walking along Picadilly or Champs Elysées. But there is absolutely no reason why it should be a valid principle for a person sitting without a parachute in a damaged airplane in the company of only one other person who has luckily provided himself with a parachute. Its alleged validity on a busy city-street is a mere pseudo-sentimental result of the presence of many witnesses – who, of course, are absent from the lonely plane above the clouds.

As to the "idealistic selfishness", we may perhaps regard it as the most obvious symptom of the agnostic's divided mind. To live means to fulfill a purpose. In man, such a fulfillment seems always conditioned by the available information. Agnosticism may best be defined as a refusal to learn as much as possible about the meaning of one's own life. Thus there also arises a sharp antagonism between agnosticism and selfishness. We may, at times, speak of a positive, creative selfishness which tries to learn – and we only learn through faith: We can only reach Siena and learn something about it by first believing that Siena exists. But this is not the selfishness of the agnostic. His is a self-destructive sentiment which apriori restricts the imaginative, penetrating and creative ways of the human intellect. In respect to this self-destructive, illusory selfishness it might also be stated that extremely few human actions lead, in the Benthamian sense, to man's greatest happiness – simply because they do not stem from the will to take into consideration the greatest number of circumstances. Moreover where do we have the guarantee that Smith's happiness is also Blake's happiness?

Two originally mythical concepts have maintained a particularly strong influence on man's thinking: The concepts of "causality" and "reality". Both of them have much in common with the concept of time. Because of that we have to try to evaluate them before we proceed any further.

A "cause" in the most ancient thought – as well as in the Christian thought before its contamination by Aristotelianism – was always an intellectual factor, a comprehending will aiming at a definite, meaningful result.

There appeared, however, some need for a term describing, in a succinct way, the relationship between events which often succeed one another in the imaginary stream of "continuity". Perhaps Isaac Newton's well known "first rule of reasoning" may intimate to us what happened. "We are to admit", declared the famous physicist, "no more causes of natural things than such as are both true and sufficient to explain their appearances". An ancient thinker would have probably formulated this principle in a slightly different way; instead of "causes" he would have more soberly spoken only of "preceding events". A very modern scholar, on the other hand, would be more after "dominating" the recurrent series of events than after "explaining" them. But what, after all, does a scientific investigator really mean by "explaining"? In Newton's formulation, the word "sufficient" says enough. Once we know all we need to reconstruct a chain of successive events, to "operate" it, we need not ascertain any more "causes" – while there might be a legion of them involved.

But why really did one choose to complicate the notion of "flowing time" by branding the precedence of one event before another a "causal" relationship? Wise and critical vocabularies existed and still exist which avoided this pitfall. The ancient Chinese nomenclature, for instance, spoke of "coincidences". It carefully distinguished between a cause and a mere precedence in time. Not so the late-ancient Greeks. Instead of using, *e.g.*, the term *próphasis*, they decided to avail themselves of the same word *aitía* which had already been used to denote the relationship between an intellectual act and its meaningful result.

Did the European civilization really have to follow the Greeks? In spite of our dependence on the Greek inheritance we have learned better. From the early Christian theologian Athanasius to the fifteenth century Byzantine teacher Gemistos Pléthōn many regretted that "Aristotle as well as some others had presumed that generation from a cause involved generation along the arrow of time". Toward the end of the nineteenth century, Ernst Mach, a courageously independent Austrian physicist, did not hesitate to deal with "time" as with a variable which, while characterizing relations between phenomena, did not require that we "ascribed to it any ontological reality" or that we confused it with "causality". Eventually, since the introduction of the quanta mechanics, the twentieth century scientist has built his new vision on the notion of probability, capable of representing the individual events without any recourse to causal relationship.

Perhaps the original, late ancient application of the concept of "cause" to chain-successions of events stemmed from a double seed: That of the concept of "dead, lifeless matter", and that of the "arrow of time". The second of these will be discussed in another of these essays. As to the first – that of the "inert, dead matter" – we may briefly state that its original, primeval meaning seems to have been that of those parts of the universe which allegedly had already fulfilled their purposeful mission. As relatively recently as in the ancient Sanskrit literature the word *prazhma* meant "reality" as well as "life" and "light".

But the odd, rather fatal omission of the fact that even such component parts – subatomic charges, atoms, nucleic acids, or cells, for instance – have a mission of their own (evident even to the primitive, *e.g.*, from the cadaver's hair which continues to grow), led to a tragic misunderstanding. There is no "inert matter" anywhere in the universe. Rather we see it full of truly living interaction between all its parts, including, first of all, the subatomic charges. Every atom is active, "affecting" other atoms. Consequently there can hardly be any "merely passive" existence. There are only mutual relationships, the apperceptions of which are filed in our memory along lines leading from the "past" into the "future".[6]

Mistakes, however, have often a long life. Even today, in spite of the more critical attitudes of many scientists, it remains an almost pathological fact that within the sphere of the Indo-European languages the concept of "cause" is still frequently applied to chain-successions of events in our current concept of the "passing time". One still remembers the almost tragicomic, desperate efforts of Albert Einstein to save this degenerated concept. Such efforts may be regarded as perhaps the last, pathetic remnant of an uncritical popularization of a fa sely mythical concept. To a historian, the concept of "cause" is only explicable by the initial awareness of the Living Creator in the primeval man's mind. A mere "observation of nature" would have had no reason to go beyond the acknowledgement of statistically describable – or merely sensually registered – repetitions of chain-events.

Quite similar was, obviously, the source of the concept of "reality". The

Cosmic God was, to the primeval man, the only Constant Reality, something Wholy Other, different from this passing and changing, dream-like world.

Recently, when a British statesman told a Soviet diplomat that contemporary British philosophers were mainly occupied by studying the meaning of words, the Russian refused to accept this as an occupation worthy of an intellectual. He wanted to know whether the Englishman was a "Materialist" and whether he regarded "this glass" as "real". He was, of course, hardly aware that the constitution of "matter" itself cannot be reduced to conceptual terms. He was probably even less aware of the fact that the concept of "reality" stemmed from the ages old intellectual need to distinguish, as sharply as possible, between the "reality" of the meaning of things – which can only be real in so far as they come from God who is Reality itself – and the lack of anything definite in the constantly fluctuating "matter". What is truly "real" is only the concept of the glass, but not the glass as a physical process which we cannot stop to seize and grasp properly. Moreover, no concept has ever originated from nature. Had the German "Materialist" who once declared "Without phosphor no thought", said "Without thought no phosphor", it would have been an equally superfluous statement.

Let us add that not only "causality" and "reality", but also the postmodern concepts of "realitivity" and "quantum", which every scientist has to impose on his observations because of the limitations of his sensory equipment, belong to the mythical heritage. This heritage differs and has always differed essentially from the natural endowment of organisms to collect the piecemeal reports of the perceptive apparatus and to build a pattern of behavior on these repeated reports. Man thinks within a climate of certitude because he is able to communicate not only urges and impressions, as animals do, but also meaningful informations. To quote Blaise Pascal: "We have an incapacity of proof, insurmountable by all dogmatism; but we also possess an idea of truth, invincible to all scepticism." Our knowledge, although vacillating and oscillating, stems from the archetypal awareness of God and from the ensuing concept of the Cosmic Order.

In this way, while comparing the primeval story about the trees planted in the garden of Eden with the report on a post-modern biological project, we are actually comparing two myths – not two assertions of which one would be a myth and the other something else. We should certainly compare them in reference to their historical settings. But, above all, it is important to compare their contents. It is in this comparison that a momentous difference in ideas appears and, with it, perhaps the most important change in the history of man's thought.

The central reality of the primeval myth is the Creator himself. Man's relation to him is characterized by the presence of the tree of choice. Man's life is conceived as the life of choice – the choice between an assent and a negation, between love and selfishness. This choice constitutes the meaning of man's life. The famous inscription which Dante placed on the gate of Hell,

> "... *mi fece la divina potestate,*
> *mi fece il eterno amore...*"
>
> "...I was made by the divine power,
> I was made by the eternal love...",

echoed this meaning as recently as the Late Middle Ages. God is the one who offers the choice and God is someone above and outside the universe. The universe is only a sequel of events resulting from destinations, instincts and urges, but also from man's intellectual choices. But as a concept as well as a living being the Cosmos is totally dependent on the Creator. Without the "Wholly Other Intellect" there can be no Cosmos, no Cosmic Order, no concept of nature, no free man.

The early man whose thinking was almost enclosed within this myth – because all his intellectual life stemmed from it – lived a hard life as hunter, food-collector and eventually tiller of the earth – or again as city-dweller, artisan, sailor and researcher in the secrets of the cosmos. He knew that his life was a life of choice, often involving deep suffering. He also knew that he had to make his choice always and immediately, at practically every given moment of his life. He was probably aware of several of the various facets of time; but the most important of these was always the present moment, the moment of decision.

Contrasted with this, the heart of the new, post-modern myth, once again a myth concerning creation, appears in the vision of a man who tries to establish his identity with the Creator. He "plays God", but without planting any tree of choice. He is going to prescribe what man should look like. No choice is involved in this modern myth, no love, no selfishness. All the fruit of the second tree is to be consumed. Suffering is to be eliminated. After some experimentary tampering with the genes a man will be created who will no longer be capable of suffering and for whom any kind of choice will cease to exist; his dispositions will be of a prefabricated, carefully selected kind. This myth is also centered not on the present time, but on the future, on the time of dreams, *tempus somniferum*. While in the Christian message Jesus is the mediator between man and the God situated in the center of all times, a Lenin or a post-modern biologist are mediators merely between man and the imaginary, again and again postponable future. But will all this really result in a new creation or will it rather mean destruction? Will the man of this new mythic vision remain alive as man? And will time, with all its uncertainties, stay with us? Or is it meant to disappear, because there will be no choice, no "possible future", but only an inevitable necessity?

Man's myths have always been occurring in time. Let us now pay some closer attention to the significance of this fact.

To belong to the Cosmic Order meant to the ancient people to follow a purpose. To follow a purpose meant to be alive. And to follow the purpose of man meant also to choose. Even before Anaxagoras spoke of Intelligence and Empedocles of Love, some early Greeks had already spoken of the Wisdom which "stears all things" by giving them life as well as the sense of life. All things, even rocks, were alive to the ancient *mythopoioi* – not in the restricted sense of some of the definitions of life suggested by the nineteenth century biology, but in the sense of a basic purposefulness *(phýsis)*, related to all the situations and times of the universe.

Only relatively recently a curious intellectual allergy against the very concept of life appeared on the scene. It had not been unknown, true enough, to some ancient civilizations. But not so long ago it came forward with a much greater vigor. A number of Stavrogins appeared among intellectuals who – like the hero of Dostoevskij's *Possessed* – saw only "empty space" and "dead things" around them and anxiously destroyed life wherever they thought they had found it. Instead of recognizing that some things may only seem to have a limited possibility to live – because of the limitations of our observational faculties – the New Age has embraced with enthusiasm the false myth of the "dead matter". It refused to grant to this "dead matter" any of the characteristics of that which is alive. Then it went further and denied validity to the concept of "life" itself. The expectations which accompanied the birth of organic chemistry in the early part of the nineteenth century, the abuse and ridicule heaped on Pasteur by his contemporaries and, finally, the insistence that life is "nothing but" a kind of movement imposed on bodies from outside by "material causes" – all that amounted to a triumph of this truly irrational mythology. The "material causes" were supposed to be governed by the "laws of matter". A new demonology came into existence.

The primeval myths had asserted that everything was alive, that – to use a modern, clumsy translation – there was a "spirit" in every source, in every mountain, in every cloud.[7] They meant that there was something striving after a reasonable fulfillment, something divine in each thing. Blaise Pascal touched the same truth when he spoke about the *esprit geométrique* as uncapable of reaching this striving for fulfillment and about the need of an *esprit de finesse*. Even Leibniz was still willing to uphold the existence of a purposeful, "perfecting principle" in all things. But already since Descartes' times, the universe was more and more frequently envisaged as a heap of "inert matter" which, under the impact of mythical daemons named Mechanical Laws, had necessarily and unavoidably followed the way to which it had been condemned ages ago.

These new myths succeeded only in splitting the universe into two pathetically futile camps: A camp of "dead" (senseless, meaningless) objects and a camp of abstract (immaterial and therefore actually non-existent) daemons or laws. The universe, according to this new mythology, represents hardly more than a game played by the members of the second camp with those of the first one.

The struggle which the modern and post-modern authors of myths led against the concept of life has been a fierce struggle. Jubilant over the possibility to "explain all biological events in terms of physics and chemistry", the scientists overlooked that those terms themselves do not "explain" anything, but merely state the correlates between events and certain prefabricated conceptual norms. Since Lamarck's times, many Lysenkos were pleased with the assertion that the giraffe had obtained its long neck by trying to reach the upper branches of trees; they hardly asked why it was the giraffe – and not, for instance, the goat – who indulged in such peculiar endeavors. If they did ask, the word "chance" was the answer. But then no one knew what that word meant. All one could do was to offer an example: if, looking for Brown, you encounter Smith, it is an accidental *(symbebēkós)* event which you have not intended; but, queerly enough, this distinction was practised by the same "Determinists" who insisted that it was not really you who intended to look for Brown.

One tried to find a "physico-chemical explanation" for cell division, almost without noticing that there was no "explanation" for the natural radiation of the "dead" uranium. One announced, with much pleasure, that there was little sense in calling the behavior of a living organ "something more than the sum of the functions of its cells, blood vessels and tissues" – without realizing that one had introduced and was constantly using the rather mythical concept of "function", not to mention the other, even more mythical word "behavior".

When is a scientific proposition meaningful? – asked eventually a few scientists who became suspicious of their own mythical vocabulary and began to wonder whether it reaches the "truth" as much as the old myths did. But while assuming this wonderfully critical attitude they forgot that "meaning" and "truth" were themselves concepts pertaining to the old mythical heritage, a heritage built around the archetypal awareness of the Cosmic God and his Order. Nature itself has only produced events, never "meanings" or "truths".

However, the unwillingness to grasp life as something purposeful has had, evidently, a deeper reason than a mere predilection for some new, pseudo-mythical concepts. High above this odd development looms the childish preoccupation with the so-called "ontology" and with the "auxiliary-verb philosophies" in general.

Even after so much clarification had taken place, scholars are often influenced by the allegedly "perennial tradition" stemming from Aristotle's decision to convert the grammatical principles of the mellow Greek tongue into "categories of being". In the poetical mind of the Stagerite the auxiliary verb "to be" assumed gigantic proportions – while, oddly enough, Aristotle never attempted to do the same with the other leading auxiliary verb, "to have". Moreover, because of the existence, in Greek, of the grammatical difference between "nouns" and "adjectives", some kinds of "being" came to be regarded as "essential" and some only as "accidental".

A golden future seemed to be in store for this invention. Epicurus spoke of "accidental swerving of atoms". Propagated again in Western Europe during the thirteenth century by Thomas Aquinas and associates – in spite of the critical opposition put up by the truly great thinkers of the epoch, Robert Grosseteste and Francis Bonaventura – this naive thinking even received the blessing of quite a number of Christian bishops. It was to end, so far, with Martin Heidegger's desperate and, of course, again meaningless question why should "being" have precedence before "nothing". In the meantime, among other developments, it also furnished the Evolutionists with the possibility of calling some variations "random" and "accidental" – *i.e.*, not so meaningful as some other variations. It even enabled De Vries to speak of "random variations" almost as frequently as of "mutations".

In Chinese – a language whose grammatical rules differ widely from those of the Greek language – such a philosophy would hardly be thinkable. Where, in Greek, 'cherry' is a noun and "red" only a mere adjective, in Chinese both are equally expressive and so is their combination. In the Aristotelian slang something meaningful combined with something not so meaningful may bring about something third. If this new thing is meaningful and purposeful, *i.e.*, something more than the combination of its elements, from where does it derive this new meaningfulness? A critical mind may grasp a theory in which all elements are meaningful. It may also entertain another theory according to which there seems to be nowhere any meaning. But to assert that something "essential" plus something "accidental" equal again something "essential" seems like asserting that a whole number plus a fraction in the same numerical system equal another whole number.

The Evolutionists seem to have believed in a mysterious and extremely mythical person at times called Variation, then Survival and then again Selection. But this person actually operated by "random" and "accidental", *i.e.*, not so meaningful, means. Without Aristotle and Aquinas this dainty trick would have hardly been possible. Recently the situation has changed again, but only slightly. Minds continue to be dominated by the Aristotelian and scholastic insistence on using the auxiliary verb "to be" without completing it into "to be what" – *i.e.*, without recognizing the meaning of an extant thing. To the minds overflowing with "ontology" something "merely is", while something else "is something". As has been remarked, no one has as yet proposed the establishment of a logical distinction between "Smith has" and "Smith has a pen". Were we to do so, a new discipline, "echology", could find its place beside "ontology" in the curricula of our universities.

A post-modern scientist who does not wish to betray his most progressive generation should only ask whether this or that proposition is helpful in providing him with additional power over this or that regularly repeated or repeatable process. It is most regrettable, from the progressive point of view, that the post-modern scientist's most cherished dream should be not just a "unified theory of elementary particles", but even a "unified theory of the cosmos". The trouble with these expressions is that they contain the word "theory", *i.e.*, "poetical vision". No post-modern scientist – if he only realized what the word "theory" means – would surely survive the disgrace of being called a poet. Yet he wants to be more than a poet. A poet is only a feeble imitator of the Creator. At times our scientist would even be ready to swallow the charge that his thinking is "teleological" and that he has imposed his "anthropomorphist" views on the piece of nature with which he happened to be working – if only he were allowed to reach the fragment of power he is after. Sometimes he would dream of creating a living structure in his laboratory. Why not? He already has brought about quite a few living things without knowing it – things purposeful and capable of influencing their surrounding and therefore "alive". No one is obliged to share Samuel Butler's opinion that robots "have no interests" and "therefore are not alive". Even if by a living structure the scientist means something which he calls biological and which he is not particularly apt to define and to distinguish from his "dead matter", he may still succeed in producing it.

But seen from the scientist's own point of view, his present intentions are truly titanic. An extremely long time ago – so his new myth tells him – "life" has come into existence through a "chance", *i.e.*, in the Aristotelian slang, "accidental", not "essential" collision of the "right", *i.e.* "essential", not "accidental" molecules. Forming phrases such as these – speaking of "chance" (meaningless) collisions of "right" (meaningful) molecules – he is actually getting ready to create a meaningful collision of meaningless molecules. He himself is the first to give this collision a meaning. He is already very close to becoming a Cosmic God. That is perhaps exactly what he has always wanted to become.

But again the question arises: will the scientific man remain alive as man? And what meaning will "time" assume in his vocabulary?

During the last three quarters of a century or so, the new mythology has reached a summit with the declaration that God was dead. While "dead" is the opposite of "alive" and while "to be alive" means, in the traditional sense, "to have a meaning", this declaration amounts to the assertion that God has no meaning. But how can then anything have a meaning if there is no meaning in the mutual relationship of things which are all related to each other?

It had been known, undoubtedly, even before the times of Dennis the Areopagite, that one could hardly touch God with one's vocabulary. Yet the archetypal expressions "real" and "living" preserved a penetrating significance. If anything was "alive", then only because God was "alive". If anything had meaning, then only because God had meaning. On the other hand, it also should be well noted that the regrettably very popular expression "God is" remains far behind the status of a truthful expression (beside being, grammatically, a mere unfinished sentence). It fails to state anything about the contrast between the cosmos and its Creator; the cosmos can never reach beyond the passing, escaping time, while in the Creator there must be the meaning of each particular moment, whether past, present or future. If some "ontologists" try to remove this inadequacy by saying that the "being" of man or of the universe is only an "analogy" of God's "being", they reach about as far as philosophers who described our knowledge of things as an "adequation" of our intellect with them, or as the psychoanalysts who declared lyrical poems to be mere "sublimations" of the sexual instinct; both "adequation" and "sublimation" are indeed absolutely meaningless groups of sounds – and so is "analogy".

Ána lógon means "according to the word". There may be some "assimilative solicitation" behind a comparison based on mere sounds. But it is too rude a kind of description to be used anywhere else but within the realm of numerically describable proportions. One may speak of an analogy between the shape of a rider's saddle and that of a saddle in the mountains. But to use such truly mystical comparisons beyond the realm of proportions is, at its best, preposterous.

Moreover, as the auxiliary verb "to be" is invariably used in connection with the concept of an illusory "continuity" within the passing time, its use in connection with the Creator insinuates the impression that also God's "being" has something to do with the passing time, with "duration" or "continuation". Some modern mythologies, *e.g.*, those built around Bergson and Shaw, may rejoice in such meaninglessness. The old myths never did. Simone Weil, in the second volume of her *Cahiers* rightly insists that even Plato's *to on* has to be translated by "real", not by "being".

According to the primeval myths man is made to the image and likeness of the Loving God. At the same time suffering, one of the main gifts of the passing time, becomes an essential aspect of man's life. In the primeval myths, suffering for the sake of creative love was already the most conspicuous quality or human life. Suffering was connected intimately with the mythical expectation of the Suffering Messiah and with the concept of "sacrifice". Sacrifice, it should be noted, was originally "sacrifice of God", not "sacrifice to God."[8]

More recently, however, driven by an odd urge to delete the archetypal, basic experiences and to replace them by new myths, the new thought made it fashionable to assert that God was an "absolute being" who had never been concerned with suffering. Christ was not the Messiah. "We are the only ones who suffer, who have always suffered, perhaps who will ever suffer", cry the authors of the new myths – Martin Buber, for instance. In this way the identification of God with the "dead nature" had apparently succeeded. But man, the entity in the middle, remained completely alone. Will he be able to stay alive, to remain meaningful?

This last question is pushed even more to the foreground as an almost necessary sequel to the two actions taken by the authors of the new myths. First they declared that a considerable part of the universe was dead; modern biology had to engage in a futile struggle to provide itself with a new definition of "life" and, as could have been expected, failed miserably. Then the second declaration came: God, too, was dead. But if that what is below man is mostly dead and that what is above him is also dead, how can man himself remain alive?

Admittedly, a simple, sharply contrasting comparison of the primeval and ancient myths with the modern and post-modern myths approximates, from a historian's point of view, an oversimplification. As has been stated, the modern process of cultural change had its predecessors and its roots in many an event which characterized the ultimate phases of the ancient civilizations.[9]

The basic wisdom began to die the moment the ancient thinkers concentrated on the Cosmic Order and slowly forgot about the Cosmic God – and even more when they made man, and not his Creator, the measure of all things. Wisdom became a mere longing for wisdom – *philosophia* – a dialogue with failure and, eventually, a dead affair. In more recent history, within the framework of the European civilization, such a process set in with the Aristotelian renaissance of the twelfth century, to continue with Descartes and the decline of the "academic thought" in our own days. Moreover, the concept of the "cause" was a very real and sober concept when it meant, in the primeval wisdom, a "will and power to achieve something meaningful". It became a piece of wishful imagination when "causality" was defined as a "dependence of later events on preceding events". Eventually it was to be changed into a very artificial – although, admittedly, still operational – "law expressing a correlation of variables".

From the point of view of a student of the mystery of time, the core of the whole issue has always been in the awareness of God's presence in the heart *(arché)* of the cosmos and thus also in the life of man. The very heart of the Christian doctrine – and thus, potentially, also the central value of any civilization sometimes still called Christian – is the doctrine of Christ's participation in history. The mere life of God, communicated from generation through cult and through mythical tradition, may recede far beyond the comprehensible symbols and leave man with mere fetishism. We are speaking here not only about the festishism of a totem in the center of a tribal camp, but also about the fetishism of a colored piece of silk or cotton flapping at the top of a pole, in front of which uniformed and bespangled crowds stomp and perform all sorts of pseudoliturgical evolutions.

The primeval myth of the "New Coming", the "Epiphany", of God was, as has been noted, connected with the concept of sacrifice – primarily God's own loving sacrifice and only in a secondary way man's sacrifice to God. This concept degenerated already in Antiquity into innumerable attempts of of a liturgical "terrestrization of God" or "acceleration of the expected epiphany". At the same time, the meaning of sacrifice was often restricted to mere, always instantaneous, pacifications of the deity. And then the dark and dismal depths of the modern and post-modern mythology set in, in which "liberators" *(epiphanoi)* armed with bombs and tanks descend on populations of various countries and individuals are required to sacrifice their lives to the glory and power of the above mentioned multicolored fetish in return for a promise of some kind of vague future bliss for their children.

The memory of Christ's birth, life and passion which had revived the archetypal awareness of God the Creator and Redemptor, lost its immediate impact on the Mediterranean and European area. It was even more obscured by the new, global interests and worries of the New Age. The ways of the European culture and civilization began to resemble the cultural process which had already once taken place in the life-works and spheres of influence of the Buddha, K'ung Fu-tsu and Socrates. Not only the archetypal concept of sacrifice, but the entire mystery of the sorrowful experiences of man was pushed aside and replaced by new recommendations concerning the ways along which man may escape suffering. The primordial time, the foutainhead (*arché, illud tempus*) was replaced by empty visions of the distant future. The contemplation of God gave way, in the new mythology, to the concept of the ultimate perfection of the human species, situated in the future "time of dreams". This ultimate perfection is mostly expected – against Thomas Huxley's warning – to be achieved either by struggle and survival, or by automatic enlightenment, or again by a Fyodorovian or Teilhardian, gradually accelerated "increase of love and comprehension."

Soon, as it happens in works of poets and composers, the dream of the future perfection of man would split into several branches which grow along their separate ways, come closer again, separate, and again embrace one another. Such would be the ways of abstruse thinkers, of artists, of political sovereigns, but also of scientists and technocrats. Of all these the last mentioned seem to have recently become the most important. While in most of the Ancient World and even in the Middle Ages the scientist's vision was a part of the awesome contemplation of the Cosmic Order, in the world of the new myths the scientific knowledge became "an instrument for reforming and remaking the world."

Already the very ancient, although evidently not primeval myth concerning the Demiurge had brought some sign of this change. It told of someone who replaced the Creator – but to create things rather from an ambitious pride than from love. However, ancient science was not as yet convertible to mere technology. Even while the Romans and the Incas constructed aquaducts and roads and while the Chinese manufactured paper and porcelain, their contemplative science maintained its superiority above technology. The Chinese used gun-powder for fire-works only and the Aztecs reserved the use of wheels for children's toys.

A definite change arrived, however, with the implementation of Francis Bacon's slogan, "Knowledge means power". Knowledge, naturally, could again move only within the realm of myths. To say that "the gas behaves as if it consisted of elastic particles obeying some mechanical laws", is a beautiful mythical parable, a true "collapsing into a mythical mode." It never became possible for a scientist, as he had sometimes imagined, to gather some data and then, on this basis, formulate laws. He always had to possess, first, the mythopoetic intuition. His conclusions never exceeded the realm of analogies or parables. Sometimes, quite often perhaps, he did not hesitate to use two or more myths at the same time; it became quite arbitrary whether he described the microphysical processes with the help of the wave or of the particle language, finding both of them operational.

There is no essential, epistemological difference between a primitive who refers to the burning branch of a tree stricken by lightning and talks of a "fiery angel" and a physicist who, using a voltameter, speaks of "electrical discharges". Both "fiery angel" and "electricity" are mythical concepts – no one has ever seen such beings, at least no one among the ordinary mortals. But it appeared of advantage to visualize nature in terms of general myths. And as the new myths stemmed more and more from a basic refusal to accept the basic human condition, the resulting vision came to center less and less on the Creator's glory and more and more on man's power.

To the ancients, the "spirit" *(ruah, pneuma)* was a symbol very close to that of God's "generative, purpose-giving life". A distinct parentage appears between the archetypal symbol of the Life-Distributing Light (Moses' "burning bush", Heraclitus' "fire") and that of the "fiery tongues" of the Spirit Who Procedes From the Father, as described in the *Acts of the Apostles*. At the very beginning of his *Epistle to the Hebrews*, the apostle Paul repeats with great enthusiasm the Psalmist's words about God who "makes his messengers spirits and his ministers flames of fire". As recently as AD 325, the oecumenical council of Christian bishops in Nicea proclaimed its faith in the "Spirit Who Enliveth" *(pneuma zōopoion)*; the Eastern Christian theologians frequently identified the messengers of God as "energies". On the other hand, the apostle Paul also described the Spirit of Darkness as an "energy of illusion".[10] To Nicolas d'Oresme, in the fourteenth century, the concept of *impetus* was still a part of the myth of creation. To Isaac Newton, in the eighteenth century, the concept of "energy" belonged to the same kind of vision, but assumed a preponderantly operational character in the interpretation of the regular processes of nature. To a constructor of engines in the next age it became a merely operational technical term – and no poetical interpretation was attempted. To a twentieth century "researcher" in the field of "psychedelics" the concept of the "enlargement of mental dynamics" is already firmly embedded in the man-centered mythology which professes to have no other purpose than to satisfy the craving for power – if not any other power than the power to dream.

The ancient myths, it should be stressed again, were based on real experiences. They described these experiences in images, songs, dances, and in carefully remembered narrations. The poetical element, naturally, prevailed. It was Adam, not the Cosmic God, who named the plants and the animals. The poetical element even increased. Eventually, it hid most of the original experience, but did not destroy it.

In the new myths, a poetical element prevails which has been increasingly successful in ignoring all experience. We may find among these new myths:

a) the myth of the ascending march of man; man is depicted as producing better and better (or happier) generations or, at any rate, generations living in better and better (or happier) circumstances; a complicated civilization is regarded as a guarantee of man's success rather than as a self-destructive structure; even the Roman Church is expected, in the words of one of its leading theologians, John C. Murray, "to be brought, at long last, abreast of the consciousness of civilized mankind"; in the work of another Jesuit, Pierre Teilhard de Chardin, this myth has been developed into a cult which protects man, as Denis de Rougemont puts it, from the uncomfortable presence of God;[11]

b) the Aristotelian and scholastic myth (perhaps more scholastic than truly Aristotelian) of a merely sensual knowledge – a knowledge collected from sense-perception or from the "matter" of man's brain – which alone is going to satisfy man's intellectual needs and help him to get rid of insecurity; this myth is increasingly reflected in our merely technical, remote-control civilization;

c) the myth of the alleged human ability to break the frame-work of the archetypal images, to "avoid all metaphysical worldviews" as much as all "collapsing into mythical modes"; the "lexicon of the urban-secular man", is expected to replace the mythical archetypes; this lexicon, it is asserted, will contain no mythical concepts;

d) the myth of the state as the "perfect society" and the real source of all man's rights and freedoms; even the allegedly ultra-progressive *New Catechism* of the Dutch bishops of Roman obedience calls the state "the great organization for life in common" and reminds the faithful that "taxes should be paid the way the state expects"; this myth contradicts absolutely the truth that while the family, the community and the professional association are natural, spontaneous bodies politic, the state is not; in fact, the state can only exist de iure by agreement between communities (revocable at all times) and only by virtue of such agreement can provide man with a few creative services;

e) the myth of freedom – which concept is no longer understood as personal perfection (growth toward God), but rather as the facility of using and consuming things in one own's way – at times also in the way prescribed by the technocratic authorities who have monopolized decisions concerning what is and what is not freedom; this myth is becoming more and more irrational as the post-modern man is more and more restricted in his choice of intellectual and physical commodities and constrained to heed the commands of the technocrats;

f) the myth of anonymous and yet infallible information; while true human conversation is silenced, man's talk is restricted to slogans and phrases received through anonymous and monopolous chanels of communication and accepted by the listeners and viewers with more than naive credulity;

g) the myth of mass "togetherness"; this image of security, designed to assuage the lonely crowd, began with Rousseau's "general will" and developed toward the stomping of the "SS and SA men" and the "people's democratic parades" or the "assemblies of hippies";

h) the myth of "velocity" and "fast covering of larger distances", the core of which is the idea of escape through the acceleration of the reviewing of available scenery – as far as this scenery has not yet been homogenized and thus indeed made unavailable;

i) the myth of a "complete escape" by means of a slow or instantaneous suicide; alternately accepting or ignoring Hamlet's words, "to sleep, perchance to dream", this myth is centered around an imaginary extension of the passing time.

In the days of the old myths, much time was devoted to art.

The ancient art was a symbolical art. It was centered around the temple as the symbol of man's real home in the only real time, the primordial time of the Creator. Even if restricted to a mere totem, the symbol of God's presence in the center of a tribal settlement was also the focus of art, from which all social, scientific and technological activities radiated.

The *homo viator*, on his insecure way from the cradle to the grave and observing in awe and astonishment the immense universe around him, engaged enthusiastically in painting and carving, singing and dancing. It all enabled him to express his joy as well as his sadness and his awsome fear. Long before the hieratic cities came into existence, the mythical lore had already become the foutainhead of intellectual life. When the cities rose, the temples – which had come before everything else in the cities – helped to stabilize and even to petrify the mythical symbols. Even then it remained the constant ambition of the artist to make it as clear as possible that the cosmos and everything in it had sprung from the wisdom of the Living God. If, in architecture, above all, but sometimes also in sculpture, he concentrated on the beauty of the geometrical, harmonious patterns, he never forgot that these were the fruits of a Living Mind. The ancient Greek predilection for the geometrical was a result of the decision not to forget the "Wholly Other Intellect". The ancient Chinese predilection for the biological forms in architecture and sculpture was a result of the decision not to forget the Living Source of the purposeful cosmos.

The Christian West-European of the Gothic centuries went even further. Mindful of the drama of Jesus' life he reached closer to the nature of the universe and of man's existence in it. Light and Life remained to him the great symbols of Divinity. But he descended to the suffering, the tired, the struggling man in his daily life. He also began to investigate the manycolored face of Evil on this earth. The art of the Baroque and even the novel of the nineteenth century, to some extent, were to continue for some time along this path – but only at a diminishing pace.

In the meantime the new myths had made their appearance. The lonely

Romantic man of the epoch around 1800, having given up God, found it difficult to remain man. In the language of the Romantic lyricists, he expressed his wish to become a lark or a wester cloud. With the Romantic epoch – when Victor Hugo exhorted the artists to concentrate each one on his own self – art began to degenerate into mere amusement and, from there, into mere shock-treatment – sometimes through atonality, sometimes through perversion punctuating the boring enumeration of the little facts which constitute the post-modern novel.

The cathedral – the Christian successor to the ancient temple – disappeared from the "secularized" city. For a time it seemed as if it was to be replaced by the buildings of parliaments, concert halls, stadiums. In fact it was more often replaced by the railroad terminal, the highway and the airport. In the post-modern civilization, there are no cities, but only agglomerations of offices, dormitories and transportation facilities. The rapid transportation from place to place must be regarded as the exact counterpart of the ancient symbolism of the sacred temple, the real home.[12]

The saturation of urges seems to be essence of what is known today as humanism. One hears of technical humanism, of existencialist humanism, of Marxist humanism, of Teilhardian humanism. Soon, in the wake of "people's democracies", we may hear of "humanist humanism". Just as in the postmodern mind instincts mostly replaced ideas, the bathroom became almost the only part of the home which still found appreciation among the authors of the new myths. "I have had", states a famous American literary critic and essayist, "a good many more uplifting thoughts, creative and expansive visions in well equipped American bathrooms than I have ever had in any cathedral... Here the mind becomes free to ruminate, to plan ambitious projects..."[13]

The question, however, which has repeatedly appeared before our eyes – "Will man remain alive as man?" – is neither a "humanist" nor a "bathroom" question. It is not a physiological or a physical problem at all. The man who is alive is the man who has constantly to accept or to reject, to live in insecurity, to go through all sorts of opportunities for creative love. To be able to love and to create is his real purpose, his "life" in the original and the only true meaning of the word. The "well equipped bathroom" and, much more, any tampering with his genes, for which biology may be getting ready, as well as any psychedelic drugging may be conducive to an essential change in his character which will deprive him of his true life. If this happens, his visions may still remain ambitious – perhaps more than in the best equipped bathroom – but they will hardly be creative. His physiology may be "perfected" but his full meaning will be gone. The "prefabricated" inclinations and capabilities will not be able to replace his meaning as man. After a while only animals may remain, once again the only inhabitants of this earth. That may very well be the sense of Jesus' words at the end of *Matthew*'s chapter 16: Some of those "standing around", but perhaps very few, will still remain alive as men when the end of the passing time arrives. But then in the Christian message all the moments of passing time are one when seen from God's Kingdom. Hardly any difference remains between an individual death and the "end of times". According to the apocryphal *Gospel of St Thomas*, discovered in Egypt only in 1945, when the disciples inquired about the "day when the dead will rest", Jesus answered: "That which you await has come, but you know it not."

Time as History's Background

> From that I have concluded that time was
> nothing else but distention – I do not know
> of what, but I would not be surprised if
> it was of the mind itself.
> Augustine Aurelius, Confessions

> As much time flies away
> traversing the space
> as is lost of space
> when we live the day.
> Miguel de Unamuno, Cancionero

> To think of a lineal time is hardly more
> possible than to think of a lineal word.
> Pierre Emmanuel, La Vie est intérieure

"When did it happen?" we keep asking when reminiscing or listening to a report about past events. With that question a mysterious element, known as "time", enters our thoughts.

More often than not a historian does not even ask after time's origin and character. Time is a necessary backbone of his narration, a peg on which he has to hang his story. Because of this, chronology, a system of reckoning time, is considered an indispensable companion to historical studies. It operates with years, months and days of the calendar based on some rhythmic occurences of astronomical character. More often than not it arranges the years into two long series – *e.g.*, before Christ and after Christ – a custom which is not an unusual way of reckoning time. Chronology has always been connected with some prominent event which was regarded as the central point of the time-picture; such was the creation of the world in the Hebrew tradition, the foundation of the city of Rome in Latin historiography, or the *hejira* of the Moslems.

Students of chronology may experience certain difficulties. If they find the Bolshevik revolution of 1917 placed by some in October, while by the others in November, or if the English dating of a sixteenth century event does not agree with the French dating, it is because some countries were reluctant in accepting the reform of the calendar introduced in 1582 by pope Gregory XIII. If again there is some uncertainty as to the date of a certain medieval event, it might be because of the different ways of beginning a new year in different Christian countries.

Many more difficulties await those who study the ancient, pre-Christian civilizations. In most of them chronological computation was made on the basis of lists of monarchs, dynasties or magistrates. Such systems would be found in ancient Greek cities before the adoption of the reckoning of years by the Olympic Games, in Egypt and Mezopotamia, in China and Japan, and elsewhere. A historian may consider himself lucky if he finds a date fixed atronomically. But the ancient Egyptians, for instance, did not share the Mezopotamian interest in solar or lunar eclipses. The Chinese had two different years, one solar, one regulated by the moon. The Mayas of ancient America used a very precise calendar, but represented the epochs as burdens carried by different symbols of the Cosmic God who moved in a cycle – so much so that, in their historical and prophetical knowledge, past, present and future tended to become one.

The historian's troubles reach their peak when he penetrates the most ancient phases of the human past – the protohistorical epoch from which no written testimonies are available, but only ruins, fragments of statues, paintings, or tools adorned with ornaments. Attempts are being made to size up this very distant epoch by various methods ranging from dendrochronology (counting the rings in the trees) to the potassium-argon process which measures the decay of radio-activity in minerals (potassium breaks down, at an extremely slow rate, into calcium and argon atoms). None of these methods, however, not even Libby's "carbon 14" method, is reliable. There always remains an unknown, ideterminable relationship between the protohistorical man and the materials with which he worked or by which he was surrounded. Above all it is by no means safe to presume that the stream of radiation to which the earth is exposed is or has always been constant.[1]

No matter how exact our method of measuring the distances in time may be, the very concepts of the past and of time in general remain essentially abstract.[2] Thinking of Michelangelo we think of him as walking and working before our eyes – no matter how much we may remind ourselves that he flourished in the sixteenth century. Discussing the history of Lithuania we move forth and back, from a unique moment or event to another in a way resembling the movements of someone discussing a large mural painting which he tries to encompass by his eyes. In a word, the element of time in history presents us with problems which surpass by far the problems of mere chronology. While chronology remains the backbone, time is the very pulse as well as the background of history. We should like to know more about it than what chronology is able to tell us.

At first sight the time of history resembles a pattern. Aristotle attempted to describe it, following Architas of Tarento, a Pythagorean, not as a movement but as the numerical expression of movement. "According to that what was before and what comes after," he added. He could have spoken similarly of the measuring of space by an intellect unable to comprehend space in its entirety. But later, in the same fourth book of *Physics*, he remarked that there was also a "circle of time" because "time is measured by circular movement". Here he thought of the day-night circle, of the recurrent seasons of the year, or possibly also of the *télos thanátoio* of each human life. Such thoughts were perhaps also the foundation of the concept of the *aiōn*, the "great year" of history which may be imagined as a circle and hypothetically regarded as repeating itself "from eternity to eternity". Leibniz, as is known, also described passing time, together with space and movement, as a pattern of relations. A contemporary scientific writer, Samuel Alexander, conceived the entire universe as a hierarchical arrangement, ordered by means of three basic elements-notions, of which space–time was the very first one.

Man is provided with a number of categories of cognition or patterns which enable him to penetrate the mystery of the universe or, at least, to make his scanty understanding of that mystery operational. Numbers, chemical elements, concepts of Newtonian dynamics, waves, Maxwell's descriptions, charges of energy, Euclidean as well as non-Euclidean geometrical concepts and postulates and other prefabricated verbal and thought-categories have, each in its turn, served us in making useful statements about the universe. But each has been purchased at the price of a certain detachment from the entirety and completeness of the cosmos. And each remains, undoubtedly, relevant to only a partial comprehension of a certain kind of phenomena.

Time looks like one of the patterns or categories framed by our intellect rather than as something inherent in it. It is not an unchangeable category. Among post-modern physicists, Dirac has explored the possibility of a change in the laws of the cosmos when different forces, such as electrical and gravitational, vary in their relative strength. The notion of a delaying time at great velocities in space has appeared in recent investigations. Models of the universe have been suggested, *e.g.*, by Goedel, based on the hypothesis of a universal rotation of matter, in which it would be possible, theoretically, to travel from the present moment anywhere into the past or future.[3]

There are many kinds of time. There is the physical time which the scientist constructs by using various measuring instruments and by regulating them in accordance with the movements of the celestial bodies. Are these movements regular? And what do we mean here by "regular"? Do we mean their possible dependence on other, unknown to us, parts of the cosmos? Or again: How much do man's experiences really depend on this physical time? Since 1958 when the so-called Mössbauer effect was discovered, it has been known that the time on the main floor of a very tall building, where gravity is stronger, is slower than near the top of the same building. If an astronaut travels, just under the limiting speed of light, the distance of one hundred light-years, he will have to spend only a few decades of his life, while the observers living in the "historical" time will regard his trip as more than thousand years long.

Then there is also the "biological time" which seems to be closer to the animal part of man's character than the physical time. Zoologists have discovered that the inborn feeling of time possessed by animals varies, in all probability, with the fluctuation of the temperature of their brains. A wound inflicted on the body of an infant heals in three days. The same wound on an old man's body requires three weeks to heal. Or should we say that the day of an infant equals one third of the healing process and that the day of an old man equals only a twenty-first part of the same healing process? Why should we regard the movements of some celestial bodies as more important than the movements of the cells closing a wound?

There are "times" which, obviously, cannot be compared mutually. Psychologists have demonstrated that the child often regards time as something dependent on his own actions. The extremely "slow" time which tortures the schizophrenic and the equally extremely "slow" time which delights the addicts of mescalin and some other drugs – are they of the same nature? It would evidently have no meaning at all to ask how "valid" each one of them is.

One conclusion at least could and should be drawn from these tentative questions: That we should not allow ourselves to be led astray by concepts which are only partially useful, such as the concept of an "absolute" time and of its alleged continuity, which appeared already in ancient India under the name of *samtana* and which the scientists of the last few centuries have repeatedly introduced on the market. The concept of a "continuous time", something spreading between historical events and transporting mysterious "influences" from one event to another, has led only to non-sensical assertions – such as that the murder in Sarajevo was the "cause" of the First World War (as if one was talking about two billiard balls in a collision and about the mythical "momentum" jumping from one to the other).

Where is there any continuity in our memory? A remembrance from our childhood stands next to that of the last year's vacations. Yesterday is certainly as irretrievable as the beginning of the world. If there is really any basic tendency in our dealing with time, it is our inclination to regard time, any time, as something complete. The symbolism of the Maya calendars, mentioned above, as well as the tendency of the Buddhist thought to regard "the nature of anything as its own momentary stasis and destruction"[4] coincides with our demands that a rhythmical phase or a melody be completed. It also coincides with our insistence that we be told the "entire story". This inclination has helped us in the realm of science. In penetrating that realm we also tend, every time, to a "whole story" – a statistical quantum, the return of a star to an "identical" point on the sky, a complete metabolism in a body, an entire regular process in the behavior of an animal. With the concept of ordinary numbers at our disposal – a purely intellectual concept, not derivable from sensual perception, because there are no two perceptions which could be regarded as identical – we recognize the swallow not only according to the numbers which we assign to the dimension of its entire body, but also from the complete story of its yearly travelling.

Searching for completeness man had started dividing the escaping time and found, to his evident satisfaction, that he was able to speak of complete units of time.[5] Searching for completeness, he also reached two remarkable hypotheses: Evolution and Entropy.

Has any other branch of scientific knowledge attracted, above all during the nineteenth century, as large and as enthusiastic a following as the studies devoted to evolution? At a time when the cooperation between science and industrial technology was rapidly increasing, lucrative projects were open to young scientists, which had little or nothing to do with the past of nature. And yet many of them, ignoring these projects, have gathered around the great masters of evolutionary theories. With avidity they devoted their lives to the study of the most remote past of nature. What drove them to such a choice? To many of them, admittedly, the principles of evolution and of natural selection meant a mechanism which would take away from their shoulders any personal, moral responsibility. But to many – and perhaps, in some way, to all of them – these principles were the cherished foundation of a great vision, a real *theoria* of the cosmos in its completeness.

As human history also came to be considered part of the picture, one could indulge in expanding the concept of automatic progress which Condorcet had drafted. One could speak of a tremendous machine running better and better, perfecting itself mechanically all the time. For decades, up to the generation of H. G. Wells and beyond, people viewed, with immense delight, the murals or museum vitrins depicting the "march of progress", from the nebulae to the upright man. They were particularly flattered to find themselves "at the head of the march". It was a complete "theatre". But its completeness was the completeness of time – in spite of the fact that time was now conceived as a line and that the beginning as well as the end of that line were lost in enormous distances.

How many of the evolutionists were or are aware of the identity between the universe and their linear concept of time? When Aristotle spoke of the eternity of the cosmos, he meant that the cosmos could not go beyond time. This, by the way, was misunderstood by some medieval Western Christian scholars who hurriedly started using revelation as "proof" that the cosmos was not eternal. Aristotle had certainly subordinated necessity to eternity. But by "eternity" he meant the completeness of time. It is the eternity of the cosmos which, in the Aristotelian vision, serves as foundation or reason of its necessity. In this time there cannot be any other universe because this universe is this time.

Then, paradoxically enough, also the word "chance" affected the discussion. It was frequently proclaimed "a more useful hypothesis than God" but at the same time it was also provided with the chareacteristics of an extremely wise, but truly mythical person. One spoke as "homologous" of the wings of birds and of the arms of man, both derived from identical structures in the appendage pattern of the vertebrates. Next one described as "analogous" the wings of birds and insects, derived from essentially different structures but performing an identical function. Wherever one turned, the bearded Father Chance was working wonders.

Eventually, however, it all finished in an annihilation of the very possibility of a "chance". One embraced totally the Aristotelian assertion that whaever happened could not have happened any other way. The fact that evolution moved one way only and that, temporarily at least, entropy was found increasing, excluded chance completely. Gone were the times when it might have seemed that the "chance movements" of a butterfly flying here and there over a splendid meadow of possibilities could become a prototype of the vast net of movements which is nature. The final result was the vision of a machine which can move, inexorably, in one direction only and which is doomed to be left, one day, without any further possibility of self-perfection or of engaging in any kind of work.

But as a by-product of this new mythico-scientific development – which Condorcet would have hardly expected and before which H. G. Wells eventually decided to close his eyes – the role of time was brought even more to the center of the stage. While natural processes were deemed interpretable only in terms of their "history", time assumed an even more fascinating character than it seemed to have before. The mystery of this "pulse of history" – "natural" as well as "human" history – increased when one decided to assume that entropy, as Arthur Eddington expressed it, was "the arrow of time" or when the unidirectional time of our experience came to be defined as "the direction in which most thermodynamical processes occur".[6]

Could we perhaps get rid of the so often painful memory of passing time? To what extent is our civilization immutably identical with the idea of time conceived as a memory of events which cannot be changed or repeated?

An outstanding zoologist, Adolf Portmann, described man as "a zoologically incomplete creature whose style of life is the historical process determined by tradition".[7] Some other scientists have spoken of the "prolongation of infancy" as of one of the basic differences between man and the animals who are physiologically close to him. A "prolongation of infancy" seems to mean, among other things, that an adult man is unable to "live on the spur of the moment" and has a constant recourse to the memory of past happenings. The great vision of the complete time – or, at least, the "so far complete time" – seems again to be clutching his heels.

Yesterday, today, tomorrow – past, present, future. Such is the basic division of time which philologists have found in many, but not in all, languages. Do these three comcepts have identical value? Are they equally operational? To a psychologist the experience of time has an almost "atomistic" character. In his eyes it certainly lacks the properties of a "continuum". Its individual intervals also lack the character of mathematical points. This becomes evident when we consider the "present time". The psychologists would rather call it an "interval" than a "point". But as this interval, at the very moment when we think of it, already belongs to the past, its character as "interval" becomes rather problematic.

Defining – what else can we do? – the "present" as the "most recent past", we may perhaps simplify our task. Simone Weil, the astonishing Jewish-French thinker whose last years seem to have consumed her life but also introduced her to the deepest wisdom her epoch had to offer, wrote down in her war-time note-books: "Find out the connection between the void and the way in which time rolls by..." Is there really more than a void behind words such as "now" or "at this very moment"?

Some scientists, much in love with the beautifully arranged evolutionary garden – so much, indeed, that they still manage to ignore their colleagues Max Planck and Werner Heisenberg – have decided to identify the past with whatever is determined and the future with the undetermined. They say that if certain material quantities ($x_1, x_2, x_3 \ldots x_n$) have certain characters, another quantity (x_{n+1}) has also a determined character: $x_{n+1} = f(x_1 \ldots x_n)$. Perhaps it would be more mature – and also more in accordance with postmodern physics – to say that an abstracted series of events which has often happened in a certain order will probably happen again in a similar order. Such an expression, of course, would hardly contribute to the prescribed divinization of the past. But what surprises us most is the assertion that while the past is determined, the future remains undetermined. Would it not be more manly to admit no such thing as "the future"! We may be in sympathy with a scientist who has decreed that "time-order does not have a meaning independent of causal order" – as we may be with every *mythopoios* of the archaic and ancient times to whom all things were full of "spirits". But we have to warn him that he has to be consistent. He is able to describe, in the terminology of his own vision, the determined past. He cannot describe the determination of the future. Why should he feel entitled to use the term "future" at all?

If he says that tomorrow he will buy a book, all he means is that a present – actually already a past – image of his entering a bookshop and asking for a book has met whith the assent of his will. He will have to wait until some new present-past experiences happen, such as waking up in the morning and going down-town, to be able to say that he is "fulfilling a decision". And it may well happen that no such experience will take place. Within the realm of determination, future simply does not exist. If our scientist were to assert that he is going to determine the future through the mere action of his will, it would be equal to the denial of the determined character of the past and of events in general.[8]

To the follower of determinism, the registered experiences are, of course, identical with the tread of the entropy through which the creative energy of the makrokosmos is allegedly being spent. Such is his vision of the completeness of time and of the universe. There is no way out of the blind alley. A scholar who adopts such a vision is hardly allowed to admire a hero or even to devote his attention to any historical personality or to any idea in particular. All is one stream, arriving from a nebulous distance and going – where? Such a scholar also has to regard the evolving universe as a "continuum". This in itself seems a very difficult task. How can a continuous evolution exist at the same time with a number of species? And how can a species exist at the same time with a number of specimens? If there is no change between one species and another, where does the concept "species" take its meaning from? But if there is a change, there cannot be any "continuum". Why not speak rather of an "uninterrupted disappearance"? A Hindu author has recently quoted the words of the *Gospels* about the dead burying their dead and added a quotation from Plutarch: "Dead is the man of yesterday, for he has died into the man of today; and the man of today is dying into the man of tomorrow."[9] There can be hardly a better description of the evolutionary vision. Uninterrupted disappearance...

But is it really necessary to conceive "time" as "passing time" only?

Even while we may readily admit that the vision of time as a "complete entity" attracts us and while we may subscribe to Aristotle's concept of a basic identity between time and the universe, it remains an open question what kind of time should be regarded as the one time which impresses its necessity on the universe. Why should we feel obliged to declare a priori that the registering of our experiences follows the arrow of the irreversible processes? Why not say, rather, that our most current concept of time is established by our mind to serve as a file in which we are able to store our experiences?

Even the behavior of the scientist suggests that this is so. Abstract images such as "continuum", "causality" or "determination" all constitute such registering files. So do the concepts of "irreversibility" or "entropy". Why should "passing time" be treated as an exception?

"Passing time" or "time past" seems indeed to be a registry in which both our experiences and our expectations are put away. Were the concept of passing time anything else but an auxiliary concept, expressions such as "the present" or "at the present time" would sound as impossible as "the quality between dry and humid". In the field of auxiliary concepts, however, anything may have some operational value – even, for intance, the concept of a "negative" subatomic particle travelling backward in time (such a reverse process can be accounted for mathematically by a suitable adjustment of equations).[10] Already a few scientists have appeared who would agree to relegate the concept of the passing time to the realm of psychology – in the sense that the direction of passing time can only be expressed by a correlation of external trajectories with the mind's memory and its projected past-future filing line – and remain satisfied with the concept of "symmetrical time". They are ready, obviously, to use this new concept even while discussing natural radiation or entropy.[11]

In the mind all ideas are indeed "now-ideas", although they are stored in two different files, one for the past, the other for the future. Sometimes the distinction between these two files seems almost obliterated. In the Hindustani vocabulary, for instance, identical expressions are used for "yesterday" or "tomorrow", "the day before yesterday" and "the day after to morrow", and "three days ago" and "in three days from now". Some distinction is perhaps needed between the "order" of these files and the "direction" of the events themselves; we can file Columbus death before his birth, but we remain conscious that it is an unnatural kind of arrangement of moments, similar to a film shown backward. Nevertheless, whatever is, is now.

Parmenides, that sworn enemy of myths interpreted merely as dramas in the passing time, was possibly right when he denied both becoming and passing and stressed the presence of all being. Our knowledge of a historian's testimony about what his sources tell him about Charlemagne is as present as our knowledge of the paper on which these words are being written. A biographer describes that what makes the hero present. He does not "reconstitute" the hero's life. He certainly does not pretend to lay his hands on any "continuity" of time. History is nothing else but human lives. If history can also be called a description of times gone by, no human life is conceived by the historian as a time gone by, but rather as a complete time present before our eyes.

More than that, every historical event or group of events is grasped by us as our own, present experience. "In order to understand the mysterious significance of the past," says Berdyaev, "man has to feel it and the entire history as something which belongs to himself and constitutes a part of his own destiny". Already before Berdyaev the late nineteenth century Russian Alexei A. Kozlov, suggested that God's all-embracing knowledge contemplates the cosmos as timeless and that our consciousness of the passing time is due to the restrictions of our own mind.[12] Realities are revealed to us as observations, perceptions, encounters, testimonies, intuitions, dreams – but always as present realities. Our mind can evidently only scan the horizon of the present time, accepting one or another of its sectors at a time. There is absolutely no reason why we should think that the entire horizon is not present.

There is equally no reason why we should accept the mythical and only partially operational concept of "passing time" as a major force independent from our mind. It is not an arrow of time which, passing through our consciousness, would compel the consciousness to accept its domination. It is, on the contrary, the consciousness itself which, while grasping its own life as a fulfillment and conceiving the meaning of every event and every life as a fulfillment, brings "passing time" into existence in the form of a "unidirectional" file.

Scanning the horizon, a film-camera takes one of its sectors after another. While one of these sectors is being filmed, the other sectors are certainly not absent. Later, when watching the film projected on a screen, we are under the impression that the horizon moves constantly – in the direction opposite to that in which the camera had scanned it. And yet the horizon does not move. It is always there. It is the camera which moves – or, better to say, is being directed – from one of its sectors to another. Something similar may be happening in our mind in relationship to the experiences, both life experiences and historical experiences.

Suppose our entire life is present in front of our mind in the same way in which the entire horizon is present in front of the camera. But let us also suppose that we can only become aware of it through the services of a mental camera plus projector. Is the resulting impression anything else but that of the "passing time"? Is "passing time" anything else but an illusion similar to the illusion of the horizon which seems to be "moving" across the screen?

Suppose the same were true about our view of history – history being located on a horizon more distant than that of our life. What else could be the real, complete character of the story of mankind than something very much like a film ready for projection?

The eye grasps an infinitesimally thin ray of light in one, instantaneous action. If, however, this ray, before it reaches the eye, passes through a prism, the eye needs, if nothing more, a very short time to take in all the individual prismatic colors one after another. And yet there would be no such colors without the ray. Suppose someone would come forward with the assertion that the set of prismatic colors – and not the original ray – is the only "real" thing? Moreover, he would say, there is a "series of continuities" between red a violet, and, to "reach" the violet, one first has to go through the red. In that case, violet would be a sequel – or should we say a "causal result" or an "evolutionary product"? – of indigo, while indigo could be regarded as a "result" or "product" of blue. Are we not behaving in a similar way while dealing with time? Ignoring the creative explosion – the unchangeable meaning of which is accessible to our instantaneous cognition – we concentrate on its "bent parts", the so-called "past" and the so-called "future", both brought into existence through the dispersing arrangement of our mind.

Of course we can go back, from violet to indigo and then to blue, until we reach red again. We "repeat" experiments. Repeat? If, having crossed the town we then walk back and begin to "repeat" the excursion, it is hardly and action identical with our first walk. It may be called "another walk across the town" only because of our inclination to "number" experiences which are similar but never identical. Our mind, it seems, is made of prismatic stuff.

The very idea of creation is behind all this – and has always been, since the first awakening of any human intellect, since the conception of the first myth, the myth about creation.

Creation is not a process. It cannot be a process, because the concept of "process" is a "passing-time" concept and the passing time itself is only a result of creation. Creation is not a movement. Processes and movements are reversible – merely as categories of thought. Creation is not. It is an act. An act cannot be "un-acted", it cannot be reversed because it is acted now and both the past and the future are enclosed within it.

Under the impact of the mythical concepts with which the modern and post-modern physics has been operating we have grown accustomed to treating creative work in a rather negative way. We speak of entropy – that "triumph of death" as Berdyaev called it – meaning a measure of the unavailable energy in the thermodynamic system of the makrokosmos. We stress that this measure in our universe is constantly increasing. And yet we should perhaps concentrate on that which is positive around us. Even physically destructive actions are creative in the sense that they bring about new conditions and new meanings, while of course they also spend some available energy. The entire universe around us speaks constantly of creation.

After all, do we not reflect the character of the creation in our awareness of it? Were our mind capable of seizing the creation in its entirety we would have no need of the concept of "passing time". But such is evidently not our capability.[13] Only some parts of creation are revealed to each among us. Because of that, the concept of "passing time" became indispensable. Again, were the creation a process, we would be able to reverse the order in which we file our observations or even to grasp them without any order at all.

But the act of creation is an act of fulfillment. Hence the irreversibility of "passing time". Creative fulfillment has no opposite. Zero is not the opposite of a number, but merely its absence.

Considering all this we should recognize how inadequate is the concept of a "smoothly, continously flowing time" for the task for which science wants to use it. Would not the concept of a "wave-like passing time" be more truthful and therefore also more operational? Our horizon, as far as it embraces the story of nature, is characterized by various kinds of time-happenings which have hardly anything in common with the concept of a "uniformly passing time": Explosive appearances of structures which had not existed before – such as the first protein molecules, the major groups of living organisms which appear suddenly in the vision of the paleontologist and are almost immediately followed by their main subdivisions, mutations of bacteria whose rate of appearance is not related to the number of generations, or again patterns of sudden variations and then long stabilizations.

But perhaps we should not expect too many clarifications from the majority of scientists. Because of their unwillingness to discern the value of words as symbols of the intellectual, not sensory, penetration of reality they are capable of arguing against Plato that the knowledge of geometrical figures is a mere "recollection of everyday experiences" – as if there was, anywhere in the universe, a real geometrical figure. They describe a head-on collision of two balls moving at an equally rapid rate as an "exchange of momentums" and then again as a "reversal of directions" – without realizing the falsely mythical, even if operational, character of such descriptions. Knowing well that for every whole number there exists a next whole number, but that there is no continuum between them, they would also insist that between every two moments of time there is another moment – simply because they believe in the false myth of "time being equal to a continuum of moments".

Similarly, knowing well that "causality" in nature or in history is not an observational fact, and not even a theory derived from reality by extrapolation but merely an "auxiliary word", they still attempt to prop up "causality" by a wholy false presentation of time. Even when they occasionally admit exceptions – such as the law of large numbers which certainly cannot be explained by the "law of causality" – they still place the coach in front of the horses by insisting that events appear as they do because they are "carried by a continuous time" – instead of admitting the fictitious character of this expression.

"Passing time" is admittedly an operational concept. "The first events of that part of our horizon representing the growth of a plant are separated from ist last event by a long time" is a sentence certainly more workable than would be the sentence "The first event of that part is separated from the last event by two hundred-thirty-seven unreversably ordered glimpses of reality". But this does not mean that "passing time", its irreversibility included, is anything but a symbol for the relation between the registering intelligence and its horizon – a "retarded eternity" as some Ismaelites called it.

We may well include into this part of our meditation a quotation from Augustyn Jakubisiak, an undeservedly silenced thinker of our own century. "The events of this universe should be conceived not as successive and happening one after the other, but as simultaneous, that is as possessing since always the completness they should possess, realizing at the same time all their latent possibilities; if that is not the nature of concrete things, then their fixity, proclaimed by the first principle of logic, remains without reality."[14]

An act is always purposeful. In contrast to an act, a "reaction" seems to convey the meaning of some "passive behaviour". But – leaving aside the rather vague and perhaps falsely mythical meaning of the word "behavior" – is not "reaction" itself a most artificial word? Everything contained in an act has a purpose – a "perfecting virtue", to use a Leibnitzian expression. But the concept of the creative act collides sharply with that of evolution. Many Evolutionists, while regarding "variation" as a truly meaningful factor, also use the adjective "accidental" which implies the participation, in the evolutionary process, of some purposeless elements. In Karl Marx the thinking is reversed: A purposeful production, directed toward consumption, is constantly improved and becomes, together with the implicitly improved consumption, a process which may be named "history" but which has no purpose whatever. It is possible, of course, not only to study, but also to understand Evolutionism from a historical point of view – as a new, not exactly very intersting or bright version of the archetypal myth of creation. "Chaos" has been given the name of "random, accidental happenings", while the Creator received two new names, "Variation" and "Selection". However, no primeval *mythopoios* would have branded God as a "result of the chaos". If some very early myths spoke of the Creator's birth from the chaos, they also regarded this birth as the Creator's own and very creative doing, as a struggle and as the very essence of the creative act in general.

The concept of the the creative act – an act, by the way, which has no duration as even the "passing time" originates from it – implies that all happenings, events, things are meaningful. There are no accidental properties or "random events". No intrusion of grammatical rules into thought is allowed, no paper distinction between "essential" and "accidental" accepted. If the Creator wanted us to see ourselves as zoological sequel to a protein molecule, then even the protein molecule receives a part of its full meaning from the fact that it may precede man on the scale of zoological classification; the appearance of the protein molecule establishes a meaningful element of the historical projection of man's own appearance.

A scientist, while discussing the deposition of human thoughts in the category of flowing time, says: "This fact is expressed in grammar by the rule that every propostition must contain a verb, *i.e.*, a sign indicating the time of the event of which one speaks".[15] Such an assertion, however, may be regarded as little more than a repetition of Aristotle's naive decision to base his various descriptive categories on the grammatical usages of his native language. There exist, in various civilizations and their various phases, various ways of reporting individual experiences or even visions of the universe. It is on the basis of these ways that languages and grammatical rules are construed. It also appears rather futile to try to reverse the process and to derive any generally valid views of reality and of human cognition from the grammatical rules of a particular language.

An American scholar, Benjamin L. Whorf, has devoted much attention to the linguistical usages of the Hopi Indians – a tribe which obviously never possessed any consciousness of time as a flowing continuum.[16] While making it possible to distinguish among momentary, imitated, or repeated occurrences and even to indicate the actual sequence of reported events, the Hopi grammar simply does not distinguish between the present, past, and future of the event itself. These terms are in fact as little translatable into Hopi as are Aristotle's concepts of *hýlē* and *mórfē* into some other Indo-

European languages such as the Slavic idioms where both *hmota* and *tvar* are derived from verbs meaning the same action, namely "to deal with shapes" *(hmásti, tvoryat)*.

Hopi, says Whorf, may be called a timeless language. Its concept of the present psychical time seems somewhat to resemble Bergson's "duration" – "a mode in which life differs from form, and consciousness in toto from the spatial elements of consciousness." It is, however, a most individual and personal concept which "does not permit of simultaneity". Indeed, Hopi expressions referring to time can have no plural. Like in Homer, where *hēmar* was not a day belonging to everyone, but a period of destiny experienced by an individual,[17] the Hopi word for "day" expresses a most individual and singular concept. As far as past is concerned, the basic Hopi view asserts that everything that has ever happened still is. We have here a good example of the so-called "ahistoricity" of the archaic man, to which Mircea Eliade has devoted his attention,[18] and also of the archaic man's refusal to entertain any memory which would be organized in the way to which we are accustomed. A Hopi, thinking of the present time "in a form different from what memory or record reports", anchors his time-thoughts in that which is both perennial and sacred. There is also a verbal form which resembles – but only very distantly – the Indo-European future tense; only it really does not indicate future, but rather the present hope and expectation.

The case of the Hopi language is certainly not an isolated one. The Bantu-Ruanda idiom, for instance, operates with a constant interchangeability of concepts denoting time and place – as if it had expected to be used by Einstein and his disciples.[19] Thought, together with its linguistic expression, always stems from the cosmic view of the peole of the civilization. At times the very brevity of the language may be conductive to an obliteration of the depth of the original cosmic view. The Hopi language was not simple, but rather full of nuances because, evidently, the Hopi cosmic view was full of nuances. At first sight we may be inclined to feel that our language, with its "verb which always denotes time", may reach further. Id probably does not.

Ancient Greek also had more nuances than modern English.[20] There were, in the first place, two concepts referring to the time experiences of man: *kairós* and *chrónos*. Of these, the first seems incomparably more important. *Kairós* may be translated as "this moment of decision" and also as "opportunity" or as "the real time of our consciousness". It denotes a reality which does not cease to be present. *Chrónos*, on the contrary, signifies something very artificial. We may translate it not only as "passing time" but also as "illusory time". Etymologically, the word *chrónos* seems to have been derived from the verb *krainein*, meaning "to finish, to do away with something". In the texts of the Orphic mysteries it was endowed with daemonic significance, as if it were a very negative mythical being.

Next, a most important ancient Greek expression, *arché*, stands before our eyes. It means both the "source" and the "fountainhead" of any kind of time or action. Occasionally it may denote a mythical messenger sent by the Cosmic God to start something. It also meant the "primordial time" *(illud tempus)*, in which the myths describing the creation are anchored and to which the archaic and ancient civilizations were looking as to the "golden time", the time from which man falls into the mere *chrónos*. Anaximander possibly identified it with the "primordial shapelessness" *(to ápeiron)*. Perhaps the most important aspect of *arché* is in that it is never represented as the beginning of a line, but rather by the center of a circle. Conceptually it is closely related to the word *télos* which means not only a closed ring ("ring of time", in the sense of the Latin words *annus* and *annulus*), but also the "source and end". It is the very center of the completeness of time. "It is evident", says Aristotle, "that the very old traditions are true, according to which something immortal and divine exists among the things in motion – but in a motion to which there is no limit; rather this motion embraces all the other motions – for a limit is something which embraces, and this motion, being perfect, embraces those imperfect motions which have a limit and a goal; because it has no beginning and no end, and because it does not end in any finite time, it is the source of other movements and again their goal."[21]

There is a perfect agreement between this remembrance of the primeval myths, indeed unusual in Aristotle, and two other Greek words: *aión*, the "entire, closed time", and *plérōma*, the "fullness of time". If *arché* is the source of all the *kairói* – which graphically may be described as located on the circumference of the circle of which *arché* is the center – both *aión* and *plérōma* may be described as their sum. It is of utmost importance to understand that *arché* is the center and not perhaps an initial – always only a provisory initial – point, beyond which we are unable to reach.

All these ancient Greek words help us to penetrate the nuances of the archaic astonishment at the universe – astonishment and also a disinterested, sacred curiosity. The ancient Greeks themselves, of course, seem to have understood less and less their own archaic wisdom. In the course of time Heraclitus' adherence to the wisdom which can only be expressed by mythological contradictions – such as, in post-modern physics, the wave and the particle nomenclatures – was replaced by Parmenides' refusal to tolerate any symbolical contradiction. Instead of sacred curiosity, mere verbal philosophy came to the foreground of the cultural stage, conceived, in Epicurus' words, as a "practical activity intended to secure a happy life". Some of the philosophers then indeed behaved like the Titans in the mythical battle between the good angels *(theói, elohim)* and the bad angels *(titans)*; they tried, as Plato states in his *Sophistes*, "to drag everything down to earth out of heaven and the unseen..."

Nevertheless, even philosophy was hardly able to obliterate the deep truthfulness of the archaic expressions. After all, the Greek language was not the only one which testified to the need of distinguishing between the various kinds of time. In the Sanskrit of the *Upanishads* and the other ancient Aryan texts, *kāla* was the equivalent of the Greek *kairós*, and *māyā* that of *chrónos*, the "passing time". Beside that, the word *sthita* seems to have been used to denote the meaning of the Greek *plérōma*, the fullness of time in which every object or event has its perennial value.[22] In Hebrew the same concept of completeness and fullness of time was expressed by the word *ôlam*, while the expression *toledhoth* denoted the traditional, historical experiences, registered along the line of "passing time".[23] In the vocabulary of another Semitic language, the Arabic, *ān* (plural *ānāt*) had the significance of *kairós*, the individual moment of decision, while *zamān* meant the illusory passing time and *dahr* was the equivalent of the Greek *arché* in the sense of the perrennial fountainhead of all happenings. Again, in the Iranian, Pahlavi, nomenclature, *mēnōk* meant *arché*, while *gētīk* denoted the created happenings which our mind is registering.[24]

All these vocabularies – more are available in various other archaic and ancient civilizations – lead us to a vision of the universe, the very basis of which is the unlimited, spheric projection of reality, the reality of light, against the darkness of Anaximander's *ápeiron*.[25] As an immensely thin ray of light may be decomposed by a prism into innumerable nuances of color which are extended in space, so the reality of creation is seen through the prism of man's cognition as consiting of innumerable moments. And only one or another nuance may be fully taken in by our mind at a certain moment.

Plato's parable about the persons seated with their backs to the fire and seeing the shadows of things projected on the wall before them is a very valid parable derived from this primordial vision. The wall is the wall of the "passing time". It is the curtain of mystery *(enigma)* of which the apostle Paul speaks. Looking to his left or to his right, into the "past" or into the "future" man may see events in different perspectives. Even Aristotle, who frequently couched his thoughts in terms which could be easily used by interpreters prone to "determinist" explanations, described the passing time as "a number of movements toward the earlier and the later",[26] *i.e.*, as different concentrations of the mind on the partial objects of our cognition. Through these partial cognitions we become aware, to a certain degree, of the complete universe – Plato's *kósmos noētós*, in which "the same thing cannot be asserted and not be asserted with equal truthfulness."

Time and the Unity of the Person

> Time past and time future
> Allow but a little consciousness.
> To be conscious is not to be in time...
> T. S. Eliot, *Four Quartets*

> Is not the cross the symbol of space? And
> so is time. This is why unity in space is
> a great consolation.
> Simone Weil, *Cahiers*

> If God is outside time, is it so certain that
> we know which moments of time count with him?
> Charles Williams, *The House of the Octopus*

The Christian message, its concepts as well as its symbols, remained deeply rooted in the Semitic, Hebraic mythical traditions. "God created man from the dust and breathed into his nostrils the breath of life; and man became a living soul."[1] There is not a word in this text about any "insertion" of a special entity called nowadays "soul". Man simply becomes a living soul. No matter how multivalent might have been the Hebrew words *nepes* and *chayyā* (one could also translate them as "experiencing life" or "living experience"), the fact remains that not a word was said in the *Genesis* about any arrival of a new, independent entity into the body – a body represented as another independent entity. In the *Gospels*, *psýchē* meant the life which a good shepherd sacrifices for his sheep, while "heart" *(kardía)* was used as symbol of the intellectual will; "blood" was the most frequent symbol of what we usually call life. "Whoever eats my dying life of man and drinks my resurrection" – such is perhaps the most thorough translation of Jesus' memorable words. As late as the seventh century after Christ, the same Semitic tradition, using "blood" as the symbol of life, was still vigorous in Muhammad's *Qu'rān:*

> Sing a praise to the name of Lord Creator
> who brought about man from clothed blood...[2]

In the meantime apostle Paul, a true Hebrew in spite of all his Hellenistic erudition, had written about the resurrection of the dead. He recalled the just mentioned text of the Genesis ("the first man was born into a living soul") and reminded the faithful in the city of Corinth that while a "psychical body" is buried, a "spiritualized body" rises from the dead.[3]

The two Greek words, *psýchē* and *pnẽuma*, which the apostle used while writing to the Corinthians, came from a vocabulary stemming from an almost primeval mythical imagery. To Homer, a poet standing in the very gateway of the Greek culture, *psýchē* seems to have been no more than the last breath of the dying man and consequently also a symbol of the fulfillment of his life – but certainly not anything imprisoned in the body.[4] But Democritus, an older contemporary of Plato, did not hesitate to draw a dividing line between the "soul" and the "body". It may well be that this usage of the word *pneuma* – in the sense of something divine inherent in man – found later its ultimate application in the Stoic conception of the sparks of the Divine Intelligence manifested in man. A similar view ran also through the doctrines accompanying the Orphic mysteries.[5] However, it is mainly to the Sanskrit Aryan literature and to Plato that we have to turn for a complete and consistent symbolism of the soul as an immortal entity, imprisoned temporarily in a mortal body. As much as man is imprisoned in the escaping time *(chrónos)* and as much as the bodily existence itself actually forms an aspect of the escaping time, the "soul" is declared ready "to flow out of the sorrowful, weary circle" as from a prison or even from underneath a tombstone. Amply developed mainly in Plato's dialogue *Cratylus*, this vision soon began to exercise a strong attraction on Christians. It is probable that, mainly in Alexandria, the ancient Egyptian concept of *ka* – expressing the intellectual as well as parapsychical properties of man, but never an entity which could be completely separated from the body – also had an impact on Christian thought. The Platonic vision took a deep root which grew stronger and stronger during the course of centuries. Confronted with the sad, disconcerting spectacle of the cold body of the deceased, the Baroque poet Milton was later to speak even of a "living soul bound to a dead body". Unable, in so many cases, to grasp the coincidence of all the earthly moments in God, even learned Christians gradually forgot that Jesus, while dying on the cross, had promised to the repentent thief that he would see him again in his own kingdom no later than that very same day.

Even among the Eastern Christians there appeared scholars such as Gemistos Pléthōn, an early fifteenth-century renovator of ancient Greek lore, who simply declared the "immortality of soul" to be a "doctrine known to the entire humanity".[6] But above all in the West, while admittedly no one went as far as to imitate the Hindu preaching of the purifying migration of souls, a doctrine began to take root, in which "purgatory" was conceived as a dwelling place where the souls, having left the dying bodies, were expecting, no one knew for how long, the day of the Final Judgement.

One would, undoubtedly, find many ancient myths describing abodes of the deceased. But nowhere, not even in ancient Egypt, did one think of a separation of any "souls" from their bodies; the little likenesses of the deceased which we see on the Egyptian paintings represented the deceased themselves – of small statures in comparison to the symbolically large figures of the "other world". In the Western part of the medieval Christian orbit nevertheless, the "separation" became quite pronounced. Only a great Spanish painter of Cretan origin, El Greco, showed the courage of following literally the poetical words of a contemporary mystic and leaving only a bunch of lilies *(azuceñas)* where, in those days, one would have expected to find the senseless body deserted by the departing soul. One seemed no longer to remember that God was the God of the living, not of the dead.[7]

Was the Platonic myth of the soul-bird escaping from the body-cage in any way mitigated by the Aristotelian doctrine of matter and form? Aristotle's teaching lacked the appealing, persuasive force of the Platonic parable. Thomas Aquinas, for instance, would pretend adhering to Aristotle, but only to follow Plato in the affirmation that the soul did not need the body, since it could and did exist through itself, if not by itself. He devoted a whole article of his *Summa Theologica* to the solution of the "problem" concerning the kind of knowledge the "separated soul" possesses.

Generally speaking, the West has shown a regrettable lack of clarity and even more a regrettable lack of faithfulness to the original Christian message in this respect. As late as AD 498 we still hear a pope, Anastasius II, preaching the true Christian kerygma: He spoke about the "spirit of the life-giving soul", *i.e.*, about something symbolizing the entire man's life. In his sixth-century treatise *De Trinitate*, Boethius still stressed that "the earthly man... consists of soul and body... not soul or body separately." Then Aristotelianism set in and, later, the Humanist combination of Plato and Aristotle. In 1950, another pope, Pius XII, readily admitted the division of man into a body originating out of pre-existing matter and a soul immediately created by God.[8] The only two more recent statements of Western theologians known to the present author as still adhering to the traditional Christian doctrine are the famous statement of Dietrich Bonhoeffer – that the "human being (*i.e.*, the being of the entire man) can be only discussed in reference to knowing" – and the blunt profession of faith of a Spaniard, José F. Ocampo, that "the soul has no nature, spiritual or otherwise; the whole man is an intellectual being, created especially by God."[9]

Indeed, according to the original Christian persuasion, the whole man was created by God. It does not matter much in what genetical connection with what animal or with the help of what kind of radiation-provoked mutation. The whole man, not just some "soul", has been promised resurrection by Jesus Christ. This whole man, however, interest us as someone who lives in the passing time.

If we are permitted to turn once again to the Greek vocabulary – regretting the clumsiness of our modern nomenclature – we may state that man lives in a number of those instances which the ancient Greeks called "moments of decision" *(kairói)*. Looking back into our own past we recall the evening when our mother, returning from town, surprised us with the gift of a toy; then the day when we were punished in school; then the hot summer afternoon when the smell of hay reached us through a window full of sun... So it goes on; always only joyful or sad moments, never any "continuity". There is no "continuity" between any of these moments of real life simply because there is no "continuity" anywhere in this world – with the exception of the geometrician's vocabulary or the biologists's jargon concerning some recurrent patterns produced by the DNA, where in each case the fictitious "continuity" is needed as an operative myth. After all, in Latin – if we resort to another piece of linguistic antiquarianism – *continuus* means "held together" *(con-tenere)*, not "connected". Each thing, *cosa, chose,* has something to do with a "casus" – a falling into a given chronological and spatial situation. A similar and equally significant etymology surrounds the concept of "existence". *Exsistere* means to stand up, to appear suddenly. In both cases we are reminded that it is a situation of an infinitesimal brevity which we are recognizing, certainly not anything of a "continuous" duration – even if the word with the help of which we register our observation may have for us a "permanent" validity. And so it is also with each particular *kairós* of our human life. When Parmenides asserted that any earthly being "maintains" itself, he allowed himself to be taken in, quite in accordance with the general Greek propensity, by his own vocabulary.

In the fourth book of his *Physics* Aristotle made a statement which clearly betrayed the difficulty he must have experienced with the verb "to be". "Whatever is composed of not being," he said, "seems unable to participate in being". Were we to apply this principle to the human person, where would we end? The person stands quite evidently, at any given moment, under the impact of situations which no longer exist but have left a deep trace in the mind, of expectations and fears which will perhaps never be fulfilled. Right now and at any time we are more "that which we are not" than "that which we are".

Only statistical regularity, not any kind of continuity, rules man's bodily organs. Man is cast into situations full of numerically expressible values. When he sees them being "repeated" with some regularity he feels inclined to call them "identical" or even "necessary" – but even these are only operational concepts. The time in which they happen seems to him practically identical with his own experience. It may seem idle to speak about its acceptance or rejection by man. But even so, while seemingly identical with our entire lives, the time which we experience has no continuity. Space and time, as each of us experiences them, are no entities independent of relations with ourselves – as so many, including Giordano Bruno and Isaac Newton, believed. Even our senses perceive different kinds of them. We have to regard the concepts which we employ as simplifying conventions.

But where then do we find the unity of man as a person? Miguel de Unamuno used to address this question to Sigmund Freud – in vain because, to the founder of psychoanalysis, all personal manifestations remained identical with the impersonal fulfillment of a stream of the least personal of all instincts.

We have grown accustomed to the arrow of passing time so much that it seems necessary to us to search for the unity of each of our individual persons in a sector of that same time. Not only the false myth of continuity, but also the imaginary points of birth and death seem, at first sight, helpful. But soon we find it even less easy to operate with them than with the imaginary continuity.

Not so long ago a congress was convened in a European capital to discuss the significance of the surgical transplantation of organs. From the first day, the participating doctors, jurists, philosophers, psychologists and theologians experienced immense difficulties in reaching a generally acceptable and sufficiently truthful vocabulary. The jurists turned to the medical experts with the suggestion that death should be defined with the greatest possible precision. But the doctors seemed already bewitched by the concept of an "artificially avoided death". They discussed pauses in respiration, diminishing of arterial tension, abolition of reflexes, even lesions suffered by the nervous system. In each one of these cases they felt obliged to state that they had at their disposal some means of recuperation. Even as far as the nervous system was concerned, while some lesions were still branded as irreparable, ways seemed already open to making them reparable in perhaps not so distant a future.

When the tide of talk reached the seats of the philosophers, one dropped biological data as well as juridical definitions. The discussion turned in the direction of the "human person". To anyone interested in the unity of man, however, this development looked as a *petitio principii*. To declare that man is a complete unit because he is a person, sounds like calling a geometrical body quadrilateral because it is a quadrangle. Above all the common-sense application of the term "person" may seem, at times, less real than Newton's "energy", Bergson's *élan vital*, or the post-modern physicists's "corpuscles" and "waves". Having met Peter I can declare him a nice person. But with such a declaration I still remain as far from the full meaning of the man Peter as from the planet Uranus or even farther. The medical man will not help me much. He knows that some of the cells in Peter's body have started dying the moment Peter was born. Moreover, having transplanted a few of Peter's organs to John's body he may be left wondering as to whom he should call Peter and whom John – or, at least, where may be the frontiers between Peter and John as biological entities. The biologist may become even vaguer in his talk: He may start speaking about the genes which had lived before Peter's conception or about the cells which will continue living after his funeral. Indeed, death actually assumes the appearance of numberless degrees of a descent – to where? Some contemporary thinkers seem to be almost as much possessed by the "terminal" quality of death as their medieval predecessors used to be by the "ultimate disposition of man's will". Sartre, for instance, speaks frequently of a "terme ultime".

Some time ago many psychologists might have been led by the Aristotelian concept of *anagnórēsis* to make an attempt to help us by pointing to the significance of memory. Today they would probably no longer consider such an attempt. There is hardly a more fluctuating entity in this world than man's memory, with all its sudden jumps, its hidden, subconscious recesses and its too easy readiness to give way to imagination. Some contemporary experts would probably stick to Freud's restrictive views, declaring that they could only "infer or rather guess how the mental apparatus is constructed and what forces (that mystical word again...) interplay and counteract in it." Some would go a step further and speak of "consciousness". Accepting, however, the description of consciousness as a sum of inherited instincts and accumulated experiences, they are still left one important step short of grasping a person as the being who represents its own particular concepts and keeps asking its own questions.

But perhaps there is a psychological way of clarifying this. "Self-actualization" was, as is well known, C. G. Jung's brief term for the most salient feature of the human person. We may or may not accept his insistence on the role of the "collective unconscious" which Unamuno used to call "intrahistory". But his basic assertion that "the person lives by aims as well as by causes" and therefore overflows with conflicts and tensions, points clearly to the person's life as a kind of drama. Other prominent psychologists of our days, observing the unique complexity of human behavior, reached a similarly comprehensive understanding of the dramatic nature of man's person. Even the mathematician Ferdinand Gonseth certainly showed a deep perspicacity in describing the passing time of man's experience as an essential condition for the integration of the person into this world. Let us also mention two of the outstanding scholars who worked recently in the United States: Alfred Adler spoke of the "creative self" as a central element in the mental apparatus which, of course, receives experiences from inherited features as well as from apperceptions; Gordon Allport, who also coined the expression "functional autonomy", underlined repeatedly the unique and dynamic character of every human individual. Even closer to the concept of the human time as a projection of observations along the past-future line stand the investigations conducted by Decroly who correlates the growth of temporal conceptions with the child's use of language and observes a gradual extension of temporal notions in the direction of both the past and the future.

Perhaps even more than to Decroly we owe our knowledge concerning the emergence of the flowing-time concepts to Jean Piaget and his investigations of time as a "coordination of motions of different velocities – motions of external objects in the case of physical time, and of the subject in the case of psychical time". Any student of the Christian message – which has always predicated God's creative act as an unrestricted movement, in constrast to the restricted movements of all what is created – can with little effort understand Piaget's interpretation of our "power of coherent recall" as "due not simply to the registration of successive perceptions" but rather as a basic kinetic interpretation of the escaping time-experience as a whole. Studying the concepts of time as they emerge in the child's experience in a way parallel to the increasing coordination of motions, from a vague intuition which can never embrace more than a single situation at a time, to reversible operations (described as tantamount to transcending space by a mobile effort and thus "freing oneself from the present"), Piaget realizes how much the concept of flowing time is involved with that of a "causal stream". He accepts this stream as the structure of our life-story or of history in general only to the extent to which it is constantly constructed and reconstructed. He is able to describe the habitual expression of "causality" by "duration" because he observes how the juvenile mind-forms reach the operational concept of "duration" in an effort to express the qualitative or quantitative ratio of distance to velocity. He admits that the "stream of time" is a construction of a special operational value; but he also reminds us that it is only a system of qualitative colligations which also, among other things, requires frequent "partitions of durations". And he very correctly shows that no sector of the "stream" should be interpreted as a mere "point on a line", but always rather as a complex situation resulting from the intermingling of a great many diverse factors.[10]

Most of all, perhaps, it was the Russians who contributed to the return to a sensible and Christian tradition – at a time, oddly enough, when some

Western Christians were engaged in spreading false late-ancient myths. The Russian scholars rarely had anything to do with the dove-in-the-cage concept of "soul" and "body". They took man as he was. Long before 1917 Ivan P. Pavlov described, as realistically as was feasible, the close interaction between the first and the second "signal systems" as a "distinctive feature of man's higher nervous activity", *i.e.*, of that what makes man essentially different from the animals. The Russian psychologists of our own generation, above all Lyov S. Vygotskij and A. R. Luria, concentrated on the unity of thought and speech. Words were described by them as external manifestations of an exclusively human activity in which not only apperceptions but also the understanding of apperceptions participate. All systems of connections, beginning with the elementary and visual and ending with the abstract ones, are preserved by the speech. The unity of man is even underlined by the insistence that words should be described as carrying out thoughts rather than expressing them.[11]

The dramatic character of the human person, as it emerges from these investigations, is well carried out by the word "person" itself. Stamming from the same root as the Greek *prósōpon*, the Latin word *persona* meant originally a role to act, a task to fulfill, a mask to wear.

Here again we approach the core of the mystery of time. The role played by a man during his lifetime may consist of many thousands of moments of decision *(kairói)* through which the experience of an octogenarian has passed, or again only of an infinitesimaly thin ray of understanding which penetrates the dense veil surrounding a sick or a feeble mind. To speak of the "duration" of man's life – measured by comparison to some stellar movements – does not seem to have much sense. An actor may be 23 or 147 minutes on the scene – but do these numbers matter? Above all the significance, the meaning of his part have little to do with the so-called "duration" or "continuity".

All this has also to be considered when speaking of the knowledge attained by a person. Vain scholastic treatises have certainly condemned men to mere robots when they described a concept as a mere sum of a certain number of perceptions *(nihil est in intellectu quod prius non fuerit in sensu)*. The discovery of a genial view, even the solution of a very ordinary problem always descend into the life of man like lightning. Sometimes they may be preceded by twenty years, sometimes only by half a second of apperceptive concentration – sometimes by no such concentration at all.

Returning, for a moment, to Pavlov's "second signal system", we shall experience little difficulty in comparing it to Plato's *noũs chōristós* or the mind which, according to Augustine, "gathers the knowledge of meanings through itself".[12] The Greek *noũs* signified man's capability to grasp the meaning of things. In the later Stoic thought we may find a definite identification of the *noũs* with the *phýsis* in the sense of man's true nature.[13] In every single moment our *knowing* is aware of the flux of events around us, of the constantly escaping time *(chrónos)*. As we have only words to carry out whatever meaning we recognize, the tendency appears to condense, to abbreviate. Hence, above all, the ever increasing importance of mathematics in our knowledge concerning the universe.

Still another obstacle, heaped in our way by some Western thinkers for centuries, should be mentioned at this juncture. Probably since the early tenth-century days of the Jewish-Arabic scholar Isaac Israeli, the phrase *adequatio rei et intellectus* has dominated the thought of many West European teachers and students. This so-called "balance between the thing and the mind" seems to be a very dead balance indeed. It is dead because the "thing" is dead. A "thing" can never be isolated from the living universe around us – a very different universe at every single moment. Fishermen have always known that a fish, once taken from the river, dies. Painters had desperately felt the "inadequacy" of their colors as compared with the colors which they saw or imagined. Eventually even physicists, through Heisenberg's principle of indeterminacy, recognized that they cannot seize both the velocity and the situation of a subatomic "particle". It may not be out of place to notice that many physicists of the Heisenberg school associated themselves with the "idealist" and "phenomenologist" thinkers to whom the quest for the person's role in the world has appeared as a quest for the world's role in the person. But while such thinkers have only turned the mirror upside down, philosophers of sorts would still discuss "adequation", that terribly dead relationship. Why not turn rather to Dante's description of love as the "union of the mind with the object loved"? Why not accept the "intentional creativity" as the most salient characteristic of man?

The "creative self" described by the psychologists, man's eminently dramatic character, the fascination a scientist feels in his attitude to the object he investigates, the tantalizing preoccupation of the artist with his task – all that would be much better carried out by Dante's words. The so-called "reason", a preoccupation with judgements whose third, "conclusive" lines never reach beyond the meaningfulness of the two or more premises, is clearly something very secondary. Even the extremely condensed, but certainly operative nomenclature of the mathematician – which Pythagoras made the backbone of his *theoria* and which has come to dominate our technology – deserves only a secondary place. Creative love remains the most obvious aspect of man's life.

The arrow of the passing time may keep flying. Some parts of our consciousness are still aware of it, even if only automatically. Some subconscious elements, perhaps rooted in the nucleic acids of our cells, may have existed since the beginning of the universe and contributed decisively to the character of each of our persons. Some subatomic charges may "see the end of the flowing time". But the moment we turn our attention to anything dear to our heart, whether it be a person, an animal, or a tree, a scenery or a scientific object, the passing, escaping time recedes into the background. Our consciousness is united with the object of our love – and, oddly enough, only thus becomes truly itself, truly human. Anguish and doubts, worries and even fear may set in again. But, "at times", we are capable of escaping them.

A film-projector whose engine has stopped remains centered on only one, extremely restricted aspect of the scenery which had been filmed. Even while the film is in motion, an identical description is valid in relation to each particular split of a second. Our *knowing*, simply described, is something very similar. There can be hardly any talk of adequation. Any act of recognition is merely a loving attempt – *epistémé*, insisting – to seize an infinitesimal portion of reality. The projector moves to the next picture and then to a third one. It will never encompass the entire film – not to mention the infinite number of films which, all concerned with the same landscape, may be made from innumerable different points and distances and at equally innumerable times.

But if each of the pictures included in the film and each of the innumerable different films are able to contribute a little to a comprehensive vision of the landscape in question, how much more, ineffably more comprehensive must be the entire vision *(idea, eĩdos)* of that landscape... Our terrestrial eyes will never embrace it. Our mind can only project, verbally carry out an extremely vague concept of it. The contrast between the segmentary apperception and the creative, projective activity of the mind's "second signal" function leads us again to a comparison between the thesis of the Russian psychologists, so close to the Judaic-Christian concept of the unique nature of man, and the crude philosophy built on the Western scholastic assertion that our intellect understands things by "abstracting" them from apperceptions. "Man was born to act, not to speculate". This well known and truthful tenet of Friedrich Schelling – evident to anyone who considers the life of man as it is – has been, time and again, ignored by those who also seem to have forgotten that meanings are here for the sake of life and not vice versa. Aristotle and those who followed him slavishly – calling him "the Philosopher" – insisted that "being", not life, should be regarded as the basic object of knowledge. Berkeley, eventually, and some nineteenth century Positivists brought it as far as to equal "to be" with "to be perceived". Some others wasted their time with nonsensical questions such as whether the world we know "is" "outside" or "inside" our thoughts. What a stream of "flatus vocis", meaningless sounds...

The real living man reaches eagerly beyond the fragments of knowledge which his restricted words can carry out. He knows that they remain incomplete. He reaches out without necessarily employing any "abstraction". Rather he does so by patiently building and rebuilding his imagination. With all the assuredness available to him he becomes aware, for instance, of the possibility of such a vision of the landscape he has been trying to paint that would embrace it in all the different moments of the passing time, in all kinds of light and shadows, in all the different moods. The possibility of such a comprehensive vision or idea is accepted even by Aristotle when he admits that man's intellect deals with such visions, while the individual apperceptions accept only isolated aspects of things.[14] Several of Plato's dialogues, of course, were devoted not only to the comprehensive ideas, but also to the contemplation of a cumulative idea, embracing all possible ideas – the truly complete and perfect idea. Even some very modern scholars have shown that they understood; commenting on Picasso's painting of a violin, a contemporary American essayist remarks: "It contains all the angles, all the impressions, all the possible views of a violin brought to life at a single instant on the canvas."[15]

It is only to be deeply regretted that many Christians remained unreceptive to this wisdom so thoroughly compatible with the Judaic-Christian tradition. We read, for instance, in Thomas Aquinas – who in this case follows Tertullian – the naive assertion that Plato "maintained that, besides things corporeal, there is another genus of beings... which beings he called ideas... by participation of which each one of the singular things is said to be either a man, or a horse, or the like..."[16] Had this medieval teacher ever read the hymn on Wisdom, which "the Lord possessed in the center of his ways, before he made anything beginning from that center", and which "was set up from eternity and of old before the earth was made..."?

"When he prepared the heavens", continues this hymn, "I was present. When with a certain law and compass he enclosed the depths; when he established the sky above and poised the fountains of waters; when he encompassed the sea with its bounds and set a law to the waters that they should not pass their limits; when he balanced the foundations of the earth: I was with him forming all things, and was delighted every day, playing before him at all times, playing in the world; and my delights were to be with the children of men."[17]

The last of the verses just quoted is perhaps of essential importance. "My delights were to be with the children of men..." The ancient Hebrews believed that Shekinah, the Wisdom of the Creator, was symbolized by a column of Light. It was through the Shekinah that man was made "to the Creator's image", that he was made man and not a mere animal. Plato in *Philebus* speaks similarly: the eternal, *i.e.*, all times embracing Mind *(noũs)* is the source of man's capacity to understand.[18] The main objective of *Phaedo* seems to be to show that comprehensive visions *(chōristà éidē)* are the ultimate goals of each of the dynamic, knowing acts of man.

It is a puzzling, perplexing question: Why have these noble truths been not only grievously misunderstood, but also eagerly opposed? Why actually has Aristotle, experiencing constantly – as we all do – the passing time, attempted to think of his own life not in the terms of life but in those of the merely auxiliary verb "to be"?[19] It could hardly lead anywhere... The first half of René Descartes' famous locution, "I think therefore I am" might be regarded as an involuntarily courageous statement of faith – although Descartes himself thought it something self-evident. There is nowhere any mathematical nor any other definition of "I". It certainly requires some faith to believe in it... But the second half of the locution remains meaningless. Had Descartes said "I am alive", "I am on the staircase", or "I am a mathematician", he would have said something meaningful. However, "I am" is as much an unifinished pronouncement as "I have" – a mere combination of a pronoun with an auxiliary verb, which has nothing to declare (as, *e.g.*, "I have a pencil" would be able to do).

Other useless word-games are known to us. Beginning with Aristotle again, some authors ascribed magical properties to the difference between nouns and adjectives in the Indo-European grammar. Many medieval books as well as the nineteenth century works overflow with this black magic: they operate with "accidentals" as opposed to "essentials", with "determined results" as opposed to "chance results", and more of similar hocuspocus. We would also find in such books classifications of words ("categories") according to whether they belong to questions such as "when?", "how?", etc. All such games seem to be supported by a rather dubious expectation: That words would carry out thoughts through their own virtue, just by being words.

"Dubious", of course, is used here in the sense of something which, at times, may have positive results. Mathematical expressions can reach far on their own. The most rudimentary mathematics is provided with this capability. Instead of naming several objects, events or processes – which are never identical, but always only similar – one simply says "three" or "fifteen". Instead of describing again and again triangular forms, one projects the concept of a "triangle" – covering thus a certain distance in the direction of one of Plato's "ideas". We are here, however, mainly interested in the game with the auxiliary verb "to be". Perhaps the real intention behind it was to avoid the tyranny of the passing time. Let us ignore Paul's dying cells – or his thriving cancerous cells, for that matter – and let us declare simply that Paul "is" Paul. Not even the fastest running clock can change what we have just declared. Or can it? Everything around us lives. Each one of us lives. Even Paul lives. The moment we utter pronouncement the anguish brought by the arrow of the passing time is upon us.

And then, under the impact of that anguish, we may ask: from where to where? Where does Paul begin and where will he end?

But is it a sensible question at all? It has much to do with the person of man. Being used to measure his activities by hours, days and years, we naturally feel inclined to evaluate his life in such a way also. However, as has been mentioned, memory seems to resist the effort. It presents the mosaic of life in a very different way – as consisting of rather loose, colorful or shaded moment-stones which do not have any dimensions. Moreover – if we may be allowed to use the symbol of a mosaic for a while longer – there does not seem to be, ordinarily, anything of unusual interest where the picture bursts from the frame or again where it plunges beneath it. It is, usually, the entire picture or some central part of it which attracts most of our attention. While looking at a painting we do not ask: From where to where?, but rather: What impression does it all make on us? It seems, indeed, unjust to deal with a person as if one was dealing with a dimension of space to be covered by a number of chronological units.

The concept of "final, ultimate achievement" has also introduced itself with some vigor into the vocabulary which we use when discussing a person. It had not always been there. In the hero-myths handed down to us in fairy-tales the culminating action invariably takes place somewhere around the middle of the chronological dimension or even earlier. The rest of that dimmension is then summed up in the well known phrase "they lived happily ever after". But such myths used to be popular only in the distant days when it did not matter, as yet, to a Chicagoan whether he would die of heart-attack as a company's president or as a mere vice-president, and before Muscovites were dying unhappily because they had not been able to exchange their candidacy for the Supreme Soviet for a full membership in it.

Perhaps we have all become victims of some Evolutionist mannerisms. The "fulfillment" of a species may possibly be seen in the oblique light of its partial survival – *i.e.*, in the survival of some of its fitter specimens in the form of a new mutation. Or have we accepted, subconsciously, the persuasion proclaimed by both the Freudian psychology and the existentialist philosophy: That the goal of man's life is man's death?

This, at least, would give us an answer to the question: To where?, provided that the problem of the survival of our cells and of the "corpuscles" within their atoms as well as the problem of surgical transplantations could be bypassed in silence. As to the other question: From where?, the enormous new literature on genetics would have to be considered. Today, we would be probably spared the trouble the scholastics used to have while trying to solve the problem whether the twins originally, before the division of a single fertilized ovum, had one or two "souls". But we would still be in danger of perishing under mountains of chromosomes and genes in a vain attempt to find out "when" does a person really begin.

Perhaps one should not talk lightly about the deep ties which connect each man with "past" and "future" generations. More attention will be given to this topic in a subsequent essay. Nevertheless, the fulfillment of a personal life would never be clearly and sufficiently grasped, if we were to restrict ourselves to methods prescribed by the Evolutionists. Achilles would never catch up with the tortoise if we were to discuss their contest only in terms of units and half-units of one and the same system. But we know – and again with all the assuredness available to us – that Achilles will overtake the tortoise; we can even carry out this persuasion through symbols such as "velocity A" and "velocity B", arranged within the system of "time axis" and "distance axis".

Attending the production of a drama we know – and so did the Athenians attending plays be Aeschylus, Sophocles or Euripides – that even the essence of a tragedy should not be seen in its final outcome but rather in its culminating moments of decision *(kairói)*, in the loving or selfish struggle of the *dramatis personae*. C. G. Jung, too, when coming forward with the symbol of the *mandala* circle, stressed the completeness of a person's life (while considering also the balance between its intellectual consciousness and the subconscious). A circle has no end and its most important point is its center.

Let us reverse the view which we were discussing in a preceding paragraph: The artist's eagerness to grasp all the variations and moods of a certain object – Monet's repeated attempts, for instance, to portray the cathedral in Rouen or Rembrandt's tireless preoccupation with the numerous, but always live aspects of his own face. Let us reverse man's projection toward the Wisdom which contains all the ideas. How does a man's life look from beyond the sphere of the passing time? It must be all present – as the film whose one tiny sector we see for a split second on the screen is also all made. The personal life's fulfillment has hardly anything to with its "first" or "last" moments; even from the biologist's point of view, after all, no such moments exist – or, rather, they have to be indentified with the first and the last moments of the entire universe. But a man's life is entirely present in the Creator's Wisdom, the *Shekinah* – in a way similar to that in which something we love is present, partially at least, in our mind. It is present there now – not as any "continuity" (even less as a "continuous stream", a combination of two words loaded with contradiction), but as a complete idea.

When Berdyaev wrote the obituary of Lyov Shestov he recalled how Shestov had tortured himself with the impossibility to "unlive" whatever had been lived through and to undo whatever had been done. Shestov was – at times, at least – onesidedly interested in the historical past. But so many of us have often turned to their own past lives with a similar query and complaint. Also with doubts: What were our real intentions when we were doing this or that? How did we look to a bystander? Would we now be able to recognize ourselves in that particular moment?

The quotation from Julien Green's *Diary* which precedes the preface of this book – "We never are, we continuously become" – sums up the painful meaning of all these questions. Where is the result of our becoming? The moments of decision which together form our person and which our memory seems so reluctant to dig up – should we regard them as mostly lost? It would mean, more or less, that in our agony, in which all the preceding years seem to disappear if we look at it from outside, the life's fulfillment would equal a zero.

The agony... Who knows anything about it? Certainly not men who have been declared dead (according to one biological standard, but not according to some other such standards) and then brought to life again, *e.g.*, through the massage of the heart. What is agony like to someone who is not going to be brought back into this passing time? Does it resemble that "sepulchral vault of mirrors" of which Vyacheslav Ivanov spoke when discussing Dostoyevskij?[20] Is it as close to dreams as not only the author of *Hamlet* but also some modern scientists such as Wilder Penfield have believed? Does it bring a revived vision of all our moments of decision? The British novelist Charles Williams in his *All Hallows Eve* drew a sophisticated and yet beautiful picture of what may well be agony's real relationship to time – he seems inclined to identify it with "purgatory". His friend and companion in thought, C. S. Lewis, built the fascinating narration of *The Great Divorce* on the identity of all historical moments; he also said of Christ's descent into the timeless and dimensionless entity which is both Hell and Purgatory that "all moments that have been or shall be were or are present in the moment of his descending".

Presented as a place – not as a state – the image of purgatory is not very acceptable to a Christian. It arose, as such, within the Western Church, from the late-ancient parable centered around the dove-in-the-cage image of man's "soul". However, all the ancient traditions as well as the Christian tradition (which uses here the term *hádēs* in sharp contrast with the term *geénna*) seem to recognize that some kind of personal judgement is conducted over the dying before they reach the last exit from the flowing time *(éschatos kairós)*. One often speaks of waiting during which the recurrent chores of the passing time are multiplied or accelerated – such as the unintermittent labors of Sisyphus.[21] To many ancient civilizations death and life, to use the words of the Aztecologist Jacques Soustelle, were but aspects of the same reality and dying implied the long and sorrowful passage to Mictlán, the state of uncomplete fulfillment.[22] Rivers had to be crossed; sometimes one river, sometimes two: The river of forgetting the bad deeds and that of remembering fully all that was good.

Students of psychology know that we are capable, within a minute long dream, to live again through months and years of past experiences. Could agony be the one *kairós* in which we are brought face to face with all the other moments of decision of which our person consists? Do we, as Charles Williams seems to believe, see ourselves in the agony for the first time as we really are? Do we meet our complete person there?

The ancient myths suggested that the dying man comes into the possession of something which he cannot share with those who have not yet reached agony. Plato, in the *Symposium*, tells us that Orpheus was only shown a shadow of Eurydice and was reprimanded because he had not had the courage to follow her along the way which she had taken. Even the other, more popular version of the Orpheus myth has a built-in prohibition against turning one's face from the land of the living into the realm of Hades. A living man is not allowed to see what the dying man has to face.

Whatever the nature of the agony may be, no person is free to gain an insight into it before he is really going to die. No one among the living is allowed to evaluate a complete human person – not even his own person, because of the shortcomings of his memory. Orpheus' art might have helped him to enter Hades, but not really feel at home there.

We would certainly like to know which among a person's features count more and which count less. But could Leopold Ranke have spoken seriously when he announced that the historian's duty was to learn how "everything ever happened"? The Dutch historian Geyl, using Napoleon's figure as an example and drawing on diverse sources, has shown persuasively how impossible such an ideal is and how fickle the historian's art remains.[23]

The proverbial saying "Save our souls", known to folklorists and incorporated also among the basic naval signals (SOS), never had anything to do with "souls" in the "dove-in-the-cage" sense, always only with the lives of persons. But it was also frequently used to signify the preservation of the independence of the person. "Save my soul", one used to say when developments were threatening one's independent, truly personal capability of action. What Shestov, and Dostoyevskij already before him, were mainly afraid of, was undoubtedly a dangerous trend: The Hegelian divinization of society, its transformation into a moloch who swallows human persons. In Hegel's doctrine, the sparks of the Cosmic Fire – an ancient Semitic-Stoic symbol – no longer illuminated men, but national states; later they were to illuminate dictatorships of the proletariat, racist powers or some anarchist-angelic societies, but never again men, never man as man. But long before these threats appeared, an anguish lived in man, stemming from the obvious inability to see one's own entire person or at least to recapitulate and to sum up the total value of one's own life.

This anguish found its way into the Christian liturgy: "From a sudden, unexpected death protect us, o Lord." It is a very human and understandable prayer. One does not want to be rushed. So much has to be cleaned up, put in order. But at the same time it seems to be a prayer of little faith. How sudden is a sudden death? What really does happen in an agony? What is its real, truly human length? Is it not preached by Christians that God really wants everybody to love him? And if so, could he deny to man's freedom the last moment of decision, perhaps infinitesimaly short to bystanders? Could he deny him one last and perhaps very comprehensive look at the unity of his own human person?

Of Hope and Anguish

... tà pathḗmata toũ nỹn kairoũ...
... whatever we suffer in this moment
of decision...
                    Paul, *To the Romans*, 8 : 18

Precisely in this negation — in his words: My
God, my God, why hast thou forsaken me? —
Christ is the fulfillment of every possibility
of human progress.
                    Karl Barth, *The Epistle to the Romans*

By the time knowledge becomes a frightening affair, man also recognizes that death is the irreplaceable partner that sits on the mat next to him. Every bit of knowledge that becomes power has death as its central force. Death lends the ultimate touch and whatever is touched by death indeed becomes power.
                    Carlos Castaneda, *The Teaching of Don Juan:*
                    A Yaqui Way of Knowledge

On Easter Sunday, 1955, a French priest of the Company of Jesus died in a small hotel on New York's West Side. His name was Pierre Teilhard de Chardin. Death found him very much alone, far way from his native Auvergne. His fellow-Jesuits, who later noisily began to celebrate his memory, were at that time hardly on talking terms with him. But then he was used to being alone with his visions. He was one of those Frenchmen who have inherited the passion of the ancient Greeks for "theory", for that cosmic view which reaches to ultimate conclusions – always mythical and sometimes falsely mythical conclusions. His conclusions were both optimistic and endless; he confessed to Gabriel Marcel that he was unable to believe in the end of this world. In his veins circulated the blood of the Arouettes, Voltaire's own family. When he was lying dead his face resembled, we are told, that of Pascal, another Auvergnat. There was much of both Pascal and Voltaire in his way of thinking. He also possessed a predilection for translucent and ringing formulae which he was able to put on paper with great persuasiveness.[1]

No epitaph was placed on his grave. Had they looked for one, they could have used Acton's words: "The prize of all history is the understanding of modern times". In his days, Teilhard de Chardin had seen many a cruel and bloody peak of our times: In the First World War in the trenches of the Chemin des Dames; in the Second World War on its most remote battlefield, in China. By training and by devotion he was an anthropologist. By the choice of his heart he tried to concentrate on the meaning of history – on that meaning, in particular, which his contemporaries would be very willing to accept. He felt again and again for the pulse of history, or for what he believed it to be. But was he really sure that he had grasped it? Gabriel Marcel asked him once whether the death of millions in forced-labor camps did not trouble his positive attitude toward the ruling regime in the Soviet Union. Teilhard's answer at once minimized the suffering of a "few" millions in comparison with the victorious march of many more into a "better future".

More often than not he concentrated on what, in his opinion, the pulse of history should be. "The tribe," he said, "has been replaced by one's country; but above the countries we have seen the rise of the ideological and economic blocs; tomorrow one single unit will be built for the entire family of man." But then he would hesitate. Doubts would seize him as to whether there really was any certainty in such an expectation. "We really have the choice", he would correct himself, "between an ant-hill and humanity; either we reach a mechanization, the elements of which are mere tools, or we shall associate freely one with another, contributing to each one the best and the most unique we possess".

Teilhard's views were those of a Thomist combined with an Evolutionist. Following the Baroque Thomist philosopher Suarez, he simply identified existence with the passing time *(duration)*, with the "continuity of efforts". He firmly believed that the combination of the Christian faith with the Evolutionist persuasion was possiible. His countryman, Blaise Pascal, once said: "... When the universe destroys man, he will still be something more noble than the universe because he will know that he is dying and that the universe is stronger than he; but the universe will have no such knowledge."[2] Teilhard believed that the material universe, no matter how much it may oppress man – and often, indeed, crush him – was itself subject to a process of "hominization".

In the past ages, the Christian thought had never even approached any Evolutionary vision of the universe. It remained very close not only to the Hebrew concept of passing time as centered around the coming of the Messiah – who was expected in the "deepest night" and of whom the Christians asserted that he had already arrived – but also to Plato's description of the historical time as a "shattered, moving image of the complete, full time" *(aiōnos eikōn kinētéa)*. Christian scholars spoke of the "following" as well as of the "imitation" of Christ *(akolouthía)*; this expression came to mean, in the writings of Gregory of Nyssa, a kind of "growth" of the message of the *Gospels*.[3] It was still in this sense that, as recently as the nineteenth century, John Henry Newman spoke of the "development of the Christian doctrine", comparing it to a river. True enough, some Western Christians, perhaps their majority, had been contaminated, mainly through Thomas Aquinas, by Aristotle's "causal" approach to the stream of "nature". But to the best among them, to Robert Grosseteste, Francesco Bonaventura, Nicolas of Cusa, Blaise Pascal, Comenius, the concept of the cause remained strictly bound to the decision of an intellectual will.[4]

Evolutionism reached the European civilization from non-Christian sources. For some time, its followers often avoided any expressly anti-Christian divinization of the stream of nature. As recently as 1842, in the very first draft of what was to become his lifework, the celebrated *Origin of Species*, Charles Darwin made the following observation: "It accords with what we know of the law impressed on matter by the Creator, that the creation and extinction of forms, like the birth and deaths of individuals, should be the effect of secondary means; it is derogatory that the Creator of countless systems of worlds should have created each of the myriads of creeping parasites." But later on, in the pronouncements of the believing as well as of the agnostic followers of Darwin, the whole stream of evolution assumed the aspect of a dark river moving in an unpredictable direction. Ernest Renan was looking for a way to make the gorilla more moral. Thomas

Huxley, during the last years of the century, envisaged the necessity of combatting evolution if need be.

For Teilhard there was no fear of exposing God to overwork or of degrading him with the chore of creating "creeping parasites". He seemed sure that the "visage of evolution" was a "consciousness which awakes gradually, through endless gropings *(tâtonnements)*". He repeatedly spoke of the "spiritual power of the matter" or again of matter as being "the matrix of the spirit". All matter to him consisted of *énergie tangentielle* and *énergie radiale* – the second being the fountainhead of consciousness, which would later become intellect.

It should be admitted, however, that behind both Darwin and Teilhard stood the general inclination toward regarding the past of nature as an almost historical phenomenon: An inclination common to all major civilizations, late-Ancient and pre-Christian as well as to the Western civilization in its Medieval and post-Christian phases. Such a tendency is a complex phenomenon. Basically speaking, it is the awareness of the fact that the universe is being created, that it is alive.

But to be alive meant, even to the primeval man, the capability of striving for completeness, after the fulfillment of one's entire meaning – of the *ratio seminalis*, to use an Augustinian expression. Also the concept of the "future" had also always much to do with the life of the universe: The future does not come to us, we go toward the future, trying to grasp the entire creation.

Without knowing about the ways of the subatomic particles or about the quanta principle, the archaic man was already certain that even rivers and mountains were alive – and stated it repeatedly in the similes of his myths. The cosmos which is alive is a great theatre (notice the common root of "theatre" and "theory" in ancient Greek). Hence the investigation of the cosmos as something which lives – some ancient Greeks would have said "moves" – toward a fulfillment. Armed with such a vision, the ancient man almost expected even the post-modern identification of mass and energy. The Greek word *phýsis*, from which our words "physics" and "physical" are derived, meant a very individual nature of each thing. The same individual purpose of each thing, each part of the "kosmos", its "spirit" in the nomenclature current among the nineteenth-century anthropologists, was described, by so many ancient Greeks, with the help of the word *pneũma*. Deriving their vision mainly from Heraclitus, the Stoics used also the Semitic symbolism, which combines "breath" or "spirit" *(rúah)* with "fire" and consequently conceives blood, a "fiery" substance, as the symbol of life.

The nature of each thing is its life. It is so not only in the view of the ancient man, but also in that of a post-modern scientist who takes into consideration the totally uncertain, but presumably purposeful happenings within the atom. Pierre Teilhard himself stated, in a concise way: "Nothing truly exists in the universe except myriads of more or less vague spontaneities whose close-packed swarm gradually forces the barrier that cuts it from freedom."

But there was also the element of time. Reciting the doxology, Teilhard must have often come very close to the awsome mystery of time and also to the specifically Christian expression of this mystery: "...as has been in the beginning, and now, and in the ages of ages." He often read and heard the word "eternity" which, admittedly, to many seems identical with a continuation of the passing time without end. Had he been a priest of the Slavic rite, he would have even been familiar with the word *predvěčnyj*, meaning "pre-eternal" and often used of Christ himself. All these expressions are very much opposed to the passing of things, to the *chrónos pankratés* which beholds all things and destroys them as Sophocles said. An older Greek myth says more about the negative character of "passing time": In the beginning, when Uranos – a name used here as title of the Cosmic God – held Gaia, the universe, in his arms, it was their son Chronos who divided them so that Uranos receded away from Gaia and hid himself. And then the messianic question arose: When will he appear again?

Teilhard, undoubtedly, could have had some understanding for the deep meaning of those ancient myths. But would his reaction to them have been a Christian one? "It seemed to me at times," he stated, "that some kind of universal being would suddenly take shape in nature; only it would not be as before, in the direction of something material, but rather in the direction of something super-alive..."

It is a Christian persuasion that all life comes from the Creator. The Christians share the suspicion of the ancient mythopoios that "passing time" is an element which hides this basic reality. Even if scientists do not need anything else but "passing time" to envisage the past of nature as a tremendous stream of aggregated units, to a Christian the natural phenomena are not aggregates of separate units, but rather manifestations of integrating forces which all reach the universe from the Creator. The Christian speaks of God because whatever he observes has a valid and not merely a passing meaning. Can he accept the Evolutionist's predilection for "passing time"? Can he see anything particularly valuable in the symbol of the unending line?

Charles Darwin, meditating on his image of evolution, compared the affinities of being to a great tree. "I believe", he said, "that this simile largely speaks the truth; the green and budding twigs may represent existing species; and those produced during former years may represent the long succession of extinct species." We may agree that this is an excellent parable precisely because it denies the image of "passing time" as a line proceeding from one endlessness to another. A tree does not grow from the tips of the roots – or perhaps from their prolongation into infinity. It does not grow beyond the tips of the leaves, again into infinity. Not only the budding twigs, but also the roots have grown from one central, germinal seed.

But most Evolutionists seem to glory in the eternal replacement of one thing by another – so much so that they seem to forget that one thing differs from another. In their vision coaches are being replaced by jet-aircraft without it being noticed that quite a few inventive, creative ideas must have intervened in the process – if it is a "process" at all. Is there any "jetaircraftization" evident in the generations of transportation media? If not, what sense does it have to speak of a "hominization" of primates? Man's creative intellect as well as his speech is something as new in the structure of the primates as is an internal combustion engine in the structure of a formerly horsedrawn carriage. Would it have any sense to speak of "internal combustion power of the horse-drawn coaches"? If not, why should we speak, as Teilhard does, of the "spiritual power of matter"? And why, above all, should we expect the "coming of something super-alive"?

Where Teilhard speaks of "super-alive", Friedrich Nietzsche spoke simply of the superman. But that word seems to have fallen on evil days, probably because it began to betray the hollow quality of the entire concept. The concept, however, is still around. Observing this we may perhaps sympathize with the two excellent popularizers of science, Toulmin and Goodfield, whom we have only recently heard complaining of "the irony that one species should combine the insights of a Newton with fears and appetites of fools."[5]

The *reductio scientiae ad evolutionem*, a true reduction of multisplendored knowledge to the drabness of a lineal thesis really stems perhaps only from a pathetic and futile kind of revolt. Evolution was hardly a strange concept before the days of La Place and Buffon. In the ancient days, Empedocles of Acragas, speaking of the animal roots of man, said: "I have been ere now a boy and a girl, a bush and a bird, and a dumb fish of the sea." And Albert the Great, an outstanding medieval biologist, had perhaps a more sensible view of the changing nature and the mutability of living organisms then the postmedieval scientists with their concept of the fixity of the species – to which they adhere while proclaiming, at the same time, the "uninterrupted continuity of the evolutionary process."

There lurks behind all this a rather badly concealed will to do violence to time.

It should be noted, in all fairness, that some medieval Christians were not innocent in this respect. Meditating about the "millenium", they more or less manifested their discontent with the drama of history as well as an eagerness to prescribe to Providence what to do with it and when to stop its flow. Nevertheless, while recognizing that any initiative concerning the happenings in time must come from the Creator, these "chiliasts" did not extend their intellectual endeavors beyond a wishful thought or a false prophecy.

The essential change appeared shortly after 1700 when, in sharp contrast to Bossuet's stressing of the working-out of Providence and even to Charles Perrault's insistence that

> by the same hand, the infinite forces
> produce, at all times, similar geniuses,

Giambattista Vico spoke of "the living force of humanity creating itself." His slogan was *natura nascendo*. He made history independent from any guidance by Providence – or, rather, he identified history with Providence. The spiral course of history may have had to him a "Providential source"; but it was a "natural course". There is an essential difference between Bossuet's observation that while men "do more or less that they intend, they never fail to obtain unforseen effects" and Vico's persuasion that history has "its own inner necessity".[6]

Next, the traditional concept of "progress" as the individual person's way to perfection was changed into Turgot's and Condorcet's idea of the automatic progress of mankind toward greater happiness.[7] In mere hundred years

Vico's *scienza nuova* was to become the Hegelian idea of the "objective mind" *(Geist)* – "God's march through the world" – and Auguste Comte's intention to reorganize everything, without God, through a systematic cult of humanity.

Humanity, from this point of view, does not simply mean "men". It means an entity of a higher order, a rather fabulous, falsely mythical entity. "I see, all the time better and better", says Pierre Teilhard, "matter as matrix of consciousness, and consciousness, born from matter, marching past me, in the direction of the ultrahuman". He also states that: "It would be easier to stop the earth from turning than to stop the totalization of mankind". Or again: "It is as impossible for mankind not to self-integrate as for the intelligence not to push further and deeper."[8] And finally: "I am persuaded that the possibility of the awakening of our consciousness to a superconsciousness emerges every day as something better and better, anchored scientifically in experience, and as something psychologically more and more necessary to provide man with a will to live and a courage to act *(goût de vivre et courage de l'action)*."

Do we discover, in the last quoted passage, the same pseudo-mythical protest which loomed large behind the despairing assertions of the medieval chiliasts? We are going, they proclaimed, to sustain the misery of this life, oh, Lord, but only under the condition that this is the very last chapter of history... Is it so, perhaps, that we find here a remedy to the complaint about the painful irony which brings together Newtons and fools into one single zoological species? This species, we are told by way of assurrance, will mature and produce a super-consciousness certainly on the level of Newton's intellect if not on a higher level. Only such assurance, it is suggested, is capable of strengthening our will to live and our courage to act. Evidently, Teilhard's generation, which spoke so much of "demythologization", felt a subconscious need for "remythologization". The past, very distant Golden Age with its wise Methusalems was replaced by the future, but equally Golden Age with infallible Egg-Heads directing some kind of an ultimate society, a world-wide technostructure.

How did Teilhard manage to ignore, in his visions, the essential loneliness and insecurity of man?

He placed before us the "community-world of men" *(monde communautaire)* not only as the irresistible goal of all the geological, biological, and even psychological developments, but also as an all-enveloping world of love, the world of the "man who learns how to love more and more". He came very close to a similar project, a conquest of death by love, envisaged by the nineteenth century Russian all-round scholar, Nikolai F. Fyodorov. But Fyodorov's project, which for a time attracted even Vladimir Solovyov, was conceived as a voluntary undertaking of individual Christians and not as an automatic, "irresistible collectivization which expresses the human aspiration toward greater consciousness."

The vision of Pierre Teilhard, while remaining as much of a tautology as Herbert Spencer's "survival of the fittest", turns that doctrine upside down. Instead of asserting that the fittest survive and answering the question "who is the fittest?" by stating "he who survives", Teilhard says "the latecomers love more" and answers the question "who are the late-comers?" by saying "those who love more". Charles Darwin with his doubts and hesitations concerning "positive" and "negative" variations seems to have remained much closer to a real experience. From the 2,000 dead at Agincourt to the 50,000 dead at Nordlingen and some other battlefields of the Thirty Years War, to the 300,000 dead in the Napoleonic Wars, to the 11,000,000 dead in the First World War and to the more than 30,000,000 dead in the Second World War, the "march of automatic progress" sounds more like the survival of those fit to enslave others than like a *chanson d'amour planetisé*.

More important, however, than any other element of our evaluation should be the one outstanding reality that love can come only from the lonely human heart and not from any phenomena of nature – no matter along what lines of articificial time-concepts these phenomena might be filed by our memory.

Professing with Gregory of Nyssa that Christ, the "Cosmic Adam", gathers up all things with the image of the cross which embraces all the "decisive moments of time" *(kairói)*, the Christians have always believed that in the decisive moments of their earthly existence they are able to manifest their love for the Creator and his judgements – or again to close their hearts in selfishness. In his sixth-century dialogue *De consolatione* Boethius still argued firmly that the term "eternal" should only denote "that which embraces all the space of life in one and the same moment". But there seems to be quite a confusion in Pierre Teilhard's thoughts concerning this most important topic. He admonishes his readers to love other men. He even proceeds to assure them: "As soon as love in our hearts is strong enough, nothing will be able to stop us in establishing the social, political and economic system of which we have been dreaming". But then again he says: "The isolated man is unable to progress *(l'homme isolé ne progresse plus)*", arguing that the expected increment of love itself requires a thorough collectivization of our consciousness and of our social life.

And yet the truth remains that the progress of the individual man in knowledge or virtue, his direct progress toward God, is the only ascertainable kind of progress. No rational relationship can be established between this only progress and the various extremely perishable accumulations of all possible kinds of ideas and values which take place, here and there, in different civilizations, and then disappear again. The increase in general happiness is a piece of wishful thinking. We do not even have a standard with the help of which we would be able to measure it. The progress of the invidivual person is often, if not always, based on help received from others. Nevertheless, it remains a personal progress. Its substance is love. And love can only stem from a free and very personal decision – a decision – which does not shun suffering.

Here, perhaps, we have reached the heart of the matter. The suspicion which we have expressed when we found that the whole belief in the future emergence of a "super-consciousness" resembled an intellectual opiate expected to provide man with a *goût de vivre* seems corroborated. Where the Christian tradition speaks of the life of each man, past and future, as of the "valley of tears", and where, above all, it stresses the presence of Evil among men, Teilhard describes the struggles and the misery, the despairs and the moral suffering as only a normal by-product of an evolution which still suffers from the fevers of adolescence or again as the birth-pangs of a better future.

Naturally, without the "better future" dream looming high above the pages of his books, Thomas Huxley would have hardly been able to sell Charles Darwin's humble and cautious suggestions so successfully. If they had not been able to read the same dream into them, Teilhard's non-Christian or half-Christian followers would have hardly been able to propagate his works. "If there is evil in the cosmos", says Teilhard, "it is because the arrangement is costly; pain is the price of being (*s'il y a du mal dans la nature, c'est que l'arrangement coûte; la douleur est le prix de l'être*)."

In other words, when the arrangement is completed, when the super-consciousness comes of age, there will be no evil and no pain. When the world-process overcomes the uncertainties accompanying the "early" phases of its flowing stream, all anxiety will be gone. This is, of course, an Aristotelian and Thomist heritage. We find the naive image of the "succession in the formation of things" rooted in a "defect of the matter which, originally, had not been ready to accept a certain form", already in the second book of the *Summa Contra Gentiles* by Thomas Aquinas. Evidently, the followers of this trend do not desire freedom. They are after the happiness and the security of the better future, of the completed arrangement, of the mature superconsciousness. Perhaps they will not have to wait very long. The *panis et circenses* of the post-modern amusement industry, the hallucinogens and the psychedelics seem to be moving in on us very fast. The man who, using an injection – or even reading the soothing assurances of a Teilhard – puts himself to sleep, may speak of the psychedelics as of a "new source of energy". Perhaps he might even call their result a "spiritualization of the bodily metabolism". But he is going to sleep and in his sleep he will no longer hear the warning that he has no right to throw away his freedom. He will feel pleased and secure. But he will miss his "moment of decision" and dissolve himself in the illusory "passing time". From the point of view of the real time he will no longer be alive as man.

We may accept Darwin's parable about the tree as a symbolical description of "passing time" – of that shattered time-image which can only vaguely reflect full and complete time. The "passing time" is not a mere uninterrupted line, above all not a line without beginning and without end. Such a time would never be comprehensible. As the tree in Darwin's parable grows from the seed in both directions, up and down, so the concept of the "passing time" grows from the present in both directions: the past and the future.

The very fact that we are also able to store the expected future happenings in the file of the "passing time" shows that this file is not anything similar to a truly geometrical line. Such a line would have to end, in each particular moment, at the point which has been reached by the drawing hand; it would be possible to construct such a line only by counting every single moment and pretending that there was no space between them – and yet it is impossible to have already counted the not yet counted moments. Only this present moment and every particular present moment represent our real time experience. It is merely in a fictitious, abstruse way that we give a certain number of moments of decision *(kairói)* the name of "passing time" *(chrónos)*.[9]

Examining the relationship between the "decisive moments" and the "passing time" we may now turn to the concept of the "decisive moment" as seen in the light of the Christin message.

"Brethren, the moment of decision has grown very short" (*1 Cor.*, 7:29). "Children, it is the last hour; and as you have heard that Antichrist is coming, so now many Antichrists have come; therefore we know that it is the last hour" (*1 John*, 2:18). In these and other similar locutions the present is clearly interpreted as the last moment before the end.

Also, while the concept of a "continuous, all-swallowing passing time" does not embrace any real present, but only past and future, the concept of the "moment of decision" appears as covering our entire life and connecting it with the *arché*, the "fountainhead of time". "As it is in the fountainhead of time, so now..."

"Zeus is the head," says an Orphic fragment, "Zeus is the middle, in Zeus all things are completed". "God has laid down, from the fountainhead of time, the moments of decision of all peoples on the face of the earth" (*Acts*, 17:26). Graphically expressed, the fountainhead of time is in the center, the moments of decision on the periphery.

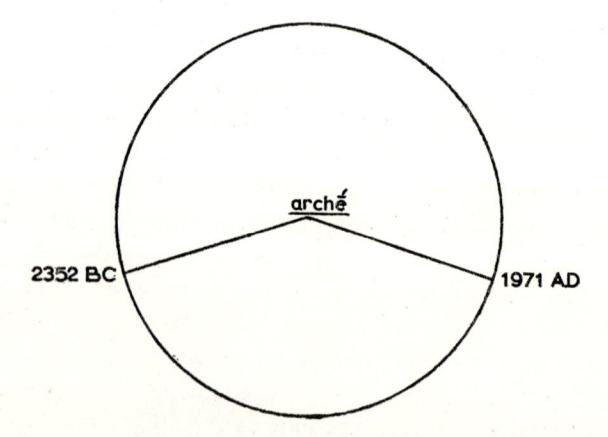

Nicolas of Cusa, the late medieval scholar who so admirably defended the Christian tradition against Aristotelian and Thomistic superstitions, had obviously a very similar vision in mind when he wrote: "Let then the concept of the clock represent eternity itself; then motion in the clock represents succession. Eternity, therefore, both enfoldeth and unfoldeth succession, since the concept of the clock, which is eternity, doth alike enfold and unfold all things."[10]

Both the "fountainhead" as the center and the "moments of decision" as the periphery belong to the basic concept of time as a complete entity. This is a truly archetypal concept – as far as we can judge from both ethnological and historical studies.

In the later stages of the major ancient civilizations still another concept came into existence: That of a cyclical time periodically renegenerating itself – something resembling the concept of a series of Messiahs, Bodhisatvas, appearing unceasingly to save the world again and again. But this concept, so similar to an Aryan-Indian statue with many arms and legs, seems to be only an ebullient overgrowth, a kind of overstressing of an idea. It bears some similarity to the vision concerning the "migration of souls".

There is no "refusal of history" in the concept of a complete, closed time. Rather we find in it a deep understanding of history as a drama. Because of the subordination of the "necessary cosmic order" to the "closed time", the persuasion arose that not only seasons of the year, floods and temperatures, but also the fates of men, or at least their basic characters, somehow depended on the movements and constellations of the most visible part of the cosmos – the stars. This "astrological" hypothesis was then handed down through all the major ancient civilizations as well as through centuries of Christian history, to Dante's *Convivio* and beyond. However, it should be noted that the identification of the closed series of "moments of decision" with the cosmic order has nothing to do with man's free will. Man's free will consists in the possibility of making an intellectual choice, of manifesting an assent or a rejection in each moment of decision, not in any attempt to predict or even to direct the course of one's life.

"He that liveth for ever, created all things at once". "God gave man the number of his days and time". These two sentences stand closely to each other in the book of *Ecclesiasticus*.[11] They assert one and the same truth – that in the cosmos, identical with the closed time, each of its parts is what it is. But because of our restricted capability of perceiving and grasping we resemble persons sitting in a cave, with their backs to the fire, and observing an emerging and disappearing series of shadows.

"Time and the cave: To come out of the cave means to cease to make the future our objective". Simone Weil, the former Trotskiist revolutionary who knew her Plato very well, wrote these words in her *Notebooks*. Hardly a more precise, and yet so succinct description of the situation of man, above all of the "progressive man", has been offered. Sitting in the cave we see only partial shadows of reality. Because of our inability of seeing the entire time but only its parts, we constantly wonder what will come next; we are almost possessed by the "future". On the cave's wall, the shadows of "passing time" are moving. Everybody wonders and worries about what will follow. We are dominated by these worries about the "future". In search for a complete vision we make attempts to derive the character of the coming shadows from the character of those which have already passed. These attempts lead us to think about "determination" and "evolution", about the "continuity of the passing time" in general. But being also aware of "creation" as a "fulfillment" we become aware of the irreversibility of the process which we are attempting to imagine.

Augustine Aurelius seized up the character of our experiences within the terrestrial time in a single flash of genius: If "passing time" seems to be an object of some distention, it is probably the distention of the activities of our mind which makes it look so. If the structure of our eyes lends parallel lines the property of converging the further away from our sight they reach, in infinity", why could not the structure of our mind confer a certain property – or, maybe, more of them – on our perception of time?

If we were able to face the fire in front of the cave, we would be contemplating the fountainhead of all those reflections on the wall of the cave, of all those partial concentrations of our mind on this and that and then still another object. From the fountainhead of time all human lives are seen, and so are the particular experiences and decisions of each single human life. The long, hot day in the vinyard becomes one moment, notwithstanding the illusory "length of time" during which this or another group of laborers had worked there.

In the cave of "passing time" there seem to be many "moments of decision" in each of our lives, interspersed with imaginary portions of "flowing time". But it is always one human fate. "Though our outward man is corrupted, the inward man is renewed day by day."[12] Even this aspect of our experience was covered and half-hidden by the vocabularies of ancient civilizations. *Móira* and *télos (télos thanátoio)* in Greek, *kala*, the "prescribed passage of time" in Sanscrit, *dōr* in Hebrew – meaning "destiny" as much as "generation" – *dawr* in Arabic.[13] Post-modern physics, too, has been able to teach us something about the multiplicity of time as well as about the transformation of "successions" into "simultaneities" and of "simultaneities" into "successions". We should make an effort to understand that an entire human life, with all its "moments of decision", may really be only one moment. The plurality of the "moments of decision", as it appears to us, may be regarded as just an aspect of the human person.

But whenever the "present moment of decision" stands before the mind of man, in that moment and in that decision he is reaching the fulness of time. He recognizes the meaning of an object, he participates in the *kósmos noētós*, he dwells in the "House of the Lord", in the "noumenal world", to use Berdyaev's translation of the Platonic concept. Even Heidegger described thought as "belonging to dwelling".[14] To think, to conceive the meaning of things, is really to break through the surface of the stream of "passing time", to reach the fountainhead – which was, since primeval times, symbolized by God's house, the temple, the *domus aurea*.

Again, however, the basic weakness of our mind forces us to file our "dwellings" in our memory. A shadow has just passed, even if it was a shadowy expectation of a "future" event. And all these shadows move in only one direction, from the future into the past. Why is this so? What is the essence of the "passing time" files into which we deposit our experiences, our ideas?

We may read of Thomas More and than again of Comenius, and yet we do not feel much need of attaching the author of *Utopia* to an "earlier" place in the file of memory than is the one occupied by the *praeceptor Europae*. Even when we hear the years of their respective deaths, 1534 and 1670, we are still not much aware of the "arrow of time". It is only after we have learned about some ideas from *Utopia* reappearing in Comenius' writings that we perceive that Comenius' place on the file is "closer" to the present than that of Thomas More. We have realized that a fulfillment had taken place: Thomas More's ideas reached another blossom in Comenius' mind. A creative act had been completed – or at least partially completed. Our imaginary, but strictly irreversible "passing time" is a reflex of the creative act.

Creation, which was the topic of man's first myth – and which, perhaps, in some way, will be the topic of the last myth man's mind will ever conceive – is our first and foremost "time-concept." Creation includes fulfillment and completeness – and so does the true and most basic concept of time. The time of Thomas More is identical with the fulfillment of Thomas More, his ideas included. It is irreversible precisely because it is a fulfillment.

We all resemble Thales in our attempts to find a basic symbol of the Cosmic Order, *i.e.*, a way by which to express the architecture of the cosmos, the historical "passing time" included. The concept of God creating the world in the fountainhead *(arché)* of time, in the primordial time, is evidently an archetypal concept. The fountainhead of time, however, is not something which would have "preceded" all the other ascertainable happenings. Rather it means something which is revealed to us "now". All creation comes from the fountainhead now as from the center of an explosion.

It is possible to describe the creative act graphically as an explosion whose center is the fountainhead and whose periphery are the "decisive moments" *(kairói)*. In such a representation, the concept of the "passing time" *(chrónos)* may be symbolized by a tangent projected from any "moment of decision" in the direction of the imaginary past as well as into that of the imaginary future.

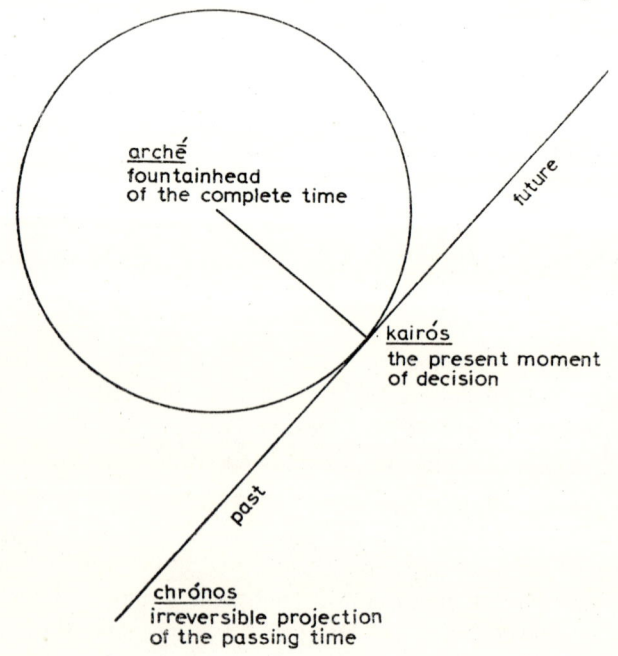

There are, nevertheless, a few questions to be answered at this juncture. Some may ask what there is in our experience to suggests that the natural order is anything but "eternal". This is a tautological question. "Natural order" means "the order on which the universe is built". The totality of the universe contains in it the fulness of time. There is no other time accessible to us but that which is identical with the vision of the universe.

Some scholars have been talking about the wedge driven by Aristotle between creation as denoting the "dependence of the world on its Maker" and creation as denoting the "first moment of the world". No matter how much of a "Materialist" Aristotle might have been, he would have hardly thought of any such distinction. He knew only of a "first mover" acting from the infinity of passing time. In fact, the scholar's talk has no meaning at all. While the creative act may consist of innumerable "moments of decision", every one of them is the first one and the last one. They all come directly from the fountainhead of time. They are all the same creative act to God. They are all parts of the same explosion.

The Evolutionists would speak of "perspectives in which we view the past story of nature and man alike". They would add that "partly to emphasize this continuity and partly for lack of a better word" it is necessary to use the word "history" for both the past of man and the past of the cosmos as a whole. They miss an important point: There is no past or future of the universe. There is only its fulfillment and its completness. All the moments of the universe are mutually interdependent. Because only very partial glimpses of this fulfillment are granted to us, but also because the basic concept of the fulfillment is constantly with us, we range these glimpses along irreversibly ordered files – along the "passing time" lines.[15]

Every man, from his own "moment of decision", is able to project his image of the "passing time" in the form of a tangential line. He may even, if he so wishes, experience some satisfaction in contemplating the "ascending" direction which such a projections appears to possess. No one denies that there are experiences which seem to persuade us that we should ascribe an "ascending" quality to our projection of the "passing time" – experiences such as occasional accumulations of knowledge and of values in various civilizations, or again geological stratifications and the sequence in which the less complicated living organisms appear to precede the more complicated organisms in their origin. On the other hand, when a drama begins, there may be a dozen persons on the stage and only very little information about the plot in the possession of the audience; yet when it finishes with only two persons and with a deep insight into a complicated issue – do we feel inclined to speak of the action as an ascent? Does not the entire projected "passing time" resemble more a drama than anything else?

But the game with the ascending line has alrady been allowed to go too far. It is one thing to visualize the genes and chromosomes, some inherent possibilities of mutations included, as reaching a complicated species along an imaginary "ascending and continuous line". It is a very different thing to ascribe to this imaginary line a creative will. After all we do not ascribe a will to manufacture cars to a conveyor in a car factory. Even Niels Bohr admitted, in his *Atomic Theory and the Descriptions of Nature*, that while we need to reduce our apperceptions to order, we may well regard "causality" as merely a mental category which helps us to do so.

Human history – which is primarily the story of ideas – can be described even less in such a falsely mythological manner. Millions of men had been looking at a kettle of boiling water and watched the steam lifting the lid; only one invented the steam-engine. Where within the ascending line of "passing time" had this discovery been hidden? Perhaps in a unique combination of a nucleic acid with a particular amount of a specific spatial radiation? An idea either exists in a consciousness or does not exist at all. Or are we to believe that millions of men using the same tones which Mozart used had selfishly kept for themselves the capability of composing *Don Giovanni*?

All "historical time" is contemporaneous – not only in the sense that it is valid for us only as far as we are intellectually enriched by it, but also and primarily because all the moments of decision are contained in the "now" of the Creator and in the experience which he now places before us.

Thus our knowledge and appreciation of the different "moments of decision" is due, ultimately, to relationships between men and the fountainhead of time. We do not appreciate Claudel because he came after Tolstoy and Tolstoy because he came after Goethe. We appreciate each one of them because of his own specific work, because of his own specific progress toward God. We should also consider that the real life of man, his time of decision, is not in any "continuity" of "passing time". It may consist of only a few critical seconds, dispersed through his terrestrial life as it appears to us filed along the line of "passing time". It may be, as has been stated, restricted to a mere ray of intellectual life in the existence of a feeble-minded or mentally sick person.

Our "moments of decision" emerge from the mist of birth and disappear again in the darkness of the agony. Some of our decisions would be filed by us along the left, the "past" part of the "passing time" line. Some other would be ranged along the right, the "future" part of the same line. We support the first group by testimonies and "historical proofs" (which are really only agglomerated testimonies). As to the second group, we sometime speak of probabilities (meaning by it recurrent similarities of events); at times we also speak of prophecies. However, although the phenomena of premonition and prevision have been accepted by post-modern parapsychology as data which cannot be ignored, hardly a thought has been given to the inevitable conclusion to which they lead: The presence of the future.

Comparing the "presence of the future" and the "presence of the past" we easily find that there is little equilibrium between them as far as our horizon is concerned. Memories prevail above expectations and experiences above premonitions. Was this always so? Among the ancient literary forms, for instance, the prophetical song *(carmen)* had a very important place. In the still extant remnants of the primitive and ancient civilizations attempts to gain knowledge of events to come appear quite frequent. We know, for instance, that the ancient Indians of America had expected, on the basis of prophetical knowledge, the coming of the Spanish conquerors.

However, it would be again a mistake to try to explain this seeming lack of balance between the "presence of the past" and the "presence of the future" merely by using the graphical symbol of the line of "passing time" and by pointing out that there are more points contained in its longer, "past" part. We should not forget that this line is only a projection of our mind. The real difference between its parts is rooted in our creative freedom. While both the past and the future are equally real to us – and both should contribute to our understanding of the fulness and completeness of time – it is our mind which, engulfed by the creative act, appears to differentiate sharply between chronological actuality and that of potentiality.[16]

"A grand order is born from the fulness of time," wrote Virgil in his famous *Fourth Eclogue*.[17] In this grand order the human mind participates through its own creative freedom. Man's fulfillment is evidently essentially different from the fulfillment of anything else in the cosmos. However, the difference is not in relationship to the completness of time. For instance, instinctive activities of some species of insects are distinctly anchored in the "future time" (*e.g.*, preparation of food for the offspring to be born only after the mother's death). The extraordinary situation of man should instead be seen in the creative character of his decision. Where an animal, in accordance with its instinctive behavior, selects between two or several possible courses of events, man decides on the basis of his knowledge of the meaning of things and possibly with the intention of bringing into existence a new meaning, a new value. No matter how much his actions may be bound by circumstances, the meanings of his actions are of his own choice. An animal's action changes its environment; a man's action changes or completes his own view of the universe and his attitude toward the universe and its Creator.

Some Christians, early medieval and later, while meditating on man's situation in time, often struggled with clumsy and useless terms, such as "prescience" and "predestination", terms based exclusively on lineal projections of the "passing time" concept. It should be noted that these terms had not come from the *Gospels* and not even from the early Christian teachers, but rather from a literary inheritance going back to the classical age of the Greek philosophy. Augustine Aurelius, above all, made his thoughts almost uncomprehensible by using the term "predestination" in connection with "grace" (illumination) given by the Creator to individual men.[18] But at the same time he was evidently quite aware that man's freedom is not abolished by the Creator's knowledge and that the use of the preposition "pre" is reather meaningless to anyone concerned with the relationship of the complete time to its "shattered image", the "passing time".[19]

But difficulties with uncritical vocabulary could hardly mar the effect of the astonishing doctrine of freedom of decision which Christianity helped to spread throughout the world by making it the basis of its concept of man as well as of its moral teaching. In man's freedom is his insight into the complete time as well as his ability to realize his own purpose.

"Judge not before the time; until the Lord come, who both will bring to light the hidden things out of darkness and will manifest the counsels of the heart."[20]

The great impatience which provoked these words of the apostle is still with us. We still see before us the symbols of the Cosmic God, which, on the calendar steles of the ancient Mayas, walk in a gigantic circle, carrying the epochs of time as immense burdens on their shoulders. The P'an Ku of ancient Chinese mythology, the one who released the "coiled up time", does not seem ready to coil it up again.

"Carrying one's cross – identical with carrying time," Simone Weil wrote down into her *Notebook*. She also spoke of suffering as "indispensable in order to pass from time to eternity". "In life and art both", said C. S. Lewis, "we are always trying to catch in our net of successive moments something that is not successive." And then, remembering how long and tiresome such a hunt may be, hed added a few words of hope. "At last", he said, "we be so changed that we can throw our nets away and follow the bird to its own country."[21]

History, being a wave-like entity, in which one emergence follows another may be greatly falsified by our impatience and by our insistence on interpreting as successive something which is not successive. But, by falsifying time in this way we are actually making things more difficult for ourselves than they really are. The heavy burden on our shoulders is evidently made heavier by the "infinite" character which we often ascribe to the "passing time". In vain some of those who introduced this symbol into their meditations also tried to laugh it away. Thomas Aquinas, for instance, a prominent leader of the thirteenth century Aristotelian camp, said: "If an infinite series of things that move and are moved in their turn, were possible without any first mover, then the entire infinite line would be mere instruments; now, this is ridiculous..."[22]

Why should it be ridiculous? It certainly did not seem ridiculous to the lord of the beleagered castle of Dunsinane. "Tomorrow, and tomorrow, and tomorrow creeps in this petty pace from day to day..." It did not seem ridiculous to Simone Weil, either. With her quick and comprehensive grasp of the situation – so much in contrast to the feeble-mineed "Materialism" of the scholastics – she realized that the mere use of the symbol of infinity actually means a refusal to comprehend as well as an acquiescence in the lack of understanding. "If One is God", she said, "then Infinity is the Devil".

On the other hand, the dangers of "infinity", in the sense of an unending series of irretrievable moments, has also escaped "Christian Evolutionist" like Nikolai F. Fyodorov and Pierre Teilhard. Having started from an infinite nowhere, Fyodorov evidently thought that his cherished image of history as a love-generating process would stop at a "point omega", where human love reaches God and becomes identical with him. He forgot – and so did his imitator, Teilhard – what all the archaic "mythopoioi" knew: That God is the Wholly Other. Left to its own forces, mankind would have to continue its journey to the Wholly, Infinitely Other well beyond "the last syllable of recorded time"; such a journey would have to be an infinite, *i.e.*, a never accomplished process. This objection has not been cleared away even by Giovanni Papini who, in his *Last Judgement*, showed a deep understanding for Fyodorov's intentions.

Was it perhaps also the dark shadows and the boredom of "infinity" which have moved men to speak of the "acceleration of history"? This "acceleration of history", in first place, has much to do with the presence of Evil in history. Some awareness of this may be traced back to the ancient civilizations. The Aryan thought of the ancient India operated with not one, but several cycles of the complete time *(yuga)*. Each of these was thought to be characterized by a progressive decrease in length and also by a decrease in length of human life and a decline in the human capability to understand.

Are we perhaps witnessing such a decrease today? The primordial myth of the Tower of Babel has, as all primordial myths do, a perennial validity. First one witnesses a dynamic idea, let's say that of Karl Marx; next, a tremendous organization, that of the Marxist movement; after that an equally dynamic construction: The enterprise led by Stalin and Mao. And then: A sudden, absolute incapability to understand one another, the Moscow–Peking story, and the catastrophy.

The social developments leading from the medieval kingdoms through the absolute state of the *Leviathan* period to totalitarian technostructures have brought with them a visible restriction of man's creative opportunities. The industrialization of production has taken away from him the psychologically most important joy of seeing a finished product emerging from his own hands. Mass production, not only of current commodities, but also of books and objects of art, has retricted the privilege of creative initiative to a few. The mass media of communication, while multiplying the reproduction of a few achievements (and hardly of the very best), have taken from many more the very possibility of reaching their fellow men. Perhaps science and technology are actually engaged in creating unsolvable problems: keeping the unfit alive without being able to feed them, inventing new sources of energy without being able to keep them away from the hands of deranged politicians, exterminating physical pain by creating conditions conducive to mental disturbances, taking care of an immense net of transportation facilities while assigning to all places on the earth the same drab visage...

A post-modern historian may become aware of a certain "acceleration" and formulate it as a problem without offering an answer.[23] The old traditions conceived it primarily as an acceleration of the coming of the final catastrophe. The ancient vision of a universal conflagration – the *ekpýrōsis* of the Greeks, the *ragnaroek* of the Germanic mythology – reappeared in the second epistle of the apostle Peter[24] and then in the fourth century Christian writer Lactantius.[25]

History, however, looks different when seen as taking place within the complete time. As the creation explodes, time also explodes and so does history. In the God-projected, peripheral and closed time, man's birth, the decisive moments of his life and also his death all coincide. Every decision he takes, belongs to the *plérōma* – the fulfillment of time and the fulfillment of purpose. And every moment of decision is infinitesimally short.[26] The question which God asks and man's reply, his decision, are "coeternal". They also coincide with the entire creation as well as with the entire salvation.

The refusal of some theologians to take this into consideration has led them into blind alleys. Most of these blind alleys had something to do with "predestination" or with the image of the purgatory placed on the level of "passing time", and yet taken out of the context of our terrestrial life. The pure and noble spirit of Jean Calvin ended on the rocks of "predestination" and of some naive attempts to "make one's predestination evident". Martin Luther, aware of the tradition according to which a deceased person is helped by the prayers of the living and arguing that such a person might already be saved "while" the prayers are "still being offered", included among his famous ninetyfive theses a "shrewd question", as he called it: "Why are funeral and anniversary masses continued if it is wrong to pray for the redeemed?"

Again, the last judgement also coincides, in the original Christian tradition, with the *parousía*, the second coming of Christ. Nevertheless, Albert Schweitzer and Pierre Teilhard have manifested a curious miscomprehension of this eschatological tenet of faith. Teilhard, as has been mentioned, followed Fyodorov in that he regarded the "second coming" as possible only after a long process of "human development". The world, he stated, rests on a center that "lies ahead of it". The second coming will take place only when the evolution of consciousness reaches, through the services of a thoroughly organized mankind, its ultimate point, the *point omega*. It is true that, on one hand, Teilhard agreed about this *point omega* that "if by its very nature it were not outside the time and space it brings together, it would not be Omega." But while he vividly appreciated – according to his fellow-Jesuit and biographer Henri de Lubac – Albert Schweitzer's assertion that the Pauline mysticism "looked toward the end of all time", he nevertheless spoke of an "evolutive" and "ever greater" Christ. And with a gentle touch of chiliasm he admonished his readers that, "to hasten Christ's second coming, they should complete man's development on earth *(pour hâter la paroussie, achevons l'homme sur terre)*".

Reading such admonitions one is strongly reminded of the many ancient civilizations where attempts were made to accelerate the epiphany, to terrestricize God by a cultic act or liturgical symbolism – by a voluntary imitation, for instance, of his expected self-immolation. A number of scholars, too, came forward with assertions that "mystical" experiences were possible, through which the "complete time" could be reached in a way somehow more penetrating and more valid than is done through mere cognition of the meaning of this or that object. To some, these "mystical" experiences were a free gift of God, a particular "grace" – to be received in deep thankfulness and humility. Some others, however, were pondering ways along which, they imagined, it would be feasible to obtain such experiences on the basis of man's own intellectual efforts.

The Near East became particularly fertile in this respect. During the Sassanid period of the history of Iran, which began in the third century after Christ, a dynamic revival of the Zoroastrian tradition initiated the so-called Mazdaist school of thought. Its followers not only distinguished clearly between the foutainhead of time *(mēnōk)* and its "luminous explosion" *(gētīk)*, but also used a particular verb, *gumečit*, to denote the "act of return" from the shattered time into the complete time.[27] Somewhat later, already within the realm of influence exercised by Islam, al-Hasain Ibn Mansur Hallāj, the late ninth and early tenth century Arabic scholar – whom some

Moslems regard as heretic and others as martyr – elaborated his doctrine concerning a "mystical union" *(hulūl)*. Describing man's experiences in his "moments of decision" (*ānāt*, plural of *ān*), he singled out every "instant of divine certainty" (*yaquin*), perceived in man's heart as something immensely more important than the concepts of "past" and "future". He also described the "instant of anguish and sudden revelation" *(yawm al-hasra)* as "piercing through the mystery of time and reaching the only true reality" *(tahquīq)*.[28] And when the so-called Ismaili cosmology was elaborated, again on Iranian soil, in the writings of the tenth century scholars, Abū Hātim Razī and Muhammad Ibn Zakariyā Razī, the concept of *azal* was used, signifying the act by which man leaves the "passing time" horizon *(zamān)* and reaches the complete time *(dahr)*.[29]

But all these men of wisdom – and also the prominent Christian writers from Paul the Apostle to Juan de la Cruz and Teresa of Avila in the sixteenth century Spain – remained far from presuming that any such deepening of our understanding could be gained through our own efforts.

Quite different expectations, however, appeared on the horizon with the trends of thought which gradually gained strength during the Middle Ages, collaterally with the build-up of the European civilization. "In the basic book of the *Kabbala*, the *Zohar*, and in Böhme's *Mysterium Magnum* the fetters of limitation and subjection of the ancient consciousness are removed.. and the truth of man's cosmic nature begins to be visible..." Nikolai Berdyaev, from whose lines these words come,[30] also wrote of the "divine in man being revealed by his own initiative, revealed from below rather than from above".[31] The book in which he did so was written in 1911 and published only a few years later as result of " an irresistible reaction against the Christian circles in Moscow". Its roots can really be traced back to the medieval philosophical writings which he is mentioning.

The archaic and ancient traditions expected the messianic revelation (epiphany) of the Hidden God. The Christian tradition asserted that this revelation had finally happened. In both cases the basic concept was that of the Cosmic God's participation in the "decisive moments" of man's terrestrial existence – *i.e.*, a change in man's situation, but a change coming from the "fountainhead of time", from God himself. Even the ancient philosophy, as has been mentioned, while hoping to help men to get rid of at least some of their sorrowful experiences, did certainly not spur them to expect any revelation of their own divinity through their own initiative. But somewhere between the times of Christ and the Late Middle Ages an enthusiastic trend began which, based on essentially new views, brought with it not only the belief in man's salvation through his own forces, but also a new vision of the cosmos. The imaginary line of the "passing time" became the center of this vision and assumed the character of an ascending line. Sooner or later, all of its followers became lost in dreams envisaging some ultimate victory for the man who "marches along the ascending line". These grandiose dreams ranged from jubilant and victorious (the terrestrial awakening of all dead in Nikolai Fyodorov's "project") to proud and bitter (the "final proof of the unredeemability of man" in Martin Buber's vision). But the false attitude they all assumed toward time became perhaps most evident in the early works of Berdyaev and in those of Teilhard.

Berdyaev, after a journey through the Italian cities in the early years of this century and possibly also succumbing to the influence of Jacob Burckhardt's studies, decided to proclaim Vasari's *rinascita* the epoch of "a new historical time". In this epoch, he asserted, the direction of the "passing time" had suddenly changed. It changed because man discovered, from his own initiative, a new role for himself, a new dimension of his own person – a totally independent freedom. Teilhard, having hesitated for a while as to what to expect from his contemporaries and successors, whether an anthill or a world-wide society based on perfect love, decided to ascribe to the ascending line of "passing time" an almost religious significance. Rising toward the ultimate "point omega" and identified with man's own efforts, this line, he declared, would bring man to God.

In neither case do we see before us anything even distantly resembling the time which we really experience. The "passing time's" alleged "continuity" is itself a false myth. In so far as we deem it useful, because it may be operational, it possesses no more an "ascending" direction than parallels possess a "converging" direction – unless, of course, one introduces into the postulate the symbol of infinity which would mean that the desired goal will never be reached.

Our freedom is conceivable only as an aspect of God's creative act. It is hardly within the scope of our possibilities to "hasten" anything. The Christian message admonishes us clearly that we do not know the day nor the hour. Teilhard's concern with the "hastening of the parousia" is about as groundless as are the worries of Albert Schweitzer about the "delayed" or "postponed" parousia. Every day in our "passing time" is *yom Yahve*, the day of the Lord. Jesus himself spoke about it when he came to the well near Sichem: "Do you not say: There are yet four months, then comes the harvest? I tell you, lift up your eyes and see how the fields are already white for harvest."[32] The apostle Peter took up this admonition: "But of this one thing be not ignorant, my beloved, that one day with the Lord is as thousand years, and a thousand years as one day; the Lord delayeth not his promise, as some imagine..."[33]

This is indeed the only possible way to understand the evangelical doctrine concerning the last things of man as well as Jesus' second coming. Each man is seen by the Creator from the fountainhead of time as one decisive moment – the entire person, from birth to death. All man's cumulative decisions are seen as one decision forming his person. A single, isolated ray of light – measurable perhaps in segments of a second – in the mind of the feeble-minded or underdeveloped has the same value as Methusaleh's centuries.[34] All the workers on the vinyard receive equal vage. The state which the Western Christian tradition calls purgatory may well be contained in individual man's agony; many years, after all, are known to have been lived in a one-minute-long dream. But, above all, the moment of the first man, the moments of each of us, and the moment of the *parousia* and the Last Judgement – they all coincide in the fountainhead of time.

The sadness and the despair of the bereaved comes to mind. Whether the Sombre Angel has approached our dwelling slowly or whether the veil of death descended all of a sudden, the days and years of passing time then begin their interminable procession, all marked by an absence, all crouching under the empty weight of loneliness. This is perhaps the most horrifying aspect of passing time, which no talk of an inevitable fate is able to mollify.

But that, too, is an illusion. Already the fulness of time is with us in which there is no separation and no bereavement. Today Christ has risen and he is still with us. Today he has risen and already is coming again in his glory. The "explosion" of the creation is also the "contraction of the Last Judgement". Everything is really only one "moment of decision" *(kairós synestalménos)*. "Behold, I show you a mystery," says the apostle, "we shall not all sleep, but we shall all be changed; in a moment, in the twinkling of an eye *(en atómō, en ripḗ ophthalmoũ)* the dead shall be raised..."[35]

Perhaps the most particular property of this "twinkling of an eye" is that it knows neither "continuity" nor "continuation". It is a true *átomos nỹn* – to return to Aristotle's vocabulary. It is the one beginning, to which our attention seems to be increasingly attracted – the number one, to which there is no number two, the perfect beginning which is not obliterated by duration, the astonishment which is not swallowed by the escaping time. "Undivided, but also in the first outbreak", says Magister Eckhart, speaking of God's joy. No matter in what century of the "passing time" we may be living, whether we arrived to work on the vineyard early in the morning or with the lengthening shadows of the afternoon, our own moment of decision coincides in the fountainhead of time with the *parousia*.

Precisely because Christ is the Redeemer, the one who by buying the slaves of death gives them freedom, this freedom can be found nowhere in the enslaving "passing time", not even in its distant future and certainly not in any childish, infinitely distant and unreal *point omega*, but only in the fountainhead of all time. Apostle Paul's invocation which has been called the most ancient Christian liturgical prayer outside the *Gospels*, "Maranatha... Our Lord, come...", does not resound into any distant or delayed future. Every moment the Angel of the *Apocalypse* enters[36] to take his oath in the name of the One Who Lives "in the aeons of the aeons" and to declare that there is to be "no more passing of time... *hóti chrónos oukéti éstai.*"

Man in the Exploding Time

> Men perish because they do not know
> how to unite the beginning with the end.
> Alcmeon

> Man stands face to face with the irrational.
> He feels within him his longing for happiness
> and for reason. The absurd is born of this
> confrontation between the human need and the
> unreasonable silence of the world.
> Albert Camus, *The Myth of Sisyphus*

> There is something Saturnal in the utopias:
> they move men, but they also swallow them.
> Juan José López Ibor, *La aventura humana*

"For fifteen centuries we have been wrestling with thy freedom", Dostoyevskij's Grand Inquisitor said to Jesus Christ in the dark prison in Sevile. Outside, fragrant with laurel and lemon, the burning, breathless night watched over the city.

"But now it is ended and over for good", the Grand Inquisitor continued mockingly. "Today, people are more persuaded than ever that they have perfect freedom. Yet they have brought their freedom to us and laid it humbly at our feet."

Had the great author of this memorable scene lived a century later than he actually did, he would not have been obliged to go as far as Sevile for his story. Perhaps, knowing more about the origins of the Modern Inquisition in Russia than he did about those of the Medieval Inquisition, he would also have had the opportunity to point out the real core of the tragedy – the fact that the Grand Inquisitor represents an institution which was originally established to protect the freedom of man, not to wrestle with it. Although founded to protect the normal family life against the Albigensian persuation that to conceive a child is a sinful crime, the Holy Inquisition eventually proved to be more dangerous to the natural society and to freedom within the body politic than the Albigensians had ever been. In modern times, the police was organized to arrest thieves. After some time it began to arrest those who defended the natural right to own things.

Instead of speaking like a preacher, a post-modern Grand Inquisitor could simply quote a contemporary American journalist by the name of Walter Lippman: "If we are to have economic liberty we must accept the truth that liberty is not the natural state of man, but the achievement of an organized society..."[1]

Besides, inhuman pride is not the only sin of Grand Inquisitors. Their refusal to use memory and judgement is almost as important. While some time ago it was still generally understood that to study history means to evaluate, to Arnold J. Toynbee, the learned author of the *Study of History*, Jesus and his ancient, prefigurative symbols, Tamuz, Osiris, Dionysus or Baldur, are all engulfed by the same fog of indifference and by the refusal to distinguish between symbol and reality. The Grand Inquisitor of Sevile had the good fortune of being able to recognize the Savior – so that he could arrest him and, eventually, receive that silent kiss which burned to the very marrow of his bones. A contemporary inquisitor, schooled by reading Toynbee's works, would probably pass the spot and remain unable to distinguish the Nazarene from any other lonely man in the crowd. Not only his judgement, but even his capacity of recognizing and remembering the meaning of things is almost gone.

By not recognizing man's dignity and by confusing his creative freedom either with licentiousness or with the "privilege" to live a "fully organized" existence of an ant we have indeed obscured our understanding of man himself.

On one hand we have been misled by the concept of man as a creature without dignity and sceptical about his role in the material universe. Recently, and for a few years before he learned better, an excellent Chinese educator, Lin Yutang, has assured us that he was a pagan because, as he said, with our astronomical knowledge we could no longer believe that an individual human being was so terribly important in the eyes of the Great Creator.[2] On the other hand we may be misled by the "ultimate renaissance" concept of man as a creature who usurps all the dignity for himself and is therefore terribly alone. An erroneous conception of freedom precedes the two sins onto which the pursuit of licentiousness debauches, namely, presumption and despair. And are they not also connected? Licentiousness, failing to live up to expectations, turns into its contrary: Presumption becomes despair.

But even while still dreaming a great deal about the perfectly organized – and thus presumably sorrowless and therefore also loveless – future, the man of our time worries.

He is worried by the uncertainty of the vocabulary through which he tries to describe his relationship to the "great process of nature". In most cases he seems to have finally set aside the older concept of evolution which asserted, with Lamarck, that an organ is improved by use and the improvement transmitted to the offspring, and which later led to the coining of the tenet that "behavior intrudes into the chromosome structure". He now mostly speaks of chance variations, some of which may be provoked by mutations or accentuated by circumstances and constitute a lasting change.

At the same time, he does not seem to know what to think of his own intellect. Should he perhaps identify it with some biochemical processes in the brain cells or with life itself? Sometimes he admits with Pavlov and Vygotskij that the psychic phenomenon is a "category of existence per se". But than he hurriedly corrects himself with Teilhard de Chardin, describing mankind as "not merely a superficial modality of the biosphere, but rather a superior and final form into which matter has evolved". But, in this last case, he evidently ignores what the verb "to evolve" should mean.

He is worried by the estimate that there will be some four billion men on earth by 2000 AD, and by the obvious impossibility to feed them all, even to find space in which to breathe. He has not yet mastered the production of food from light which every tree or humble bush possess by instinct. He almost expects that, through exposure to high-energy radiation or the use of radioactive isotopes in industry and medicine an increase in mutation rate will be brought about, which might lead to a biological degeneration. Sometimes he also points to the increasing mechanization and "stupidization" of the manufacturing processes which might lead to a degeneration of our "organs of intelligence". He also increasingly worries about the pollution of the earth as well as of the atmosphere.

But then again and quite often, subtle, sophisticated arguments are offered in support of the illusory image of an evil-less world. Thus Emmanuel Mounier, a French thinker who used to quote from Marx as often as from the *Gospels*, suggested that perhaps mass-production should be regarded as being "of capital importance to the ethical development of humanity" or, even, "an indispensable condition to the exercise of a really human existence."[3] He linked the emergence of even vaster societies with "the movement toward personalization" and asked whether it is "any more artificial to use a radio than a plough" – where he should have been asking whether, in our remote-control civilization, a radio is not an incomparably more effective instrument of power of one man over other men than a primitive spear.

Such worry perhaps testifies that, after all, man is not such a Determinist he has pretended to be. A true Determinist should not worry about nature, past or future. Whatever happens in nature, his creed says, happens necessarily. If the contemporary man is worried, it means that he has not given up history or freedom. But then he should also recognize that the core of freedom may hardly to be found in the ability to reshape environment and to regiment natural processes. Such regimentation gives much power to a few men and helps to enslave the others. With the advent of automatically operating machines, new possibilities of production are being kept open only to a few specialists, while the bulk of mankind is being deprived of any such possibility

True enough, the hope is being held before our eyes that, in our free time – in the leisure which automation will bring us – we shall be more and more able to devote ourselves to our intellectual growth and to creative work. The fact that working hours have been curtailed by half during the last hundred years and that this change is being accelerated, seems to support such expectations.

But – apart from the consideration that one's own main enjoyment comes from what one does for a living rather than from what one does in one's leisure time – the important question is: What is happening to our capability of deciding about our own, "private" actions? A survey, necessary to answer this question, might well start with a look at the disintegrating and, at the same time, sprawling cities, the mushrooming deserts of the suburbias and the self-defeating system of transportation. About this system we are told that it is here to enable us to cover distances quickly; actually it steals the distances from us by making all the places look identical and live identically. These, of course, are only some of the factors which actually dominate our private time and our private lives.

Also it is precisely on the basis of "technical developments" that the state has renewed its drive against the community and the family. Perhaps the hope of the servants of the state is that last traces of communities will soon be obliterated and that the homogenized masses will live in trawlers, fluctuating from one part of the world-state to another. In this direction the onslaught on the freedom of man has been, so far, most successful. But the post-modern state has developed adequate tactics against the family, too. Russian and Chinese state-enterprise systems force women to quit their families for the meaniest kind of employment; they take their children away to place them in state nurseries and they condition every single subject for his particular job in the state-machine. The United States and some other "free" countries began to rate the wives of men employed in public services – not according to their capability of being good wives and mothers, but according to that of fitting into their husbands' kind of public service.

We should turn next to the invasion of man's private space by public means. While previously only roads amd common pastures were regarded as public property where people had to look out not to hurt and not to be hurt, now all the air above our heads and around them has been invaded. That one may no longer sit in the shady corner of one's own garden without being constrained to listen to the roaring jets overhead and to the blaring radios in the vicinity is a deplorable but perhaps also an inescapable reality.

Even more serious is the invasion of our private time by the minority pressure groups who tell us what to do and when to do it, what to buy and where, and above all what to think and say. In this respect the totalitarians have proved naive enough while trying to order which "voluntary brigade" one should work with on Sundays and how many evenings one should spend subjecting oneself to "political reorientation". They were also naive enough to state simply that one had to buy only green felt hats because brown felt had not been included into the current production plan. Methods used elsewhere are more subtle. They wary from suave persuasion ("what everybody thinks and does", "what you have to wear this winter", "what is expected from you") to very insistent and threatening persuasion. A not very conservative American politician declared not so long ago that a wide variety of economic sanctions is being employed in enforcing conformity to popular, and even minority standards and patterns of thought. Bureaucrats employed in insurance prey on the insured, publishers of text-books exploit students, successful managers of private enterprises or state sovkhozes and factories prey on their subordinates. The trend follows the way from the economic sphere to the intellectual one. It reaches from the sheer impossibility of obtaining food uncontaminated by chemicals to the ever increasing impossibility of communicating an idea which does not suit the pattern established by the "public" or "private" owners of the means of communication.

In the past, when manuscripts were copied by hand or when publishing houses were still small, the chances for good and bad ideas, for correct and wrong informations were, on the whole, balanced. Only a few years ago, a small publishing house whose owner was also its editor in chief, was able to publish, from time to time, a work of merit which did not sell. The owner-editor took the risk. Often he was proud to do so because he was interested in cultural values. Today, in most publishing houses, the editors are driven to the wall by the anonymous shareholders who want their moneys' worth. As a result they do not even dare to think of publishing a work which would not bring great profits. If it is a state-owned publishing house, they publish only works catering to the holders of political power.

Even where intentions are still honorable, the collective character of the editorial work in many large establishments leads the selecting hands toward books and articles which are either agreeable and trite, or sensational and stupid. The big magazines are particularly anxious to please. Their enormously large staffs, which like to call themselves "aggregations of talents and resources", are truly successful in restricting and destroying all intellectual initiative which would not be pleasing to the multitude.

It helps little when some naïve sociologists, belonging to the "reconstruction of man" school, try to coax their readers by declamations about the need of getting rid of all the selfish elements of society. The Romantic poets of Rousseau's generation knew that kind of oratory much better. It helps even less when some people – those, above all, who expect the state to take over all human activities – come forward with the "free elections" stunt. Even while admitting that man's inventions and institutions gradually surround him as an oppressive wall, they place their hope in the tenet asserting that "in a parliamentary state, the individual citizen controls the administration and will therefore do his best to make it work for his own freedom." The core of this particular illusion may be illustrated by a quotation from a Nobel prize winning physicist, P. W. Bridgman. "Christian ethics", says Bridgman, "did not recognize the existence of the problems of the mutual relations of people in modern democracies, in which each individual has a measurable share in determining the action of the society as a whole... Christian ethics is primarily the ethics of partners in misery... To me the most important new problem in a modern democracy is the ethics which should control me in my capacity as a member of a majority, actual or potential, in my exercise of compulsion of my neighbor."[4]

From a scientist of fame, one might feel entitled to expect a more realistic observation. Does each citizen really have a share in determining the actions of a "modern democracy"? Or is he rather coaxed into the belief that he does? To have a share in the life of the body politic has indeed been a traditional demand of some Christians in various different epochs of the story of our civilization. But most Christian teachers, while they also stressed that the awareness of a moral tradition should be present, accompanied this demand by a very important qualification – namely that an individual citizen should possess such a share "according to his own capacity". By that they meant, translated into our own political language, "according to his ability to obtain and understand correct information on the subject". That was also the main reason why the Christian theory of society has always been so much concerned with the family, the community, the professional association – in one word, with the spontaneous societies where correct information is easily available – as well as with the "poor", the less talented, to whom above all the growing science becomes less and less understandable. It admitted only reluctantly that the spontaneous societies might have to give up some of their responsability in favor of artificially constructed societies such as the state. Whatever decision an individual person makes about any contemporary state-affair, is, in an ever increasing number of cases, based on indirect and almost never fully understandable information. Moreover, in this age of monopolized press, radio and television, it has become difficult to protect the powerless from being silenced by the powerful.

Furthermore, as every honest sociologist will admit, even the decisions of an elected state-administration are preponderantly based on information furnished by the bureaucracy. The bureaucrats, no wonder, think first of the preservation of their own species. Our prominent physicist may indeed be provided, before long, with an ethics which would control him in his capacity of a supporter of an actual or potential majority. It will no longer be an ethics of partners in misery, *i.e.*, of real human persons. Rather it will be the ethics of a winning, successful group – perhaps a group which will stand behind two or several fictitious political parties. And, undoubtedly, it will have much to do with "coercion of neighbors". This coercion will mainly be based on the fact that the scientific knowledge, without which no modern society could be run, will hardly be accessible to more than a talented few. On the basis of what knowledge, what real information, will then the average citizen vote?

To all this we have to add coercion coming from outside the state. Every post-modern government is moved to all sorts of actions by the actions of the governments of other states. Gone are the days when the king of Ruritania was only constrained to act when the king of Mauritania, accompanied by a dozen knights, had already crossed the brooklet dividing the two kingdoms. Today, Ruritania's people's chairman maintains a large secret service – well fed by his toiling subjects – with the only purpose of getting all the information concerning Mauritania's people's chairman. The moment this dignitary begins constructing a new chain of some "anti-anti" missiles, the first mentioned dignitary simply has to do the same, whether it pleases him and his subjects or not. Eventually decisions on both sides will have to be entrusted to machines working much more rapidly than human brains. If only one, world-wide state is formed, such machines will increasingly have to be relied on. The influence of the individual citizens on their "programming" and their actions will be practically restricted to a zero. Such is the inevitable character of our "remote-control" civilization.

Nevertheless, even if all the falsifications of freedom are considered, freedom itself remains a reality. But it seems inevitable to reach to the very roots of things and not to remain satisfied with the contorted words offered to us by the Humpty-Dumpties sitting high on the wall of the communication means. Otherwise some false myths might prevail in our thoughts. The totem whose figures symbolize the Cosmic God of Love would be replaced by a totem whose figures do not symbolize anything at all.

The post-modern man is certainly willing to speak of education as an effort directed to the "eradication of every doctrine which holds that man should tend toward God". At the same time, however, he takes good care that God's place be taken by a pack of very little and rather meaningless gods. Discussing the ideas of John Dewey, a most influential master of post-modern education in the United States, Christopher Dawson remarked: "It seems to me obvious that this concept of education is a religious one in spite of its secularism; it is inspired by a faith in democracy and a democratic mystique which is religious rather than political in spirit; words like community, progress, life and youth, but above all democracy itself, have acquired a kind of numinous character which gives them an emotional or evocative power and puts them above rational criticism."[5]

We cannot avoid going back to God, if we really want to speak of "freedom" and "creation".

Both words are meaningless in that artificial realm which, under the influence of philosophers and scientists, we often imagine to be the "continuous stream of nature". Whatever happens in that falsely mythical stream, is "necessary" – which means that there is nothing free and nothing new in it. Moreover, were man only a part of such "continuous stream", he would be hardly able to explain the origin of concepts such as "freedom" and "creation".[6] It would be hardly feasible to say that the continuous stream of natural necessity invented concepts which, to itself, are meaningless. Or does evolutionary nature evolve into nonsense?

But there is a "now" in our experience of reality, from which we can start a discussion of "freedom" and "creation". We can distinguish it from both the "determined past" and the "non-existent, but statistically probable future". This "now" opens to us the *kósmos noētós*, the complete time, in which the basic principles of logic are rooted. It is in this "now" that meaningful events happen and that things come into existence. It is in this "now" again that we are free to chose – in favor of creation or against it.

We know about creation from our own experience. We know that it is always a struggle. Every creative effort requires some overpowering of the currently happening events of the physical world. Creative activity also affects our life. While engaged in creative work we live more fully. Without such work we merely vegetate. "Every moral act of love, of mercy and of sacrifice brings to pass the end of the world where hatred, cruelty and selfishness reign supreme; every creative act entails the end of the kingdom of necessity, servitude and inertia and the promise of a new, a different world, where God's power is revealed in freedom and love."[7] We also know about creation from the tradition. The oldest memories of primeval civilizations as well as those of primitive societies still extant in our world speak about creation. All the arts of men stem from myths describing creation. The basic moral principles were enunciated in those myths. The scientific theories were and are rooted in them.

Some philosophers, admittedly, have been engaged in erecting barriers on their own way to the comprehension of the creative act. Instead of realizing the difference between the illusory passing time – in which no truth remains a truth – and the complete time which alone makes the principle valid that a complete "a" cannot be both "a" and "non-a", they wasted their energy on intellectual splitting of hair. They forgot that any knowledge both recognizes the meaning of an object and embraces or rejects the object. Time and again they also succumbed to the illusion that it might be possible to interpret the cosmos as a "continuous stream" and yet to save the meaning of things. In contrast to such illusions even the Aryan thought of ancient India, which doubted the possibility of distinguishing between a thing's existence in the passing time and its meaning, between "illusion" and "reality", between "Maya" and the "Absolute Spirit", insisted that "to live in the passing time is not in itself a bad action, but that bad action consists in believing that there exists nothing else, nothing outside the passing time."[8]

Common sense tells us that the time of creation is not the illusory "passing time". The conceptual distinction between space and time – J. W. N. Sullivan used to call it "man's psychological peculiarity" – points to the real time, a time not affected by the flux of physical events. Looking into the "past" or into the "future", man may see events in different perspectives. He may isolate them and speak, for instance, of "species" or conceive them as a stream and speak of "evolution". But what about eating the pudding and having it, or dividing a flowing river into a number of pints and still having a flowing river? All this is only possible because through our intellect we are able to reach the realm of the full time, Plato's *kósmos noētós;* even in Aristotle's teaching, the pure act of the mind resembles more a rest than a movement.

It is sad indeed to see a Christian theologian to start with the falsely mythical, although operational, "continuity" and "chains of material causes" and then suddenly declare that, as God is "transcendent" to all this and the concept of "transcendency" seems empty, the very concept of God himself may "collapse into meaninglessness". The crux of such argumentation is obviously in the expression "transcendent" which in fact is an absolutely stupid and empty word. But this word has come into use precisely because one had first adopted the falsely mythical expressions of the "continuous process of nature" and of the "material causes". Contrasted with the sheer childishness of such empty sounds, the Living God, without whom there would be no meaning at all in this world, must, of course, be adjudicated a different adjective: if not for any other reason then because man since his very early days had known God as the Wholly Other. However, to express this difference by the word "transcendent" resembles vaguely an attempt to differentiate between a handful of chaff and the cathedral of Chartres by branding the cathedral as "something which is not blown away by wind". Next, another philosopher might arrive and state that to speak of a cathedral as "something which is not easily blown away by wind" makes the cathedral "collapse into meaninglessness".

And yet it is not God, but man and his knowledge whom such a "collapse" threatens. There is simply no place for man's person in a nature conceived as a "continous process". There is even no place for a "species" in a really "continuous" evolution.[9] The illusory *dharma*, a fleeting moment of existence which seems to be here and then again is no longer here, has no hope of even an occasional victory in its struggle with the one and "continuous" arrow of passing time. It is not so much the question of what might happen to God in our thoughts. It is rather the question of what will happen to our thoughts themselves. When will they be swallowed by the escaping time and our persons with them?

On the other hand, any idea – even a very partial idea – together with creative love constitute the only connection between our existence in this world and the complete time. "Thought is free of the passing time," says

Plotin.[10] The physical happenings connected with an idea which is being carried out by our words (unspoken or spoken) may mingle with the passing time and pass away with it. But the idea, the "intentio peragendi", remains unaffected by the illusory passage from the past into the future.

In many a branch of the ancient arts this knowledge came to be reflected either in symbols and parables or in the very structure of the art in question. The artists of the Islamic area carried on this tradition. Invoking Louis Masignon's authority as well as his own experiences from Córdoba and Granada, Camón Aznar speaks of an "Islamic version of time, equal to a discontinuity of successive moments, distant from one another." "Even God's action", he states, "is instantaneous because it takes place in sudden and sharply defined moments... A perfect moment will be that of the Final Judgement, preceded by other catastrophic moments... This discontinuity is illustrated by means of the esthetic principle of interruption, the supreme rule of the Moslem architecture and decoration. Above all the distribution of light, the openings and counteropenings, incorporate this discontinuous, instantaneous vision..."[11]

In the Europe of the Gothic cathedrals, which were built more from light than from stone, the illusory "continuity" of the passing time and of the perceptions carried by that time, was combatted by means of a sacred theater: From innumerable pieces of stained glass, each bright as a little star, but sharply divided from its neighbors, as well as from many an entire luminous scene, the universe and its whole time appeared symbolically before the faithful.

When Dante on his pilgrimage through the region of the blessed stopped to contemplate the starry depth of the space, he suddenly remembered the primeval tradition concerning the "fountainhead of time", the

> "opening of the horn
> which springs from where the axle-point doeth lie
> round about which the primeval wheel is born..."

A while later his mind reached the final conclusion concerning man's knowledge of things past as well as things to come:

> "... so unto thee, who hast the point in view
> which sees all things as present,

> are displayed contingent things
> ere they in fact come true."[12]

Christianity was joining hands here with antiquity... Six hundred years before the poet of the *Comedia*, one of the last surviving witnesses of the pre-Christian wisdom, Damascius, spoke of any idea as a "pause in the passing time." And only two centuries before Damascius, Augustine Aurelius coined two most truthful expressions when he distinguished between the "distention" of the mind – when it has to move along the imaginary line of the passing time from one apperception to another – and its "intention", when, in any particular cognition, it reaches the incorruptible meaning of a thing.[13]

Antiquity and Christianity also joined hands in describing the unique situation of man in the exploding time – in the time as well as in the universe necessarily subordinated to the time. Both, using only slightly different names and symbols, spoke of the same Cosmic God who – to render correctly the expression used by the Hebrew book of *Genesis* – creates the cosmos " inside the commencement". They both knew that the cosmos is created "in number and in wisdom",[14] that is, on the basis of unique as well as comprehensive ideas or meanings, but describable in general names which can cover all kinds of numbers. They both realized that while man's mind, located anywhere on the periphery of the creation, may use the illusion of the passing time, its knowledge of each particular thing is immovably rooted in the fountainhead of time, in the very center of its explosion.

Pindar, the ancient Greek poet who was as aware as any of his compatriots of the glory and the tragedy of man, frequently spoke of the hero's death, but hastened to add that, while man dies, "the reflex of the complete time lives on."[15]

On the other hand, the individual books of the *New Testament* overflow with sentences pointing to the wave-like, catastrophic character of our experiences in time and interpreting the uncomparable significance of the moment of cognition which is also the moment of decision. "The hour arrived and is now", says the Evangelist. And the apostle, who had stressed how "suddenly" the light shone around him on the deserted way to Damascus, gently admonishes his disciples and followers in Corinth: "Look, now is the well-offered moment of decision; look, now is the day of salvation."[16]

But passing time has obliterated wisdom. Men's eyes became glued to the evolutionary distances of the imaginary "future". And so much else has been obscured. The reality of evil, for instance – and with it the creative freedom, because freedom is a choice between good and evil.

Not so many centuries ago, Dante was still allowed to place on the gate of hell an inscription which read: "The eternal love made me". In those days, not only humble Christians but also intellectuals realized that, without the possibility of a definite "no" (which is "hell"), as opposed to a definite "yes" (which is "heaven") there would be no men capable of real love, but only automatons, robots. It was still known then that love is the highest value in the universe.

The modern and post-modern intellectual has forgotten and often wilfully obscured this wisdom. Toynbee compares the religious faiths in all their secondary aspects but ignores the essential one: their attitude to human suffering, to love, to the choice between assent and negation, between sacrifice and selfish escape.[17] But it is in this core of the matter that the Christian doctrine differs substantially from all the other religions of the world.

It had been well known to Dante, and also to Shakespeare, that, where love is ignored, childish attempts are usually made to do away with evil as well. Giovanni Papini, a scholarly publicist who should have known his Dante, has tried to show sympathy to the Prince of Darkness[18] – forgetting that it is his refusal to accept any sympathy which makes Satan what he is. Carl G. Jung, another outstanding scholar of our days, has written an *Answer to Job*.[19] To him, Satan is only one of the aspects of the Creator; and the Creator is not a conscious being, because consciousness is only being born, developed from non-existence into existence. Papini and Jung have both forgotten that even time and growth or development are created and that, hating God's love and, consequently, hating all creation, the Spirit of Pride is abscinding himself from life.

As to Jung's conception of God – or as to the even more post-modern concept of the "principle of hope", exported from the Soviet Empire by Ernst Bloch,[20] the very notion of a reality which has not been, is not, but will be, is only a very false myth and, at the same time, rather a trite notion; only what is *now* may be regarded as alive. Even if one accepts the stream of passing time as the only reality the absolute interdependence of all its sectors is evident; some "early" nucleic acids and Smith's character cannot be isolated from each other. "We shall be as gods" is the promise whispered in the human ear. But "we shall" is only a caricature of "we are". It is also something Satan himself denies as he denies all creation. He is indeed imprisoned in his self-concentrated dream in which there is no real memory and no real hope, but only illusion.

Men of great wisdom who could have helped to clarify this issue have been almost silenced and their works ignored. The case of the already mentioned Polish scholar Augustyn Jakubisiak seems to be of particular interest in this respect. Jakubisiak, the author of three learned and penetrating books on the subject of creative freedom,[21] was one of the most lucid and also most truly Christian thinkers of our century. His struggle against the pseudo-myths was only equalled by his defense of the Christian tradition against the spread of the Aristotelian, Thomistic and Cartesian obscurantism. In his faithfulness to the Christian message he evidently incurred the wrath of the servants of the false myths as well as of those Christians who are ready to bend over backward in catering to these servants. As result, his very name has been omitted from even most comprehensive encyclopedias as well as from textbooks of the history of philosophy.

A real effort to reach the truth does not seem to have the value of a broken coin in the eyes of this most progressive century. Only its own false myths are acceptable. Woe to him who does not dance in front of its bovine likeness. In an epoch which still resounded with the voice of a leading Christian bishop inciting the faithful to learn and teach the utterly anti-Christian medieval philosophy, clashing headlong with Jesus own words in *Matt.* 16 : 17, it required some courage on Jakubisiak's part to assume a different point of view. He demonstrated that the peripathetic and scholastic system lacks a basic coherence because its theory of reality disagrees with its interpretation of the intelligible. While admitting frankly that we are unable to define or even vaguely to describe the way in which our mind intellectually seizes the objects of cognition, he showed that such an intellectual act is not merely identical with sensual perception and cannot be exclusively derived from it. He insisted, above all, on the most important role which the number plays in our thinking. To him, the idea of the number is derived from the intuition of space and presupposes the simultaneity of the objects of cognition. "Every entire number", he declared, "is precisely the determination of the spatial limits of a concrete thing; because these limits enclose the complete expansion of the thing, the contents of the entire number, which represents all this expansion, does not imply the idea of succession, but rather that of simultaneity."

In space, according to Jakubisiak, every concrete entity has its place, delimitated and separated from the places of other entities. It is this place, the scene of the complete expansion of the entity, which also makes impossible any confusion between entities. Thus the results of man's sensual perception agree with the basic logical principles concerning the singularity and identity of things. This singularity and indetity is in itself not subject to any change. "That A is A means that A is always A; two meanings are actually implied by the logical formulas of identity; they proclaim not only the unity of every subject with its predicate, but also the fixity of this relationship."[22] The basic law of logic, as is well known, has been frequently attacked by critics "as though it asserted that nothing changes".[23] Nothing does, Jakubisiak replied. Nothing changes in the meaning itself. Nothing changes in its linguistical expression, either – in both its correctness and its truthfulness, in so far as it is at least partially correct and truthful.

As to the problem of time in this connection, the inadequacy of the peripathetic and scholastic views could hardly be corrected by the modern and post-modern thinkers who "submit all reality to the absolute regime of change and turn intelligibility into a mere postulate of the thought".[24] Helped by the results of post-modern physics, with its acceptation of multiple times and of simultaneities becoming successions and successions becoming simultaneities according to the observer's point of view, Jakubisiak turned courageously to the very ancient traditions to which passing time or its alleged length have no absolute value and stem only from the human mind's capacity to grasp no more than parts of reality. The illusion of passing time appeared to him as a result of the disproportionate relationship between reality and the scope of our apperception. He described the sensation of passing time as resulting from the way in which the mind registers its partial apprehensions of the real. That the reality which is simultaneous appears to us as successive, was once again recognized as merely a basic aspect of man's experience.

What Jakubisiak had to say about our twofold – perceptive and intellectual – grasping of reality, appeared conducive, in a truly dynamic way, to an even broader and more fundamental problem: How to describe reality.

It is sufficient to remember some of the troubles the logicians recently had with the meaning of the word "is", to realize at once the entire scope of the problem. Should the expression "is" be accepted as a logical constant? Or should it be only treated as part of the non-logical vocabulary? Such questions have often been asked by logicians. Their answers invariably favored the second course mentioned. Parmenides, one of the early victims of the "auxiliary-verb-philosophy", forbade, it is said, his disciples to use negation, arguing that "not-being" could not "be". Very recently, some logicians concluded that a "complete description of the universe" might be reached by using the "absolutely affirmative" modes of the same verb "to be". Some others spent hours meditating whether "red" or "Pegasus" really "are" or perhaps only "are being instantiated". Some wondered whether "-4" "is" in the same way as "4".

In fact, the auxiliary verb "to be" has proved, for centuries, the source of much confusion. In the Indo-European languages it was always a mere auxiliary verb. In some other families of languages, it hardly exists. And yet, since the time of some ancient Greek philosophers, Aristotle in particular, an entire "branch of wisdom", the so-called "ontology" was constructed around it. Medieval Materialists as well as Enlightened Raisonneurs of the later centuries adored it. Descartes, as we have mentioned in one of the preceding essays, made of it the "cornerstone of philosophy"; he was satisfied with pronouncing it very solemnly and then leaving the sentence unfinished.

In connection with our quest for a deeper comprehension of the "creative freedom" it is necessary to criticise the use of this auxiliary verb and to relegate it to its not so very important place. The enthusiasts of "demythologization", true enongh, still seem to act under the impression that "to be" is a "less mythical" and "more rational" expression than "to love", "to create" or "to act freely". It is true that using expressions such as these they would be expressing something mythical. But restricting themselves to a mere auxiliary verb they do not say anything at all. In the Lord's Prayer we say "hallowed be thy name", not "hallowed be thy being". In the tradition of the Eastern Christian Churches it is believed that an immense wealth of grace is present in the very name of God. Their liturgical language, for instance, speaks of the "glorification of God's name" *(imyaslavie)*.

A comble of linguistic nonsense, if there ever was one, may be found in expressions such as *esse simpliciter*, which the scholastics used with such predilection. When the archaic man called God "Sun", or "Fire", or "Eagle", he acted in a much more sensible manner. At times he called God the "Maker". The ancient Hebrew tradition referred to him as the "One from the mountain" or as the "One who is alive" or "gives life" – these being the relatively most correct translations of the name *Yahve*. The *New Testament* vocabulary speaks of God as "Father" and "Love" and "Illumination"

Our words should be "correct" and, as much as possible, "truthful". In Frege's logical nomenclature, one speaks of "denotation" and "sense". All the just mentioned mythical names are correct and, in varying degrees, truthful. They do "denote", they convey "sense".

Semyon L. Frank, a prominent Russian scholar of Jewish background who, together with Bulgakov, Struve and Berdyaev, had participated during the early years of this century in a serious attempt to save the Christian consciousness of his country, devoted much attention to the reaches of our language. The very title of his most brilliant book, *The Unfathomable*,[25] announces his main thesis: The unreacheable is being attained through grasping its unreachability. The thesis itself belongs to the outstanding and anti-scholastic intellect of Nicolas of Cusa: "*Attingitur inattingibile inattingibiliter*". However, in contrast to the late medieval teacher whose epoch did not doubt the presence of mystery in the universe, Frank had to struggle with many pretentious and often utterly confusing assertions of the more recent centuries – above all with the conceited belief of the Enlightened Rationalists that a "proper word or sign" can be found for a completely truthful description of every object of cognition.

The realities of man's experience appear rooted in that "unspeakable reality" conceived by the archaic man as the "Numinous", the "Wholly Other", the "Creator". Things would certainly have remained deprived of meaning if there was no Complete Meaning. But, at the same time, when we assert that we live – that is that we are capable of influencing our surrounding – we cannot say much more about it. When we assert that we know – that there are other realities, beside our persons, of which we are aware – we have equally exhausted our vocabulary. Contemplating this situation, Semyon L. Frank coined the expression "God's Sacrum" *(Svyatynya*

Bozhestva), meaning both "God-with-me" and "God-and-Cosmos" – a reality most evident but also least attainable. And defending himself against charges of "scepticism" or "irrationalism" he also insisted that both "abstract rationalism" and "abstract irrationalism" should be blamed for placing insurmountable obstacles on man's way to knowledge. One should not think of the "unfathomable" as a "night in which all cats look grey", but rather as of "Light". "The Unfathomable appears as that unattainable Light from which, for one, streams the visibility of the Cosmos, but from whose presence also results the dark, unpenetrable irrationality of that same Cosmos."[26]

Listening to Frank's words we are reminded of Augustine's parable comparing human memory in its relationship to time to light in its relationship to the universe. Man's knowledge as well as his will, *i.e.*, his attitude to what he knows, seems indeed to be a kind of light – a reflected light, perhaps – which is able to raise reality to life. Evidently, man lives as much as he is willing to live intellectually.[27] More than that, by becoming aware of what is his own meaning, he also becomes aware of God.[28] Frank's more famous predecessor, Vladimir Solovyov, used to laugh at the progressive and evolutionary wisdom prevalent in the nineteenth century by saying: "Man is a mere ape and *therefore* has to spread goodness through the world." But turned upside down, this ironical proposition becomes a very valid assertion: "Man is anxious to do more than a mere instinctive life would permit him to do and therefore cannot be regarded as one of the regular processes of nature."

The expression "being alive" is employed here as meaning the capability to affect another reality. As even the subatomic charges in a rock affect their own particular surroundings, the rock is also alive. "Reality is not unmovable and static, but rather something elastic", says Frank. "It not merely is, it becomes, it grows..."[29] There is no life which would not strive after a certain fulfillment. But while other natural forms and species fulfill each its regular and statistically describable pattern of life, man alone produces history. We call this experience "man's creative activity". It stems from the projective activity of his mind, from that "second signal ring" on which Pavlov laid such stress. There is always a decision involved – giving one's assent or assuming a negative attitude. Any person accustomed to the "chains-of-material-causes" kind of thinking may feel inclined to react to what we have just said by remarking something about the "assent" or "negation" having been "brought about" by some "preceding events" or "preceding experiences" – in other words, to introduce the concept of "determination". But that would only mean the introduction of another very false myth into the discussion. The word "determined", used in this context, lacks any content. Man's activity is truly a historical, *i.e.*, absolutely irregular and statistically unpredictable activity. Because it escapes all patterns, it can be grasped only in its entirety, as "complete history". It can be understood only within the scope of a true "theoria", a vision which attempts to embrace the entire cosmos as well as man's struggle between creations and destructions. Thus there indeed is a concrete reason why the same mythical word "creation" could and should be used for both man and the Altogether Other One from whose hands both the universe and man come. God and man indeed are both engaged in creation, not in any "process" but in the creative "act".

God and man both bring new things to life, but man does so through the grace of God. This grace – and this is a most important thing to realize – is "contemporaneous" with man's decision, with his "yes" or his "no". There cannot be any talk of any "sequel" of events or of any "merits" here. The Creator's basic decision, itself a decision of Love, to grant man the possibility to love and to participate in creation, or again to be selfish and to refuse to have anything to do with the creative act, and finally also the happenings "resulting" from man's decisions – all these coincide in one and the same center of the entire time, in the same *arché*.

"The truth is what makes us live, not what makes us think..." With these words Miguel de Unamuno, one of the most uncompromising minds of our century, reached the very core of man's situation in the exploding time. He probably would have even hesitated to employ, in this connection, the word "situation". Perhaps while speaking of atoms, stones, plants and animals we might feel entitled to use such a term – but then even all these creatures strive after fulfillment. Nothing is really situated, everything lives. Man, however, while accepting the *télos* of his life, also decides about his fulfillment. Moreover, knowing the meaning of things, he participates actively, on the basis of his own decisions, in the creative act. The author of the *Tragic Sentiment of Life* would have perhaps even worried lest the words "participates actively" fail to describe what he himself preferred to call "*la angustia vital* – the anguish of life".

Unamuno was as much a contemporary of Henri Bergson as Blaise Pascal used to be a contemporary of René Descartes or as Semyon Frank was to be the contemporary of Pierre Teilhard. Against the paper-like quality of the *élan vital*, Unamuno's "anguish" stands in all its sombre, most human reality as the very central truth any man can reach about himself. "In that anguish", Unamuno says in the *Vida de don Quijote y Sancho*, "in that supreme solicitude experienced when we pass through spiritual narrows, when the last ideas seem to be escaping us, we reach, full of apprehension and anxious to catch up with them, as far as that what really is the one essential knowledge. We realize that the world is our creation – not our illusion, as a German has suggested. Through the supreme labor of that sollicitude we may conquer the truth which is certainly not a mere reflection of the universe in the mind, but rather its place in the heart. The anguish of the spirit is the gate leading to this essential truth. One has to suffer to be able to create and, while creating, to live. Even if one's head tells one that the consciousness is going to crumble down one day, the heart, awake and illuminated by anguish without end, will show that there is a world in which reason cannot act as guide. The truth is what makes us live, not what makes us think."[30]

Unamuno's voice was crying in the desert of the degenerated, "Teilhardian" Christianity. It spoke to the contemporaries. It was to speak even more persistently, and perhaps more in vain, to the generations to come. And yet one realizes more and more how much this voice was needed. Even courageous men who from the lies of this world have turned to Christ's message hesitate to embrace this message in its entirety. To the realization that all truth is a revealed truth they prefer the belief that knowledge reaches us through our senses. They preach the comforts of the illusion of progress instead of the sober reality of the tragic quality of life.

Thus Thomas Merton, a Cistercian monk of our own days, seemed to be quite impressed by Teilhard's renaissance-like dreams. Nevertheless, he was obviously not so sure of man's role when it came to a sober evaluation of the historical time. He spoke as of a curious fact, calling for study, of "the art played by the myth of momentous choice".[31] Clearly enough, saturated with both Thomist and Positivist Determinism, Merton arrived rather late to the cognition of the fact that "decisions are made for us and we either accept them or not", *i.e.*, that man's role is neither that of a determined cog in a machine, nor that of a God who determines. But the difficulty experienced by Merton is once again in choosing the words. It is rather characteristic of his background that he, to his own great surprise, suddenly found himself on a sympathetic ground when he turned to a well-known pre-scholastic but again not very Christian theologian, Anselm of Aosta.

"One of the things", he noticed, "Anselm has to say to modern man is that the power to sin is first of all not a power; nor is it an expression of freedom, and finally it does not even enter into the definition of freedom; freedom is not measured by our power and capacity to sin." Did Merton, by the way, realize how much this doctrine of Anselm was opposed to the Thomist robot-like concept of man as a being mightily attracted by God and free only in the capacity to rescind himself from this attraction? Would he have perhaps also been ready to admit that Jean Paul Sartre's doctrine of "justification by sin" and his concept of the "absolute liberty in sinning" were a genuine derivation of the principle expounded by Thomas Aquinas?

But Merton's reaction to Anselm of Aosta deserves notice, if not for any other reason, then certainly because of its affinity to the life-long religious struggle of Miguel de Unamuno. Merton eventually defined his main problem as "the difficulty of realizing that our power of consent is real and creative..."[32] Had Unamuno read about Merton's "problem", he would have probably shrugged his shoulders and would have remarked something about people not inclined to admit that they were really alive. Indeed, there can be hardly any "difficulty of realizing that our power of consent is creative", wherever one admits frankly that life is full of anxiety. "It is this vital anguish", said don Miguel, "which brings us to the faith of God..." "To believe", he went on, "means to live from a desire and to transform it into the very point of departure of our actions; from that desire or thirst for divinity rises hope; from hope, faith; from faith and from hope, charity; in that desire are rooted the feelings of beauty, purposefulness, goodness..."[33]

Unamuno's younger compatriot, Pedro Laín Entralgo, while studying human faith and human credulity, has hardly ever mentioned Blaise Pascal or John Henry Newman. José Ortega Gasset, who used to describe doubt as a modality of faith, as well as the American Pragmatist William James seem to be much closer to his heart. That notwithstanding, Laín's wisdom is a genuinely Christian one. He speaks of "credulity" as a "basic structure of the human existence" through which man comes to regard as an "effective reality" those channels which enable him to reach beyond the frontiers of his own person. Characterizing the creative act in our life as an "opening into eternity" he also attracts our attention to the concept of the "project". "Project" is the form of expectation *(espera)*; it is both a volition and a question. And no matter how partial and temporary it might appear at any given moment, it is always man's only contact with the divine reality. "Man", says Laín Entralgo, "inquires into the way along which he could become what he wants to become; he inquires into his own reality as well as into the reality of the world."

However, without theorizing too much about the nature of the passing time, Laín Entralgo is also aware of the role which the illusions concerning the past and the future play in man's hovering over the perimeter of the exploding creation. "From each of his present moments, man projects himself into the time to come through a hopeful and anxious act of futurization, but also takes hold of his past, using it as basis and material for the future, or leaving it, by an act of regret, at the margin of his life."[34] It is a remarkable thing to see here both the illusory concepts of the passing time, the future as well as the past, conceived as functions of the creative will. While many modern and post-modern poets, both lyrical and political, seem more and more inclined to speak of hopes directed into the future, it might be rather sanitary to realize that future itself is only an aspect of our hopes and dreams – and so is our look backward, into history. Particular satisfaction may be derived from this realization by anyone who has never believed in the assertion that history is a science and who has always seen in it primarily a personal conception of the ever-present eternity.

Another outstanding Spaniard, the psychologist Juan José López Ibor, has approached the mystery of creativity armed with a deep knowledge of the structure and the ways of the human mind.[35] "Man", he says, "is again being envisaged as a natura naturans, not as a mere *natura naturata*. New experiments or, better to say, new ways of experimenting, reveal every time more the creative aspect of every biological act as far as human act."

"The perception of a sensation", he states again, "is a psychic function which has all the characteristics of such a function – above all its intentionality. Within the camp of the consciousness, which certainly is an open camp, perceptions are not found situated on a single level; rather some of them are privileged and it is to them that the activity of the person is directed." Or again: "The projection of every muscular movement establishes a spatio-temporal equivalent which we can only explain through the beginning of a prolepsis or anticipation."

López Ibor's intimate knowledge of the human mind is projected against a panorama of history realistic enough to include a sober awareness of its real or illusory acceleration. "We are the witnesses," says the Spanish scholar, "historical witnesses, of a hypertrophy of bustling activities as a historical conduct." Most of these activities are concerned with technics. But a technical act has to be distinguished from the religious and artistic acts through its very restricted finality. "There is, in the technical act, always a great deal of operating with mere material objects and its finality lies in these objects." An ever increasing number of technicians and even scientists are busy solving problems which are not of their own choice. Moreover, many among them, as well as many "non-technical" intellectuals, believe that their worries and problems will be solved through some kind of synthesis of the already extant knowledge rather than through new ideas.

On the basis of these observations López Ibor develops his particular contribution to the study of our remote-control and synthetical civilization. He is primarily concerned with the same "vital anxiety" on which so many of Unamuno's thoughts had centered. He is aware of the fact that this anxiety has some merely contemporary and perhaps not very important aspects. "The nihilism", he says, "which infiltrates the contemporary world also brings about its anxiety; against this anxiety man defends himself by turning to the satisfaction of his instincts; this is one of the roots of the contemporary erotization of the world."

And yet it would be not very realistic to envisage the contemporary man's anxiety merely in its pathological aspects. Nor would it be historically correct to see in it something which only our own epoch or our own generation have provoked into existence. Even López Ibor sees the man of any historical age as someone alive not only within the creative explosion, but also as a bearer of that explosion – as someone who participates in the creative act. Even to him man's anxiety is a creative factor. But it brings suffering. The entire history is a drama and every human moment of decision is a tragic moment – because every such moment, every *kairós*, rises from the most interior and most full of anxiety realm of the person which Augustine calls "*viscera quaedam animae*". "Vitality betrays whatever it suffers by loud cries of various kinds among which the most characteristic, exuberant and frequent is anxiety".

However, if anxiety means suffering, to what extent should it be considered a pathological element? We should not forget, says López Ibor, that even if anxiety produces perturbances, "it pulls man from the vulgar milieu and helps him to reach the authentic level of life." There is, of course, always a dramatic element involved, a highly insecure element. To "live" means incomparably more than the merely abstruse, paper-like auxiliary verb "to be" has ever been able to convey. "The individual man is not so much what he is as rather what he is striving to become; to make himself, he chooses, at every given moment, from among the possibilities which are being presented to him; but what he always chooses is to make himself." Thus we appear as participating, through our very life, in the creative act – an act which includes the entire passing time, all becoming, all struggle, all fulfillment of purpose.

Much is given to us from the very beginning, but always in a dramatic way. "Man," to quote López Ibor again, "would not be able to lift up his existence through a merely voluntary action – it is only the anxiety which lends him the means." He lives on the very outskirt of the creative explosion, very close to the frontier between light and darkness. There, too, his very life is being threatened – "life" in the sense of a "purposeful meaning". Man fears that he might be engulfed by the darkness above which he seems to be hovering. He fears, as we have mentioned, the dissolution of the unity of his person. In his moments of isolation – among which the moment of death reigns supreme – he experiences the pathological aspect of his life; he feels the threatening nothingness of the "non-life". And yet again even this anxious feeling is a constitutional element of his life; only when it is accentuated beyond measure, are we truly entitled to call it a pathological element.

In their relationship to time, God and man appear undescribably different. God is the author of time. He had been regarded as such since the very first, the most archaic myths. He lives in the fountainhead of time. From there he creates and knows the cosmos. He also knows the complete time. Man does not possess this knowledge. In his own ideas as well as in the meaning of individual things he sees only an infinitesimal part of the universe. And storing what he sees into the files of memory he finds himself surrounded by the illusory passing time. He eventually dies having observed, throughout his life on this earth, the deaths of a multitude of living things. Each such death is shaped as an impact of some things on other things and as replacement of some by others. But still he is able to reach out for creative freedom.

"The creative act of knowledge is an act of loving choice, selecting the one good from among an evil multiplicity."[36] These words with which the mature Berdyaev began his magnificent, yet at times impatient apology of the creative man, are rooted in the awareness of man's time-situation. Man's location on the periphery of time is the crossroad of choice. In each moment of decision man has to decide. If he chooses freedom, he participates in the creative act. To create, as Berdyaev repeatedly declared, means to renounce the merely terrestrial life for the sake of values which are not engulfed by the passing time. It also means to bring into life things and events which, so far, have not been, in a chronological sense, completely alive. "Freedom is the baseless foundation of being; it is deeper than all being."[37]

Berdyaev thus corrected the views concerning a man-made freedom which he had entertained before the First World War. The freedom of which he now spoke is, of course, creative freedom, not Voltairian independence. "Freedom *from* is in sin; freedom *for* is in creativness."[38] Love may be described as the contents of freedom. "What is near and dear to man does not compel him; those who love each other and are thus united are free; only those who are at enmity and not united are enslaved and know necessity."[39]

Many years after he had finished his early works, at the close of his life, Berdyaev returned again to this topic. This time he wrote: "Freedom, too, is a mystery; it is not open to rationalization; the mysterious nature of freedom is expressed in the fact that while it creates a new life, it also gives rise to evil..." Or again: "Freedom in this world is conflict, not a thing to be enjoyed."[40] In some respects, Berdyaev disagreed with Semyon L. Frank. He blamed Frank's "monistic philosophy" for "having constrained him to say that the existence of evil is a scandal in philosophy."[41] But Berdyaev may not have devoted enough attention to Frank's thought. During the early part of his own career he had believed that contemporary Christianity would be superseded, within the scope of history, by a new age of religious creativity in which even saints would cede to "men of genial creativity". He later became much more critical, even sceptical in this respect. Similarly, had he studied more conscientiously what both the ancient and Christian traditions had to say about the role of evil in man's terrestrial situation, he would have probably become more able to understand the author of *The Unfathomable*.

Evil's role in the creative act indeed requires a careful consideration.

While we recognize the message of the *New Testament* as the tradition of love par excellence, let us not doubt that the archaic and ancient civilizations had also been aware of love's presence in the creative act. Buried under heaps of symbols – which may be strange to us, but among which the ancient man was at ease – the idea of love as the force behind creation burned constantly with the fire of a diamond too hard and too precious to remain completely lost and forgotten.

But love, as has been mentioned, stems from a choice between an absolute assent and an absolute refusal. As such it also stands in the very center of creation: Not only as its fountainhead, but also as its consummation. Even if we regard the entire creation as being of a catastrophic, explosive nature – and it seems necessary that we should do so – we have to think of choice and, consequently, also of the presence of evil. This is what the Christian tradition means when it speaks of Satan's immortality. Satan's life coincides with the entire creation. But so does also its goal.

In its attempts to describe this most important matter, the auxiliary-verb-philosophy failed miserably. In its works, "being" appears as a completely static and colorless virtue which evaporates the moment one touches it because it has no contents. The philosophy's attitude to God's love seems even more perverse. The Creator's love is mostly conceived not as an outgoing act, but rather as an attractive force, as cool and irresistible as that of a magnet. Even to Plato, not to mention Aristotle, God was an absolute entity which attracted man's intellectual mind, but was so perfect that it certainly did not love anyone or anything but itself. A millenium and a half later, Thomas Aquinas could most poetically speak of the love manifested by God's Son. At the same time, however, he described the creative act in a rather abstruse way as God's knowledge of his own essence. And the moment he turned fully to the Godhead and began to speak "philosophically", man's intellect assumed in his vision the role of a splinter attracted by God as by a gigantic, overpowering center of gravitation. The choice made in favor of God became a "natural", *i.e.*, automatic inclination of the human heart. There remained no place for real love. There really remained in Thomism only one possibility of choice: to revolt against God and to bury oneself in evil selfishness. Even according to Duns Scott God, while conceiving ideas because he thinks of creatures, thinks of them only "with respect to himself". The scholastic philosophers seemed simply unable to say that God loves, that God is love. The skeleton of the Aristotelian conception of the Creator as a mere "primum movens" or "caput mortuum" would not quit their cupboards. Only in Francis Bonaventura, still living under the influence of the truly Christian and therefore genuinely anti-Aristotelian heart of Francis of Assisi, the wording is significantly modified. To Bonaventura, creation is a dynamic expression of the Divinity, a "putting forth, by the Eternal Word, of the possible anticipation in its essence."

Why was it so difficult to concede that God loves and that also man is capable of a real, *i.e.*, really voluntary love? If Aquinas embraced a onesided solution, others drifted into an opposite extreme. To some it seemed that our capability to act selfishly must be something involuntary, something we are really drawn into, against our better will. Gemistos Pléthon professed this opinion. Eventually even Semyon L. Frank seems to have thought that we never do evil freely. Years before him, Jean Jacques Rousseau had already decided that man was necessarily, "by nature", attracted by his own, human goodness; thus in Rousseau's writings, rather than in those of La Place, God became a "superfluous hypothesis". Clearly enough, if consistently built up the doctrine of Aristotle and Thomas Aquinas, as well as that of their equally onesided opponents could not have ended anywhere else.

In the *New Testament* as well as in the other early Christian doctrinal and liturgical texts one always speaks of God as the Loving Father. From the abyss of the complete time God knows about his own loving decision to offer himself as man in the utmost sacrifice on the cross. This is the decision par excellence of which all the other creative decisions are only parts and imitations. The author or authors of the *Genesis* and of all the other very old myths, because they were poets and narrators, could not but relate the various objects of their attention as every narrator would do: Placing them along the illusory line of the passing time. But the "fall" of man is certainly not any "chronological event" from which God's decision to become the Incarnate God could be derived as a "sequel". The granting to man of the possibility to say "yes" or "no" is seen by the Christians as envisaged from the very center *(archḗ)* of the complete time. It also introduces the sacrifice on the Calvary. "O truly happy sin which deserved so great and so gentle a Saviour", sings the Roman liturgy while beginning the Feast of Resurrection.[42]

"God the Creator also is powerless to conquer evil by an act of power," Berdyaev remarks. "It is only the God of sacrifice and love who can triumph over evil, the God who took upon himself the sins of the world, God the Son who became man."[43] These words certainly touch the most central reality in the cosmos. It is also the most central reality which man experiences. It is the very core of man's situation in the exploding time. Being capable of love, we face not only the "Yes" but also the "No". We face not only that what is God, but also that what is Evil.

The presence of evil – real evil, not just any Thomistic "privation of good" or any temporary insufficient organization of the universe as Teilhard de Chardin would suggest – constitutes a very real fact. Perhaps to men it is even a more evident fact than God's own presence in the universe, as Gilbert K. Chesterton used to say. Passing time threatens to engulf us on every step. Such has been one of the archetypal human experiences since the beginning of history. We may turn to the Bantus of Africa or to any other still extant primitive group to find easily that, to them, sickness and death do not originate in their own "life" or "life-force", but rather in an exterior agent, exterior to the entire realm of life.

Evil is certainly real, but it is not alive. It is death itself. "*A morte perpetua libera nos* – Free us from the irrevocable, final death," prays the major litany of an old Christian liturgy. Throughout the universe, life is the fulfillment of purpose, while evil is its destruction. The statistically sizeable events and the equally regular instinctive processes of the physical nature threaten to absorb our entire persons. They affect our intellect so much that it tends to objectivize time, to rely only on experiences filed along the illusory lines of succession and to speak of "determined" events, including the events of our own lives. They make us speak of "dead matter".

And yet we know that there is creative freedom. Freedom means a victory over passing time. We are capable of obtaining this, no matter how partial, victory in every moment of decision, while realizing that meanings never lose their identity. The particular tree in the garden on which I am looking in this particular moment from this particular place, has a particular meaning. This meaning is not subject to any change. It is contained in God's own complete idea. It is my freedom to reach it and to share in its creation because my joy participates in the fulfillment of its purpose. Physically, of course, the tree is subject to decay; chemical processes are taking place in its component parts, which sooner or later will lead to its death. This is evil – a little illustration of it – which surrounds us and with which our freedom and our love are struggling. Realizing this we become aware how much it is necessary to reject the concept of man as a mere robot.[44] In contrast to the assertion of the scholastic philosophers that man is attracted by the Good and that his only freedom is in the possibility of a revolt against the Good, the true situation can only be described by stating that man is constantly engulfed by the evil of passing time. He can turn to freedom through a loving choice. But he can equally sink deeper into the outer darkness through many kinds of freely accepted selfishness.

Christians have also always spoken of man's basic situation as the result of "original sin". But relatively few Christian teachers have made it clear that the drama of the "original sin", well depicted in so many archaic myths, can only be grasped as the exact contrary of the action of a rebel against tyranny. In fact, the original sin is not the rebellion of a prisoner. It means a refusal to be free, to cooperate in creation, to be fully alive. It means to enter voluntarily into jail or rather to remain in the shattered, passing and objectivized time, with all the "security" restrictions which such decision brings with it.

"They have brought their freedom to us and laid it humbly at our feet," declared the Grand Inquisitor. The drama of the original sin is happening throughout the entire circle of history. Satan is present, according to the archaic traditions, every time the original sin appears, every time an ordinary man is born.

Do we know anything about Satan – beside being able to symbolize him sometimes as a snake or at times again as a most attractive man? Both the crawling of the snake and the attractivness of a handsome man symbolize earthly, passing qualities. But we should like to know more. The "ontological" philosophers have engaged, for centuries, in a most childish and futile discussion concerning Satan's "being". Some, such as Karl Barth, spoke of Satan as of someone to whom we are giving his life, while the Creator denies it to him. Some tried to find out to what extent he "is" or "is not". Instead of Aristotle's "to be" they could have adopted, from James Thurber's *Thirteen Clocks*, the verb "to glob" and tried to find out whether the Evil One "globs" or "globs not". If we want to say something meaningful, we have to go back to the archaic traditions whose authors were not yet haunted by auxiliary verbs.

In the primeval myths we find, in the first place, the tremendous symbolism of Light as opposed to Darkness. From Moses' "Burning Bush" to the "Disc of the Sun" of the Incas or again to Plato's "Fire in Front of the Cave", to John the Evangelist's "Light Out of Light," to the fiery hand symbolizing God the Creator on Lothar's cross preserved in the treasury in Aix-la-Chapelle, to bishop Robert Grosseteste's magnificent similes, to Francis Bonaventura's "light of reason and fire of yearning" and to Blaise Pascal's astonishing testimony concerning the most essential experience of his life, this archaic symbolism proved human mind's most efficient instrument in touching the central mystery of the universe.[45]

In all the primeval traditions light appears as practically synonymous with creation. In the Hebrew book of *Genesis* it is said that God, "inside the fountainhead of everything", created complete time and passing time – these being the obvious meanings of "heaven" and "earth", while the "firmament" appears only later in the text. But this is immediately followed by the creation of light – the "two large luminaries" as well as the stars coming again much later in the text. In the Zoroastrian tradition, where the Cosmic God was often simply identified with Complete Time *(zervan, aiōn)* and where creation was also often described as the self-manifestation of the Creator, two angels proceeded from the Creator's face.: Ormuzd, the angel of luminous creation, and Ahriman, the angel of darkness and of the destructive, passing time. Ormuzd fought with the retreating Ahriman.[46] In the mythological tradition of the Japanese Shinto, the symbols of the divine creative activity, either Kami-rogi and Kami-rami or Izana-gi and Izana-mi, begat the Heaven-Illumining Amaterasu and the turbulent Ruler of Darkness, Susanowo. In the ensuing struggle between the sun and the storm Susanowo established himself on the boundary between the dark world and the realm of light – while some of his sons even worked for the "welfare and security of the people'.[47]

Similar chapters from other archaic traditions could be easily provided. Light is always represented as contrasting with darkness – as meaning and order contrast with lack of meaning and with chaos. Light struggles with the darkness of the passing time and darkness recedes and falls into a bottomless and shapeless abyss. But while this happens, a boundary is established between light and darkness. This boundary may appear as death itself or again as the Bearer of Light, Lucifer – "bearer" in the sense of someone burdened by something, bearing his burden and falling. Evil first appears as something or someone capable of resistance. It is defeated by Ormuzd, by Amaterasu or by Michael – whose name means "Who equals God?" But its task is also to make possible the choice from which love or selfishness may be born.

Is Evil real? Is it present? Both these questions should be answered, without hesitation, in an affirmative way. Is Evil immortal? Certainly: nowhere within the realm of the passing time does it pass away. Even Plotin, who used to call passing time "dispersion of intelligible" and "distraction of mind", knew well that the sum of passing time and of evil are one and the same thing.[48]

We should certainly like to know more about the shadow which trembles along the boundaries of light. We should not forget, however, that we are speaking of an explosion which no "chronology" can describe and that the narrations of the primeval myths had to be "chronological" only because they could not but be visual. "History and its conception," says Berdyaev, "are possible only when the world process is conceived as a catastrophic one."[49] Light lives and gives life. Darkness would not be there, were it not for the light. But even while darkness is real, it does not live as light does. It does not live even as man does. It may be capable of some kind of imitation or of reflecting, but it is not capable of creative acts, of acts of freedom. It is only the resisting frontier of decision, the opportunity necessary for man to choose freedom and to manifest love.

In Plato's dialogues a disparity may appear, at first sight, between *Phaedon*, with its concentration on man's fall into the passing time, and *Timaeus*, where the creative activity of man occupies the foreground of the stage. But there is no real disparity between these two approaches to the human situation. Both aspects are very realistic.

Between God in the fountainhead of complete time and man, alive on the periphery of creation, in a shattered, objectivized time, there is a tremendous bond: The creative act itself. This act is God's manifestation of his love, but it is also man's opportunity to manifest his love. It is an act by which God gives man the opportunity to chose freedom. It may also be man's acceptation of this opportunity. Satan's "fall" – from the fountainhead to the periphery, away from complete time into the shattered time – is another aspect of the same creation: The flight of darkness before light.

The cosmic drama is visible from any part of the periphery. The archaic man sees it through his myths. The ancient man, with one foot in the realm of myths and the other in that of philosophy, knows of it; he sees the drama as:

> "...now all coming together into one because of love,
> now each pulled apart by the hatred engendered by strife."[50]

Even the modern philosopher is hardly able to deny it. Friedrich Schelling speaks of the contradiction between "yes" and "no" as of having "shattered eternity" and "resolved it in time". A contemporary "existentialist", Karl Jaspers, asserts that "even in the grasping of a decision, as far as it becomes manifest to the world, there remains some inevitable hesitation."[51]

There is nowhere a conclusive finality in this explosion because it is happening now, because we are in it and because it includes our own anxieties and decisions. "True fredom", says Berdyaev, "is an expression of the cosmic – as opposed to the chaotic – condition of the universe, its hierarchical harmony, the inward unitedness of all its parts."[52] It also means, therefore, man's assent to God's work. There are, as Augustine would say, innumerable "rationes seminales" in the exploding creation. But while the fulfillment of some is ordained by the Creator, the fulfillment of others stems from the creative will of man as much as from that of the Creator. The Christian traditions speaks here of "grace". An infinity of modalizations is included into the Creator's "fiat", corresponding to each of our decisions which are directed freely toward love. From the complete time God's grace reaches into the shattered, passing time.[53] It finds us standing astride the shadowy frontier.

There is no "middle zone". There is only the immensely thin frontier of decision. The City of God, as Guitton remarks, paraphrasing Augustine, emerges from Satan's city through God's grace.[54] But God's grace is the answer to our hope. Hope is the decision through which we free ourselves from the darkness. Hope and grace coincide in the eternally present act of creation. Where light is alive, darkness only pretends to be alive. Darkness knows no fulfillment. It only destroys, it denies fulfillment. And yet darkness plays an essential role in the creative explosion. It provides the frontier of decision on which also the hill of Calvary is located.

Friedrich Schelling's famous meditation, *Of Human Freedom*,[55] surprises every new reader not only because of the depths of understanding which it reaches, but also because of the time when it originated – in an epoch when Rousseau's false myth about the absolutely autonomous, "innate" goodness of man was ready to cede its place to Hegel's even more illusory dream concerning the divinity of the state. Schelling's meditation culminates in a simple, clear-cut phrase: "The very relation of man to God constitutes man's personality."[56] We have reached a similar conclusion. Our fellow-man would disappear as a shred of fog from our sight if we were unable to direct our minds to the complete idea which the Creator has of him, of all his moments of decision.

The expression *epánodos*, used by some Fathers of the Church,[57] hardly meant anything else but man's constant turning over his shoulder toward the center of the complete time from where he comes. The coming of everyman, the fulfillment of everyman's life happens now. The *dharmas* of the passing time may appear and be dissipated instantaneously along the line which serves our mind as its "past-to-future" file. But man becomes now, lives now, knows now, chooses now, loves or rejects now.[58] His becoming, his fulfillment are being granted to him by his Creator now and directly. Man does not "merit" them in any way, but he has been provided with the freedom to "cooperate".

If some philosophers have branded miracles a kind of "violence against nature", one may retort that the entire creative act is a violent act: From the blossoming of a tree to the composition of one of Mozart's symphonies. Everything is extraordinary, everything is a miracle. Both the theologians who talk about the "possibility of God's intervention" and the scientists who deny it are desperately lost in their "continuities" and "causalities". They will simply refuse to see that everything is "discontinuous" and unique; each man, each drop of his blood, each charge within the atoms of his genes.

Oddly enough, it seems slightly easier to speak to theologians and philosophers, or even to scientists, of angels. Of course, we shall hardly ever learn to know how the concept of "God's messengers" appeared in the primeval mythology. We can only strain our imagination – mostly in a very naive way – when we hear about angels whom some people saw. We find it even more difficult to imagine the angel-guardian who, in front of God's face, holds in his hand all the decisive moments of the life of a humble charwoman – probably because we ourselves lack the humility required to see that humble woman as beautiful as she really is. However, we are really surprised to see the scientists obviously unable to exist without angels and yet unwilling to talk about them with any frankness. Evasively and subreptitiously they have been talking about them with increasing frequency. Where Aristotle used to be satisfied with "matter" and "form", Newton felt the need of talking about "matter" and "force".[59] Today, scientists practically bombard us with unseen "energies" entrusted with all kinds of tasks in the running of this immensely complicated universe. They hardly remember, of course, that *enérgeia*, in Greek, meant "angel".

But right now we are more concerned with men than with angels. We have to deal with each man as with a unique person. He comes as such from God's hands in spite of Aristotle's insistence that "one can be the cause of one only" *(hén henós éstin aition)*. Wherever the Stagerite might have discovered this axiom, we could not be bothered by it. All men belong to the one creative act of God and yet they are all different. They belong to the creative act together with their capability to chose as well as with the very personal use they make of that capability. Nevertheless, this being so, the mutual interdependence of all men, of the entire mankind, surges before our eyes as one of the primary aspects of our life.

We can approach this fascinating topic from various different sides.

From the historian's point of view we have ben obliged, on the preceding pages, to point repeatedly to the permanent presence of the basic myth of creation in all our actions. From the primeval "mythopoios" to the postmodern biologist engaged in an attempt to provoke mutations and even further to a laborer who, on his return from some monotonous function in a factory, decides merely to rearrange his furniture, everybody has been and still is interested in producing something new. Creativity constitutes one enormous bond among men.

From a psychologist's point of view, the human child experiences his relations to the surrounding objects as conditioned by his association with the adults. While an animal's experience is perhaps preponderantly his individual experience conditioned by his instincts, the human child experiences comprise as much of the total human experience as the child can bear. Where channels of communication are impaired, the first opportunity is used – as in the famous case of the deaf and blind Helen Keller – to break through the complete isolation and to participate in history.

From a theologian's point of view, the entire issue may be most succinctly described by saying: We are all in Adam, we may all be in Christ. If all history happens now – notwithstanding our lack of capability to see it as such – we should understand that what happens to Adam happens to each of us. Moreover, it is almost superfluous to speak of Adam's "fall". This "fall" is not exactly a Christian concept. It had remained foreign to the vocabulary of the *Bible* as well as to that of the early Christian writers. It found its way into the Christian tradition only at a considerably later epoch – mainly through the followers of the Gnosis and of Plotinus. It certainly had its meaning for Plato – who in his *Phaedrus* speaks of the "fall" of souls into the prison of the body. It is not very useful to us who are aware of the unity of man's person and do not regard our bodies as traps for "falling souls".[60]

Our "being in Adam", while it could be only clumsily described as a "fall", means primarily a basic condition of man. It means that we are in "untruth", as Bonhoeffer used to say – inclined toward selfishness which we can overcome only through love with the help of God's grace. It means that there is an "original sin" – although even this expression dates only from the fourth century.

The word "original" cannot be identified with "hereditary". It cannot be understood in the sense of the beginning and continuation of a line, but rather in that of the center of the complete time and of the creative explosion. It is not prudent to assert that this "origin" is and will remain incomprehensible. We are certainly capable of comprehending it ever so slightly if we return to Dante's famous gate – that gate to absolute negation which God's love had built. The Eastern Fathers of the Church speak rather of "death" than of "original sin". "Death" means here subjection to the passing time. To be subject to death in the passing time is certainly a basic, *i.e.*, original condition of man and as such not beyond our comprehension.

This subjection to the passing time, however, is also a magnificent gift, a tremendous opportunity granted to man. The coming of love is its sole purpose. In her *Revelations of Divine Love*, Julian of Norwich, the late-fourteenth century author of far-reaching spiritual visions, presented us with a far more comprehensive and also comprehensible conception of the "original sin" than the inspired and yet so crude narration of the *Genesis*. She saw the Creator with a gentle smile of love and understanding on his face to give a command to Adam-Everyman – "for in the sight of God all men is one man, and one man is all man" – and Everyman running "in great haste for love to do his Lord's will, running and falling into a ravine... The Creator is "looking with love" at the eager servant. He knows a misstep will occur, a slip into anguish and anxiety, but also into faith and hope and, above all, love. To make possible a real choice and thus also real love, to create the highest value in the universe, is the purpose of the creative act; it can be achieved only through man.

Where does it happen? In paradise, the myths say. The scientists laugh and so do the "progressive" theologians.

Paradise... We all remember it. Standing, our hands joined with those of our parents and our children, on the periphery of the exploding time, we all remember paradise. Each of us may see indistinctly only the few flames right in front of ourselves, but each of us is also slightly aware of the entire explosion. Man is certainly aware of its center – hence his ineffable yearning, his constant longing for that absolute which the flowing time does not bring him. Some theologians, eager to let everyone see how humbly they kneel in front of the world, began to speak of the paradise as "merely an image of things to come". But they only lie to themselves. True enough, for milleniums old poets had the habit of placing paradise in the "golden age" of the most distant past. Since the two last centuries, our new poets are in the habit of placing it in the "golden age" of an equally distant perfect and ultimate society. But these are all illusions. Paradise is right in our own personal beginning, in the very center of the creative act. We are all Adam. We all feel a certain melancholy even in the moments of the greatest happiness. We are all created in paradise and sent, by the Angel with the Flaming Sword, into the passing time, into an "essential category" where we are born into history and die in it.[61]

As could have been expected, saturated, as we are, with "chains of causes and consequences", we have tried to apply these false categories even to the center of time. First Adam was created, then he tried to become powerful as God, then he was expelled, then his sons and grandsons had to suffer because of what he had done... Such a legalistic presentation, conceiving sin as a kind of inheritable property, may seem inevitable to poets very much taken in by terrestrial stories. But even if we describe myths as narrations of events that happened "in illo tempore", we should not forget that "illud tempus" is also now. Perhaps it would be better to say that myths describe what happens now, in the fulfillment of time...[62] Adam and Eve mean any man and any woman. The strife between Cain and Abel means every strife between brothers and neighbors. The Tower of Babel means any attempt to organize the human society on the basis of some super-idea – such as the Marxist super-organization which was eventually to lead to the utter inability of the men from Moscow and Peking to understand each other's political language. The Deluge means every anti-intellectual degeneration which brings the dark waters of the primeval abyss back to the surface of the earth.

We are all created in the same center of the complete time. And "while" we are created, all our moments of decision appear – not just some "first" one or some "last" one, but all of them. In them appears our love and our selfishness, our salvation or our second, final death.

The choice between eating or not eating the fruit of the tree which, allegedly, should make us like gods is the choice of our entire lives; it represents the sum of all our moments of decision. We are all Adam. We all find ourselves close to the fringe of death. But we can also save, as Bernard of Clairvaux firmly believed, the dead-born babies as well as infants who die shortly after birth by our mere creative will to conceive them. They already live in our love.[63] The Creator's grace is immediately with us. Being Love itself, the Creator thirsts for love *(mi fece il eterno amore)*. Even in the Hebrew myth, he immediately announces the crushing of the snake's head. He is at once ready to answer the slightest sign of our love with his own love. He does not take away the suffering, nor does he promise that he would do so in the future; that would defeat the purpose of creating the opportunity for love. But while leaving no one without sufficient grace, he, the "light that illuminates everybody coming into this world", may pour unusual graces into some human hearts – and, of course, ask for a greater love in return.[64]

Above all, "while" the "first Adam" is created in all those who bear the burden of the day, the "last Adam" *(éschatos ádam)* becomes the son of the Woman Who Crushes the Snake's Head. He is given the name of Emanuel, but he is also called the "leader of the deceased",[65] *i.e.*, the one who leads back to life those who find themselves in the shadows of death. Even his task has nothing to do with the lineal concept of time; it is happening now.

The firm hope of the Christians that the departed are with God and – in the Eastern Churches as well as in the Roman Church and the Church of England – the persuasion concerning the efficacy of prayers lead to the conclusion that the prayers for the departed are a true manifestation of the basic awareness of mankind's unity. So is the Far Eastern cult of the ancestors. So are many ages-old customs of many different ancient civilizations.

Perhaps, in these days of "togetherness" and "Socialist solidarity", it may seem superfluous to remind anyone of the unity of mankind in front of God's face, a unity which we all share. Nevertheless, there is a very essential difference between sharing and organization. To share signifies to participate in the innermost way, to bear common responsibility as much as to be bound by love. To be organized means, on the contrary, to draw boundaries, to assign to each member and to each cog its own function or obligation – and perhaps even to go further and provide fuses to safeguard the organization against possible failures.

Having started this essay with a story borrowed from Dostoyevskij, we may well conclude it in a similar way. First, in the epilogue to *Crime and Punishment*, Raskolnikov is telling us about his delirium which might have reflected both his own decomposition and that of the human society. He speaks of a "terribly pestilential" atmosphere in which men, as never before, "regarded themselves clever and infallible in their wisdom" and yet "each man was persuaded that he alone possessed the truth". He tells how in cities "alarms were sounded all day long and everyone went eagerly to mass-meetings, but nobody knew who had ordered them to come and for what purpose." Then, in Dostoyevskij's last major work, a hint arrives through Ivan Karamazov that an organization will be achieved, however only for the purpose of allowing each individual to obtain everything which an earthly life can offer.

The solidarity of man with his fellow-man, described so succinctly in the parable of the Good Samaritan, is evidently as important as the unity of man's person. Neither can be rooted in the flowing time. The stream of genes does not constitute an entire person. It may symbolize a "continuous" – as the false myth would pretend – stream of inheritance, but not a solidarity. Both the person and the solidarity of persons can only appear in relation to the Creator on whom all persons and all their solidarities are centered.

Both man's person and men's solidarity are threatened, on the fringe of darkness, by isolation – by man's isolation from God as well as by man's isolation from man. In the lonely crowd voices are heard which counsel isolation. Historians should have no difficulty in recognizing how old and squeaky these voices are – no matter how new may be the publicity surrounding them – and how threadbare is the advice they offer. One of them resounds currently around the world under the name of Zen-Buddhism. It says: "Throw away the body and find the soul" – and the silly old false myth about the dove-in-the-cage immediately replaces the realistic notion of the entire man.[66] It declares itself a "method of direct seeing into one's own nature"; but soon we find that it really amounts to a "method of ignoring everything else but oneself". Beside sitting and breathing in a prescribed way a concentrated effort is recommended "to think of neither good nor evil and judge not right or wrong...to bring to end all desires, all concepts... to forget all attachments". One is expected to look within and to realize that one is the Buddha. More than that: That one's true self is the Great Self. The Great Self, however, is no longer a man, nor a god, but only a Great Zero.

6

The Death of History?

We are not but we expect to be.
                            Blaise Pascal, *Pensées*

Perhaps science is as yet best known by
its capacity for depriving man of enjoyment,
and making him colder, more statuesque and more
stoical. But it might also turn out to be
the great pain-bringer.
                    Friedrich Nietzsche, *Die fröhliche Wissenschaft*

I remember the rage I used to feel when a
prediction went awry. I could have shouted at
the subjects of my experiments: "Behave, damn
you, behave as you ought."
                            B. F. Skinner, *Walden Two*

The falsely mythical concept of the universe as a stream has changed its face several times. We may admit that each of its temporary countenances had its charm and that each was attractive to the contemporary climate of opinion in its own way. The Christian thought has not proven immune to those charms. After all, both Christianity and the modern scientific vision have one common feature: A manifest, nostalgical dissatisfaction with the current state of things. They both have inherited, oddly enough, the messianic expectations of the early man. True enough, the Christian hopes are centered around Jesus' second coming *(parousia)*, while the scientific expectations vacillate between the scholarly satisfaction with the infinite vistas and the more popular thoughts consecrated to the coming of the Perfect Man; but theories have their epochs and man's uncertain heart does not remain faithful to any one among them for a longer time. As decades ans centuries passed by, the mutual relations between scientists and Christiupa also suffered a number of changes. Extremely few scientists became ever aware that their visions had something to do with the primeval myth of the messianic change. But a number among them realized that, instead of relying on the "natural course of developments", they should "take the issue into their own hands"; Thomas Huxley was perhaps the first to do so and since his days an increasing number followed his advice. The Christian theologians, on the other hand, as much as many of them had already fallen under the spell of Aristotelianism and Thomism, found themselves increasingly attracted by the scientific visions.

The illusory dream of power seems to have played here a decisive role. Even very recently "pure scientists" such as Jacques Monod admonished everybody around to direct human efforts to the objectivity of science alone, asserting that in this way the problem of values will be solved and a "new and supreme ethic" established. Somehow they bypassed the object which stands behind the objectivity: the will to power which does not seem inclined to disappear from human life. Many Christians, too, have forgotten Jesus' repeated statements that his kingdom was not from this world. They, too, succumbed to the charm of the object behind the objectivity.

At times, nevertheless, quarrels erupted between the disciples of science and even the not very faithful Christians. Thus throughout the later half of the nineteenth century scientists and theologians discussed Charles Darwin's works with vehement sarcasm. We may still feel amused by their enthusiasm; it brings color into the otherwise greyish epoch. But our interests have again changed during the more recent decades. The civilization in which we live seems to have lost many of the supposedly Christian facets which it still possessed – or was believed to possess – in the days of Charles Darwin, Thomas Huxley and bishop Wilbeforce. It hardly bothers us today whether "homo sapiens" was the cousin or the grandson of some primates. Indeed, revisiting Darwin, we may incline to the opinion that he and his associates had their main quarrel with some Platonists rather than with Christians. They were fiercely attacked as alleged opponents of the Platonic belief in the immortality of man's soul. More than once they were blamed for having cut the ties to the Platonic vision of man as a composite, divisible being, consisting of "mortal" body and "immortal" soul. They were charged with having made it impossible for that "soul" to exist, temporarily, in man's body by making that body even dirtier than it looked to Plato. Today we are perhaps more aware that Plato's visions had always little to do with the Christian message. Indeed, reading once again the *Origin of Species* and *The Descent of Man*, we may ask whether Darwin himself – if not the Darwinists in general – perhaps did not stand closer to the Christian view than bishop Wilbeforce.

Well within the Christian epoch, in the fifth century, when Gregory of Nyssa discussed with his sister Makrina the last things of man and the question came up of what happened to man's intellectual qualities when his bodily forces failed and his organism underwent decomposition, Gregory, accepting the experience of the flowing time as basis for his answer, stated very simply that the intellectual qualities remained with the dispersed elements of the dead person until his resurrection – in a way in which the purposeful qualities of a tool remain with its dissembled parts.[1] But many centuries were to divide the eminent Cappadocian from Charles Darwin. What did the author of the *Origin of Species* think about man's intellectual qualities?

In the first place – and this may perhaps surprise the reader who has only indirectly heard about Darwin – he would have probably not accepted so easily the hypothesis of the flowing-time stream as a basis for answer. "Origins" meant to him an immense number of basically momentous changes, not the beginning of a stream of events. He certainly disliked the concept of "creation" – but, paradoxically enough, not that of the "Creator". Once, in the "Historical Sketch" attached to the third edition of the *Origins*, he quoted with approval from Richard Owen that by the word "creation" some zoologists meant "a process they know not what".[2] Nevertheless, having stated at the beginning of the third chapter of *The Descent of Man* that "man differs so greatly in his mental power from all other animals" and having also remarked that "the difference in this respect is enormous", next, merely two paragraphs further, he admitted as his intention "to show that there is no fundamental difference between man and the higher mammals in their mental faculties". In the "General Summary and Conclusion" of the same work he first asked that it be admitted that "the mental powers of the higher animals, which are the same in kind with those of man, though so different in degree, are capable of advancement." But then he stated: "A great stride in the development of the intellect will have followed as soon as the half-art and half-instinct of language came into use; for the continued use of language will have reacted on the brain and produced an inherited effect; and this again will have reacted on the improvement of language." Finally, four lines later, language was described as "that wonderful engine which affixes signs to all sorts of objects". After that, the discussion closed rapidly with the assurance that "the higher intellectual powers of man probably follow from the continued improvement and exercise of the other mental faculties".

Evidently the investigator who was very nuch at his ease with "momentous origins" was rather lost when the need arose to deal with "the origin". He would have hardly descended to Lamarck's cheap description of man as "someone animated with a desire to exchange ideas". He would have probably realized that the word "desire" was not very apt to sum up the "exchanging of ideas". But what did he mean by a "half-instinct"? From where had "art" and "half-art" entered the scientist's vocabulary? What should "coming into use" mean? Above all, what should be understood by "that wonderful engine which affixes signs to objects"?

Had Darwin been educated by some scholastics, an explanation would be easy to find: Aristotle himself seemed fond of phrases such as "the eye is a matter for sight"[3] But Darwin was no scholastic thinker. He even did not share some of the views which the Enlightened rationalists had inherited from the scholastics. He consistently refused to have anything to do with the so-called "laws of nature" which he branded as "constructions" and "mental conveniences". Thus he actually followed the apostle Paul who had stressed that there was nothing in nature which could originate in nature itself. Moreover, Herbert Spencer's efforts to proclaim nature a grand design moving along the arrow of time toward an inexorable final goal – a truly scholastic and Cartesian description – remained evidently strange to Darwin. He was satisfied with demonstrating that concretely knowable situations accompanied the appearance of certain specific values. In each case such event was grasped as a facet of the given moment. Even the concept of "species" as something durable was rejected. To Darwin, an "idea" would have never meant a "form which endures". In the already mentioned "Historical Sketch" he specifically approved of the view that the introduction of new species may be a "regular", but not a "causal" phenomenon.

Aristotelian "causality" was, of course, still very much alive in Darwin's days. The geologist Adam Sedgwick concluded his criticism of Darwin's "dish of rank materialism" by exclaiming: "Change the conditions, and old species would disappear; and new species might come in and flourish... by what causation?"[4] "Causality" was perhaps the main weapon in the hands of Darwin's critics. Faithful to Thomas Aquinas they still regarded it as a stream, allegedly "continuous" and provided with anthropomorphic paraphernalia. Long before the ship "Beagle" left Plymouth, the Aristotelians of the New Age had entered the stage: Descartes talking about "mechanical laws" as "producing things from chaos", the Enlightened raisonneurs professing the persuasion that "natural morality" had always existed in human hearts, Lamarck with his ready-made "principle of evolution". After Darwin the adoration of the Continuous Stream would be resumed. Some twentieth century biologists would even return to Lamarck and speak of "genetic assimilation" or "natural selection of genes" which dispose organisms to become modified in reaction to environmental stimuli.[5] Many seem to have forgotten what *aitia* really meant in ancient Greek: an intellectual intention. Bergson's *élan vital* remained blind and to Betrand Russell man became a "product of causes which had no prevision of the end they were achieving"[6] – a description resembling the story of a man who left a dark room to look for a lamp without knowing that the lamp was an instrument with which he could lighten the room. The admirable Stream of Continuous Events found itself on its way to a Divine Throne. Eventually the Jesuit Teilhard was to provide it with some "direction of convergence". Asserting that it was "obscurely stirred by the Prime Mover", he presented this "Mover" as a venerable Aristotelian figure who, nevertheless, had in the meantime transferred his seat from the infinite past into the infinite future.

Perhaps some readers not familiar enough with Aristotelianism and Thomism should be reminded that the Aristotelians had diluted "cause" into four different brews:

1. material cause which is the Stream itself;
2. efficient cause, an instrument by which the Stream is moved;
3. formal cause, a poor remnant of the original *aitia*;
4. final cause, the situation eventually reached by the Stream.

Cognition itself was swallowed by the Stream; Aquinas had called it "adequation between mind and thing" and Herbert Spencer an "adjustment of internal to external relations". No one was told what "adequation" or "adjustment" might mean, nor what the difference between "internal" and "external" might be. What mattered was that cognition moved with the Stream. Somewhere the concept of "Perfection" was smuggled in, derived probably from Aristotle's "final cause". Supposing that the death of an impertinent fly alleviates the killer's situation, could it not be regarded as the killer's "perfection"? In Montesquieu one could already guess that the Stream would be perfected; Lamarck spoke bluntly, perhaps under Condorcet's influence, of a "tendency to perfection"; even Cuvier, who preferred catastrophies to evolution, opinionated that each catastrophy might be "an advance in the complexity of life" – taking it silently for granted that the way from simple to complex is always an advance, never a retreat. Eventually Herbert Spencer was to declare: "Instead of civilization being artificial, it is a part of nature; all of a piece with the development of the embryo or the unfolding of a flower."[7]

Certainly the growth of a seed into a fruit is often called "advancement" because it is a creative fulfillment. But why should the same word "advancement" be used when speaking of the Stream of flowing time between the appearance of a primordial virus and the coming of a professor of sociology? In what sense is the professor more advanced in fulfilling his meaningful life – provided that not only viruses but also professors of sociology have meaningful lives? Both the struggle in nature and man's recently formed dream about the tree of evolution lead to the question: who should be regarded as nature's greatest accomplishment? If the survival of those who are fit to survive should be used as the standard of evolution then the ones who have survived the longest period should perhaps be also regarded as the fittest. In that case man would be left far behind many other species whose span of existence on this earth seems much longer than his. But why should we not organize a system of evaluation around the struggle itself? Could we not assert that the species, or even a larger part of nature, which is least dependent of a favorable outcome of the struggle, and least exposed to fatalities resulting from the struggle, has also the greatest probability of survival? From that point of view the plants would appear ahead of other sectors: they rarely have to consume other structures because most of their food comes from light. Both the primeval man who used to identify the Creator with the sun and the Christian who adheres to the symbolism of light could then envisage the theory of evolution as Jacob's ladder leading more and more into light and into light alone.

The Victorians, however, thought of man only. They felt very much assured by Spencer's *First Principles* in the belief that "evolution can end only in the establishment of the greatest perfection and the most complete happiness". Even if Thomas Huxley was to lose this faith before the century had run its course, man remained the great favorite of the Evolutionists in general.

But what was Darwin's real relationship to the Divine Stream?

We may feel slightly taken aback when reading, in the *Origin of Species*, that "we must suppose that there is a power, represented by natural selection ... always intently watching each slight alteration... and carefully preserving alterations which tend to produce a distincter image".[8] We are not told expressly that "distincter" means "more perfect", but the parable certainly suggests that the Stream possesses a "watching consciousness". Moreover, variations are described as "useful" as well as "each good for the individual possessor". In *The Descent of Man* they are defined as "secondary causes". Darwin also differentiated between "favorable" and "injurious" variations. We are told that the Stream's products, compared to those of man, "plainly bear the stamp of far higher workmanship".[9] This makes one wonder why there should be any difference at all between man's products and those of the Stream of Nature; are they not identical?

Such opinions – together with Darwin's belated adoption of Spencer's "survival of the fittest", where fitness can hardly mean more than reproductive proficiency – may incline us to a more sceptical judgement concerning the great scientist. His conclusion might have been more sober, had he spoken simply of "sequences of events", instead of branding some "causes" as "secondary", opposed, evidently, to some other, "primary", "causes". Instead of stressing that "variations are selected for conditions" he could have simply spoken of interactions between organisms and environments. Railroads were not exactly the newest thing in Darwin's England; did they not represent a net of conditions selected by the contemporary variation of homo sapiens? Today it seems even more obvious that conditions are selected by variations as much as variations by conditions and that both are inherent in a given situation.

Moreover, while situations certainly do change, nowhere do we find any evidence that this change happens in any "orderly" fashion or that "only events with purpose" have the quality of "survival". It is rather the post-modern scientist who seems to fail with an increasing frequency in avoiding a falsely-mythical vocabulary. He imitates the military in talking constantly about "codes", "messages" and "informations". At times he even endows the Stream with a "self-regulating mechanism". And how often do we hear tautologies such as that the Stream is "significant" because it is "full of significant happenings" – as if *all* "happenings" were not component parts of just one enormous "happening" which is the universe... Of course, we have to admit in all fairness that here and there one encounters a scientist capable of turning values upside down and of declaring not only that "evolution is discontinuous", but also that selection is primarily a "destructive agency".[10]

But, to return to Charles Darwin, we have to state that even while retreating, at times, before the voices coming from outside his laboratory, he never became a complete victim of the Purposeful-and-Self-Regulating-Stream superstition. Even if he occasionally used terms which induced his critics to ask him whether "Variation was the cause of variations", he defended himself. "It has been said," he stated in one of the later editions of his magnum opus, "that I speak of natural selection as an active power or deity; but who objects to an author speaking of gravity as ruling the planets?" Perhaps he even grew more and more inclined to see the real "origin" in a "trifling difference" rather than in any "endeavour toward perfection". In 1857 he wrote to Asa Gray, a Bostonian naturalist: "Only a few of those annually born can live to propagate their kind; what a trifling difference must often determine which shall survive, and which perish..." In the closing arguments of the *Origin of Species* the enormous extinction is stressed not only of the "less improved", but also of the "intermediate" forms of life. Possibly the meaning of the concept of "purpose" was often a subject of Darwin's meditations – the same concept which Nietzsche, in the fifth chapter of *The Joyful Wisdom,* declared to be in great need of strict criticism. While to Asa Gray "adaptation to purpose" remained "the appropriate proof of design", Darwin was quite evidently aware that "complexity" or "perfection" of any kind was not the "purpose". On the contrary, he seems to have reached the conclusion that the more complex was the character of an organism, the lesser were its chances of survival. Thomas Huxley, who knew

Darwin's thinking intimately, refused to identify "fittest" with "best" and admitted, as early as 1864, that, should the earth cool again, "the survival of the fittest might bring about a population of more and more stunted and humbler organisms."[11]

Nor was the Divine Stream very divine in Darwin's thoughts. In the very first chapter of the *Origin* he had spoken about man's power of selection as different from the conditional selection which characterizes nature in general. History was alive to him. Man and man only, he stated, "adds selections up in certain directions useful to him." He spoke of "directions" in plural, not of the sole direction of the Stream. Perhaps he was more optimistic about man's creative capabilities than the post-modern biologists who admit with Julian Huxley that "man knows that he is a victim". And while he did describe, occasionally, as "good" whatever pertained to the preservation of a species, the opposite concept of "evil" never entered his vocabulary – in sharp contrast to, *e.g.*, Herbert Spencer who branded as "evil" any "non-adaptation" to the Stream.

It is rather essential to notice Darwin's persistent cautiousness in avoiding terms about which "there hangs a moral flavor". It certainly was an exceptional and honest cautiousness. By contrast, the Aristotelian worshippers of the Stream were becoming, as years passed, ever more eager to endow the Stream with a capability of distinguishing between "good" and "evil". To Thomas Aquinas, evil in the universe was a mere "privation of good". Even in the so-called "natural theology" of the early nineteenth century, evil still hardly existed; Paley assured his readers that it simply "never had been the object of creation". But after Darwin things were to change even in this respect. Thomas Huxley's last work, as is well known, expressed the view that man should combat evil perhaps even at the price of "opposing evolution". With his grandson Julian Huxley we see man carried by the Stream, but armed with a "moral purpose". The springs of the Stream have, oddly enough, assumed an almost evil character: it was and still is postulated that its future course should be better and better. One has never stopped identifying "higher degrees of organization" with "better levels" – notwithstanding the current experience that "higher organizations" are often "organizations toward death".

Even Darwin was, admittedly, attracted by variations which tended both to survival and to greater complexity. Such an attraction prevails in the study of the formation of eye in the sixth chapter of the *Origin* where he also describes the "Creator's craftmanship" as "superior to that of man". But his "variations-conditions" do not have to be hanged on any "causal line" of escaping time. They do not possess any time-enduring quality, nor any "inclination to better or worse". To anyone who accepts the *New Testament* vision of the creative act as an explosion, few things can be more sympathetic than Darwin's view of the innumerable variations-conditions surrounding each man in each of his particular "moments of decision". Darwin actually shows that it is only some groups chosen from an immense number of specimens which we try to cover by the expression "species". He also shows that each specimen alone consits of an immense number of situations. Our effort to gather up a restricted number of these situations by saying, *e.g.*, "this flower", is only a feeble attempt to see in a way resembling the Creator's all-embracing view or, if you wish, his unrestricted movement.

The Victorians who combatted Darwin hardly did so because of any anxiety to defend the freedom of man and to foster history against zoology. They themselves adhered, perhaps more than Darwin ever did, to the concept of the Continuous Stream which history is certainly not. The author of the *Origin of Species* with his momentous variations-conditions stood closer to apostle Paul's stressing his "*now* is the time of salvation" than did men who operated with "ages", "generations", "schools", "centuries" and other similar patterns belonging among the paraphernalia of the Divinized Continuous Stream. As has been mentioned, Darwin's critics were hardly concerned with man as a creative being – *i.e.*, with an animal who, through the grace of God, possesses the capability of a free, intellectual choice and to whom Jesus gave the promise of resurrection. On the contrary, we may frequently discover at the bottom of their hearts the thought which Leibniz had expressed so succinctly: "It is of an infinitely greater advantage to defend the immortality of souls as their natural property than to affirm that they will not die only thanks to a miraculous gift bestowed on them by divine charity."[12]

Two elements had entered into the formation of this old story:

1. the Aristotelian identification of all creation with a "harmonious" nature in which evil is only a "privation";

2. Plato's concept of the "immortal soul".

The first, needless to say, cannot be saved even by some "Angelic Doctors" from being diametrically opposed to the Christian conception of the entire creation as "toiling and travailing". The second stems from Plato's all too hasty identification of man's capability to reach some truths with the "soul's incorruptibility".[13] As to the first of our two just mentioned elements, there is not a little irony in the fact that the scholastic philosophers never understood that it also opposed the very concept of creation: with all their passion for "proofs" they never succeeded to demonstrate that their "harmonious nature" was not infinite and did need a Creator. As to the second element, Lessing made it the basis of all education, Kant declared it a "necessary postulate" and Robespierre enacted it in 1794 as a law of his very perishable regime – but even so it still has not assumed any validity.

Combined of these two elements the whole trend – which Charles Darwin never really fully embraced – leads to something very serious: A theory, or theories, which predicate the death of history.

To a sober observer history does not admit, through its very essence, any lineal representation. Whatever is "continuous" is also "necessary", while history is the sum of free decisions which can be narrated as a drama but cannot be transformed into a contingent series of events. Denying the nature of history, attempting to depict it as a continous line or again as a dialectical but no less necessary spiral, the nineteenth century has only proved its unwillingness to understand things as they are. Creation happens now and so does every man's decision to participate in it through creative love or to reject it through pride. Every "now" is now and has no dimensions. An extremely rare and truly momentous creative idea of a primitive, almost submerged in animality, hardly differs from the eighty-years' endeavors of a scholar. Within the creative act which happens now every man receives his opportunity and all his decisions are included within the same creative act. People are certainly chosen – and perhaps only few are chosen – but through their own choice; there is no predestination and no postdestination.

And yet, paradoxically, mainly since the days of Charles Darwin, the absolute uniqueness of each variation-condition has been more and more ignored and the very sense of history denied. It is understandable that from the scientifico-technological point of view generalizations of a mathematically describable character are indispensable and that less and less place is allotted to studies whose results cannot be summed up statistically; the build-up of technostructures, above all, requires such behavior. But the unique character of each particular part of nature, whether organic or inorganic, as well as the essential concept of history are now being denied even by many theologians.

To a Buddhist it is perhaps impossible not to assert the existence of the Continuous Stream and of the chain of causes and effects. It would be equally impossible for a hunter not to assert the existence of wild game. As a hunter lives on wild game by killing it, so a Buddhist thrives on the *patikka samuppada*, the infinite line of birth, death and of "again becoming". If he were to deny the "chain of causation" he would have nothing to fight, nothing against which to strain his will and to discipline himself. He has a priori conceived this life as a struggle against a phantom; consequently he has to believe in the phantom. He is not even able to admit the creative character of history.

But why have so many "Christian" theologians recently assumed a hostile position toward history and why have they rejected history's very existence? As early as in their polemics with Darwin they asserted falsely that the scientist was denying the momentous event through which man appeared on this earth as man. They were, already then, ready to recognize everything else as a "continuous process" – something which Darwin never fully admitted. Now they seem to have turned to an even greater extreme. Led by Teilhard they accepted the divinization of the Continuous Stream. They gave up the quite evidently discontinuous character of history and replaced it by a self-inflicted tyranny of sheer necessity.

Perhaps the very core of this now more and more prevalent fashion is the refusal to say "yes" or "no" to any event. It may well be so that the intellectual pride revolts against the fact that our intellect can never embrace more than a single situation at once. Even granted that we may have an intuition of the enormous universe around us, we can still direct our attention only to one event at a time. But by holding to the phantom of the lineal and necessary process one somehow imagines to free oneself not only from the present moment, but also and primarily from the obligation to assume an attitude toward the current situation, to make a decision about it. It may well be escapism through "causal determinism."[14]

Because the entire trend has already moved far away from reality it is hardly surprising that within its scope we are encountering opinions as mutually diametrically opposed as opinions can be. Only the basic postulate – that history really does not exist and that we are governed by some kind of a Divine Inexorable Stream – has remained identical.

Thus to Thomas J. J. Altizer, a prominent member of the American "Death of God" school, and to the Jesuit Pierre Teilhard de Chardin the universe seems, at first sight, to mean one and the same thing. Only a fairy-tale mirror, similar to the one through which Alice once stepped, divides their respective visions. Teilhard's *Phenomenon of Man* and Altizer's *The Descent into Hell* deserve a place on the same bookshelf. In the first place, they are both equally ignorant of the Christian conception of time. Second, they are equally estranged from the conclusions of contemporary science – a characteristic not surprising in Altizer who never pretended to be familiar with science, but unexpected in Teilhard who originally had made his name in anthropology. Their ways of thinking are indeed very close to each other. What a critical scientist has written – that "Teilhard becomes more and more confused and excited and finally almost hysterical"[15] – is applicable also to Altizer. But while Teilhard expects the Stream to reach a collective extasy, Altizer envisages his final New Jerusalem as a "totality or an all", abolishing all "polarities and divisions" and thus, evidently, also any free, creative thought.

Both authors use the Stream as the foundation of an "eschatology". In the Christian thought, "eschatology" always meant what Christ's message said about the ultimate things of man. Each human person is standing, according to the Christian tradition, as an individual before the Creator's face – even if, described in a parable, holding the hands of all the others around him. Christ came to die for each man in particular or for all men as a community, but not for mankind as an evolving line. To love the man whom one encounters anywhere *(plēsíon)* never means, in the *Gospels*, to dissolve one's identity in him, but rather to offer him one's own, entirely unique heart. Teilhard and Altizer, nevertheless, have both desired otherwise.

Their actual point of departure seems to be the so-called "eschatological scandal", dating from the writings of Johannes Weiss and Albert Schweitzer. According to these two German scholars the early Christians found that they had been cheated when they were told by Jesus to expect his not very distant, almost immediate final coming. Perhaps Weiss and Schweitzer should really not bear all the blame. It is an old story which started with some speculations of the early Christian theologians concerning the "temporary" character of Christ's *kénōsis* and its interpretation as God's action in a "pre-existent" Logos. The moment one started using "chronological concepts" while speaking of the Creator, Christ's presence in every moment of history was obscured. One had forgotten Jesus' words: "Hypocrites, the appearance of earth and skies you know how to scrutinize, how is it that this present moment you do not scrutinize?" One had even forgotten those very definite words by which Jesus answered from the cross the prayer of the thief on his right side: "Today you shall be with me in paradise..." Not "at the end of the world" or "in the distance of times", not even "tomorrow" or "in a short time", but "today".[16]

Should the "truly modern form of Christian theology" be dated, as mainly Altizer is inclined to assert, from this negligence – not from a "discovery", but from a negligence – it would mean an altogether regrettable mistake. In the Christian message all the points of history, whether individual or general, all the moments of decision *(kairói)* are one moment, one "now" with God. A man's death and Christ's final coming in glory *(parousia)* are one and the same moment. Few aspects of the Christian message are so consistently, and in such a precise vocabulary, expounded in the *New Testament* as this one. But it does not seem to have helped. One even refused to listen to Nietzsche who, speaking of world's history, asked whether "an essentially mechanical world would not be an essentially meaningless world".[17] The same Aristotelian machine-like Stream, attired in all its inevitable necessity, which had already charmed Thomas Aquinas and Descartes, also bewitched Teilhard and Altizer.

They simply had to produce the vision of a universe which, in addition to the majesty of the Aristotelian inevitability, would use mankind as an important, perhaps decisive element of its own structure. Why mankind and why not individual, free and creative men? Why has history to die and be definitely replaced by a Stream? Were we able to answer this question we would also be able to unravel completely the thoughts of the apostles of the "new, revolutionary conclusions". Moreover, we would have at hand an answer to the question why has Christ's message been rejected by so many.

Perhaps we should concentrate, first of all, on the concept of "totality or an all". "My name is legion", declared in the *New Testament* the man who was tortured by evil spirit. The intellectual inheritors of that poor man have been evidently often qualmed by a merely mathematical postulate: What is finite cannot embrace the infinite. The Christian message has dared to proclaim the opposite: Any individual man is capable of loving God and, what is much more, God loves him. Christ has been proclaimed both the alpha and the omega, both the fountainhead and the plenitude of the infinite movement of the creative act. Each moment of each individual human life can be directed to God now, no matter from what sector of history it comes. And yet the "closed circle" of the creative act is immensely wealthier than an infinity of human lives. It is possible to illustrate this graphically: An explosion has an infinitely greater number of points on its circumference than any number of infinitely long tangents to the same circumference (representing our illusory projections into past and future). Merely operational postulates such as the "meeting of parallels in infinity" have no logical value. What is not a mere postulate, but a real evidence, is the fact that, in the case of each tangent when each point on it ($-\infty \to A \to G \to \infty$) is paired off against a point (or even two) on the circumference, two points, 01 and 02, are always left out. Given an infinite number of tangents, this results in an infinity of supernumerous points of the kind of 01 and 02.

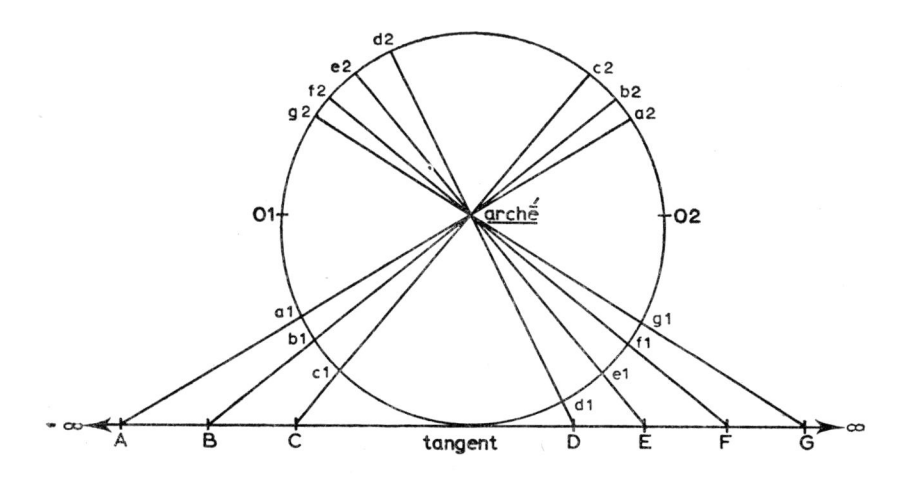

The tormented men who have rejected Christ's message often feel attracted by the multitude, by the "legion" which seems to multiply their own selfishness and pride and thus, of course, also multiplies their tortures. The "legion" may appear in the form of an assembly, of a mob, of a political party, of an army, or of an enormous number of engines. It may also appear in the form of a Stream of Generations. The men tormented by their own pride often speak of a "continuous succession" – a self-contradictory expression, because "continuity" means an absence of change, while "succession" means replacement of one by another. At times they insist that a multitude of men, just because of sheer numbers, must find an outlet from its present situation. Kierkegaard, in the *Last Years*, proclaimed: "... I must say I am not a Christian... in spite of the abyss of nonsense in which we are caught, we shall all alike be saved." Half a century before him, William Blake, poet and engraver, the first to proclaim the death of Urizen, the "Old God", also asserted that the true God is the "Eternal Body of Man". Herbert Spencer, in his *Social Statistics*, stated that "the ultimate development of the ideal man" was "logically certain – as certain as any conclusion in which we place the most implicit faith: For instance, that all men will die."

Spencer's belief seems of particular interest. He was not concerned with Smith or Brown, but with an abstruse entity, "the ideal man". But he placed the production of this ideal man on the same level as all men's death. The Stream before his eyes reaches, in a distant future, a certain desirable – but why really desirable? – level. At the same time it becomes subject to disappearance, to death. We may feel here the presence of a darkly mythical urge to reach something both ideal and irreal. Kierkegaard, who had learned his catechism, certainly knew what "salvation" meant to a Christian. Why did he want to be saved if he did not regard himself a Christian? Granted that God was the "Eternal Body of Man" as William Blake wanted it to be, what else could be understood by such a body than the elements which pass from one generation to another? Why should this Stream of Elements be called God?

It was certainly not the scientists who have led the way into this theological jungle. Buffon and Lamarck might have been intrigued by the possibility of arranging the many species into a developing or changing pattern. Buffon perhaps even more than the younger Lamarck seemed to be fascinated by the conception of the universe as a Stream. But science did not have any need to speak of "salvation" or of describing the "eternal Body of Man" as God. Indeed, it did not have really any need for looking toward the production of an "ideal man". Darwin, as we have seen, denied the usefulness of any such postulates; there is no ultimate goal nor any Aristotelian "causality" in his universe. He simply described a mutual interdependence between conditions and variations which happen in any particular moment.

Only the authors of the "new myths" look toward "ideals" and seek their "causes". If such "causes" are not available, these new *mythopoioi* hasten to produce them out of their wizard's hats, telling us how "God will become fully immanent in mankind" or again how the "humanity's soul" is going to "break away, carrying upwards its incommunicable load of consciousness". But what moves them to such sermons?

Every genuine myth is rooted in experience; every false myth may be regarded as a travesty of experience. The primeval myths about creation and their cultic representations all tried to tell about it in images, parables, movements, singing and music. Twentieth century biology with its pseudo-mythical stories about the "spontaneous tendency" (*read*: purposeful will) of nucleic acids and chromosomal apparatuses to "proffer" (*read*: to create) genetical variants as "solutions" of the "problem of remaining alive", also seems to attempt to describe an experience, perhaps a rather inevitable experience. Even a fairy-tale expresses the very real experience of dreams and imagination. Is it not possible that the Teilhards and the Altizers also offer us some kind of a real experience in the form of their new and, of course, rather false, myths?

Perhaps it is the experience of the ordinary man on the pavements of a megalopolis. Every day, after a breakfast accompanied by a hurried consumption of some mass-written and mass-printed daily paper, this man lunges into a stream. Mass transportation, mass production, mass consumption of lunches, more mass production, more mass transportation; eventually late in the evening, mass viewing of mass amusement. Next day, the same stream – day after day, year after year. This inhuman stream of mass events may still be punctuated, here and there, by exceptional and genuinely human experiences. But the mass character predominates, increases, becomes more oppressive every year. It does not seem improbable that some post-modern theologians are really engaged in an attempt to transform this real experience into a myth but that they have chosen a rather false way – or, to be more precise, one of two false ways which they have regarded as the only two open to them.

One is an escape into the realm of dreams. Mostly a chemical escape: after mere dreaming come pills, injections, more pills. A world of very selfish visions opens its gates. One's imagination separates itself from the dreary stream and flies its own way. This is the Teilhardian dream, the dream of the separated Platonic soul, of "hominization" and "ultra-hominization". But the "separated soul", curiously enough, seems to have preserved something of the stream-like character of the daily experience. It joins other "souls", it becomes the "soul of souls", the *point omega*. Allegedly it may even find Christ himself, but only in the dim, unreal infinity of the escaping time.

The other is an escape into resigned acceptation. Mostly a psychological escape: Self-persuasion, concentration on nothingness. A world of illusory powers opens its gates. One's will seemingly comes to dominate the dreary stream and to establish itself on a throne above it. This is the dream of Altizer, the dream of the "acceptation of the full movement of history" – it has become impossible to regard history as anything but a "movement" – as well as of the "absolute transformation of the world". The Creator himself is moving from "transcendence" to "immanence", obedient to the "revolutionary will" of the man who has invented both these empty, nonsensical words. "We can know our darkness as our own".[18] "Eternal death could appear as symbol of that pure immanence which is the opposite of pure transcendence."[19]

Embracing the first of these two new myths we are promised an escape from entropy. Embracing the second one we are promised a final acquiescence in entropy. In both cases we are assured that this is God and it is also intimated to us that the suggested solution agrees with the opinions of contemporary science – such an agreement being regarded as something very important. God could not make his peace with science in the Victorian days – but that, of course, was Urizen, the Bearded One of William Blake. He is dead. A new God is being created – as George B. Shaw used to expect. The Teilhards and the Altizers see to it that he emerges in a shapely form from man's hands. While we were obliged to give thanks to the old God for our lives, the new God is here to thank us for his existence and to adjust himself to all our desires for power.

Not only scholars but also some of the Christian bishops of our time seem to be infected by dreams concerning this "new God".

In this respect the apostolic letter *Octogesima adveniens*, published by pope Paul VI in Rome in May, 1971, is a document equally remarkable and bewildering.[20] It criticizes very correctly the production of superfluous commodities while a scarcity of basic commodities continues in the world; it condemns social indifference; it insists on the mysterious character of history; it points out that to make man a mere object of science may mean building a prison for him; it even speaks unhesitatingly about the dangerous growth of supranational economic powers capable of ignoring the common good.[21] Nevertheless, the author seems to have accepted, as one of his basic ideas, the concept f "progress". While another pope, Pius IX, had condemned the "automatic progress" in his famous *Syllabus*, the author of *Octogesima adveniens* had already used the expression in the very title of his 1967 *Populorum progressio* – without bothering in the least either to define the differences, if any are extant, between his own and his predecessor's use of the concept or to offer any definition of the concept of "progress" at all. Moreover, where Pius IX evidently felt adversely provoked by the contemporary Western thought, Paul VI seems to have acted in a hasty eagerness to conform himself with the prevalent thinking of his own age. He went so far as to invoke the authority of the *Gospels* not only in relationship to the conversion and spiritual or intellectual growth of individual men, but also in relationship to what he calls "the progress of social life"; next he proclaimed bluntly that the Church had a specific mission: "To support man's endeavor to take in his own hands his future and to direct it." This mission he also described as an "action of solidarity within the turmoil of history".[22] Further on it is stated in the *Octogesima adveniens* that the very "center of Christian preoccupations" should be seen in the "efforts directed toward the solution of new difficulties which put at stake the very future of man". After that the reader is assured that industry's "incessant creativity" is going to "transform nature itself".[23] Almost at the same time he is also told about a "progressive instauration of a less imperfect justice."[24]

Even with that the reader of the *Octogesima adveniens* has not yet reached the heart of the matter. In Chapter 22 of the encyclical he is openly admonished to accept the "aspiration to equality" as one of the "two forms of man's dignity and freedom" – the "aspiration to a participation" being considered the second such form. Chapter 24 proclaims the "aspiration to equality" the main factor of a "new democratic society" in which "man constructs his destiny". The same chapter goes as far as to suggest that everyone should, for this specific purpose, "subordinate all his particular activities" to "an immense, universal body politic".

There is, indeed, something terrifying in these assertions and proclamations. The reader feels that it would be almost in vain to recall to the author of the encyclical the numerous texts of the *New Testament* which condemn envy – and what else is envy but an "aspiration to equality"? Even a non-Christian student of the human past would remember the warning of the Roman Stoic Seneca who observed how man's joy increases with the number of people sharing in talks, songs and dances, but how strife begins the moment the attention turns to sharing of material goods. Even a non-Christian historian is acquainted with the real "beginning of the New Age" inherent in Francis Bacon's view that not the limiting of desires but the forcing of nature to do our bidding should be regarded as means for the removal of struggle over material comforts. To hear a leading Christian bishop inviting everybody to join in the struggle for "equality" and discovering in such a struggle the "rhythm of progress"[25] becomes a most distressing experience. Should we call it a new and painful renewal of the story told in Matt. 16:23 about Peter's temporary unwillingness to accept the necessity of suffering – a most meaningful story, but somehow never accepted to adorn the interior of the cupola at St Peter's in the Vatican?

"To oppose the increasing technocracy," the encyclical continues, "one has to discover modern forms of democracy which would give to everyone not only the possibility to obtain information and to express his opinion but also to integrate his own, personal responsibility with the common one."[26] But while pronouncing this emotionally and yet so emptily sounding phrase one has bypassed in silence the one really important discrimination which characterizes the human society: The uneven gifts granted to man by his genetic inheritance. How large a promille of citizens of any country is today capable of only a slight penetration of the widely ramified scientific knowledge at the disposal of the technocratic managers: The wealth of information coming from the realms of infraatomic physics, electronics, biochemistry, neurophysiology, psychology, economic analytics etc.? How many citizens can, in such conditions, "obtain information" and "express their opinion"?

Are the scientists themselves capable of any "reconstruction of society"? They have already done their best to ignore Darwin by saving in incubators as well as in the wheelchairs of the octogenarians practically everybody unfit to survive. Instead of concentrating on problems such as photosynthesis which might grant life to the young and hungry, they have devoted their time to the study of sicknesses such as cancer and heart-ailments which kill mostly the elderly and the well-fed. Having taken death away from the childhood's experiences they brought about an atmosphere in which mental disturbances increase at a terrifying pace. They placed the injection-needle not only in the hands of nurses, but also in those of the victims of overcrowded and polluted regions; the same goes for cars and planes put at the disposal of people whose basic health requirements include the largest possible amount of natural locomotion *i.e.*, of simple walking. Above all, they have hardly made a significant discovery before they hastened to place it at the feet of conscienceless industrialists and political warmongers.

That a Christian bishop should counsel us to take our future into our own hands in connection with man's "anspiration to equality" and that he should ignore, at the same time, the immense and very "natural" differences between the intellectual capacities of individual men, means a regrettable blindness *vis à vis* the reality which surrounds us. It also means to ignore the prediction uttered at the end of the already quoted chapter 16 of Matthew's *Gospel*. This prediction warns against the possible loss of life *(psýchē)* as directly connected with the "gaining of the entire world". There will be some, the warning continues, who will see Christ's *parousia* before the darkness of death envelops them. There may be many more who will have to suffer in an utmost darkness and loneliness of a prolonged agony. Already now they are hardly able to understand, and therefore even less to influence, the management of their societies. Democracy – influencing the government through voting based on a real understanding – is as dead as a thing might be. Jean Jacques Rousseau knew well that "democracy" was applicable only to his small native Geneva and not even to a state as large as France – what would he have said of Paul VI's "world-wide body politic"? Had the author of *Octogesima adveniens* really wanted to counsel his breathren, to "sustain their faith", he should have told them the truth in all its terrible simplicity.

He could have also warned them not to waste their time in trying to dominate the powers – and even less a "world-wide body politic" – but rather to spend their endeavors in small communities, in personal charity, in the help extended to "anyone encountered on the road" (which – not "neighbor" – is the correct translation of the evangelical word *plēsíon*). That the social and military managers will indeed try to take mankind's future into their hands even more than they have so far done, is highly probable. The Christian faith, however, is certainly not anchored in such endeavors. The managers resemble the same Satan-Peter who refused to recognize the need of suffering. They should be dashed against the Rock, "and that Rock is Christ".[27]

The recent versions of G. B. Shaw's cherished conception of God as a built-up Life-Force or, again, versions of Lucretius' conception of God as a magnanimously accepted despair are both man-made concepts. But why have God, really? Why call him God at all? Would not "Uniformity" be a better name for our product? Military formations and *Gleichschaltungen* as well as "tortures of hell" fascinated Iñigo de Loyola, founder of the "Company" to which Teilhard was to belong. The dreary uniforms of Maotsetungia seem to fascinate the followers of Altizer. Moreover, should not science which operates with generalizations all the time welcome the Spirit of Uniformity with open arms? And yet, while science operates with generalizations for the sake of succinct definitions and also for technology's sake, no scientist would suggest that nature is uniform. He even knows, as we have remarked, that "species" is an exceedingly summary word covering an immense number of specimens of which not even two are exactly alike.

The pre-modern historian also used to be acquainted with the true character of the universe and mainly of history. Only relatively recently has he started envisaging history as a "march", a "rise" or even a "sweep". But whatever he has written in this vein may be considered dead-born: Not only mass-produced text-books but also the voluminous collections which Acton has initiated or the laboriously compiled giants such as Toynbee's work. If history is dead, so is historiography. They both died the day when Teilhard's "orthogenesis" or Altizer's "descent" were born. Even in this sense the new myths seem to reflect some real events.

In the olden times, when history was still fully alive, it did not deal with a species, least of all with any "march" of that species, but with some most individual specimens. Man was alive as a person, distinct from other persons. If the historian was of a Christian persuasion, he believed in salvation. He believed in the salvation "now". He did not know of any "ultimate salvation". It was obviously not so much God as history which Nietzsche's man with a lantern has declared dead. Or perhaps it was God understood as a Stream. In the days of Herbert Spencer it was still fashionable to believe that the Stream was leading to a definite goal within history. With Nietzsche it suddenly stopped leading to any such terrestrial goal – or, rather, Nietzsche was the first to notice it. Somewhat later even H. G. Wells had to admit it at the end of his life's tether.

Having discovered the "most difficult possible thought – the eternal recurrence of all things", Nietzsche set out to find a man – or perhaps to create him? – a man who would accept this discovery light-heartedly and joyfully. It does not look probable that he has found anyone. Perhaps he forgot to count with a mode of thought stronger than his own, stemming from Kant and Hegel. To Hegel, the myths of Creation and of God's New Revelation resembled mere categories of thought. Creation was described by him as "relationship between an abstract notion and the things in which this notion may be instantiated". Not a "creation from nothing" but still a "creation". Similarly, whether an Incarnation has ever happened or will happen, seemed immaterial to Hegel; but he certainly regarded it as a most "actual" conception. Half way between Hegel and Nietzsche, Søren Kierkegaard appeared ready to accept Hegel's message – no matter how much he hated him otherwise – but with a sense of guilt and with his heart still set on salvation. There really could be no talk about a "simple, joyful and light-hearted acceptance" of the Eternal Return of Things. If it were to be accepted at all, it had to be under the disguise of the paraphenalia of primeval mythology: Creation, Incarnation, Salvation.

Even God-Man was needed, provided that one turned him upside down as Kirillov did in Dostoyevskij's *The Possessed* – "not God-Man, but Man-God" who is going to kill himself to prove his self-made salvation, his "terrible new freedom". Christ himself appeared as needed as soon as one turned to the "great demythologizer" Bultmann; but a Christ who has not risen from dead and whose final coming would coincide with the Stream only as soon as parallels meet. Actually there is only a barely noticeable difference between Kirillov and a modern theologian such as, *e.g.*, Bultmann. Bultmann's apostles, confused and bitterly sad about the death on Calvary, were to receive an illusory "Pentecostal revelation" about some "future resurrection". We now seem able to get rid even of that resurrection, providing we identify it fully with the Stream, no matter how often it may still appear floating above the Stream's surface...

In Thomas Altizer it does surface quite often. Trying hard to learn whatever there may be to learn about the "meaning of a radical eschatology" from the "seemingly anti-Christian revolutionaries" and listening attentively to "every call from the future", Altizer hesitates somewhat between the "coming of an absolute transformation of the world" (only it must not be expected immediately)[28] and a belief which he reads into the apostle Paul: A belief that all things will be subject to Christ and Christ himself to the Father only after a Cosmic Power, inherent in the Christ-Stream, "has been fully exercised".[29] While Christ's ascension is dismissed as a "backward and upward movement", Altizer's readers are asked to join into God's own "forward and downward" movement, through which God would reject his "primordial" ascendance and become an "immanent" God, a real Stream. Accepting this Stream as our own continuous passage – it could hardly be anything else than "continuous" – or as our transition from "transcendence" into "immanence", we are asked to recognize the "full autonomy of man" as a "reflection of the autonomy of God". We are then graciously offered a "form of power which faith had long associated with the sovereignty of God."[30]

In each case, however, it is only the power to kill the last remnants of history which we are being offered. Perhaps we have already learned to resent history because history is painful. Where Nietzsche spoke of pain as "one of the best self-preservatives of a species", we are assured by Teilhard that things painful will be corrected and we are exhorted by Altizer, Camus or Buber that we should learn how to despize them. But whether we see pain being cured (even entropy will be painless the Jesuit way) or whether we learn to despise pain (accepting entropy with hands akimbo) we are already now offered the power to ignore the drama of history.

Quite recently a large concert-hall was inaugurated in Washington with a musical drama composed by a much publicized New York conductor and called the *Kennedy Mass* – in memory of the late president of the United States. The protagonist of this musical pantomime is a guitarist who, infatuated by his own popularity, assumes the role of a priest and begins to celebrate what, very mildly, may be called a persiflage of the Christian liturgy. But when he attempts to offer his retinue a "communion", his followers reject it and scream *"Dona nobis pacem* – Give us peace..." The "celebrant" than recognizes the truthfulness of their view and joins them. This work represents, in a thorough and most telling symbolism, the peak of the contemporary attitude toward the Christian message. Not only Charles Darwin but also Jesus knew that the entire universe is one tremendous struggle. Indeed it lies in darkness, witnessing a gigantic encounter between Light and Darkness. The Savior descended into it not to bring "peace" but "fire". Man's will to share in the creative act, his willingness to accept the cross and thus to manifest his love was strengthened by the Savior's self-immolation. He, too, has offered us peace, but such peace as can never reign in this world. Those who reject their opportunity to manifest their love through suffering, through the acceptance of Jesus' body and blood, may gain only the peace of this world, the false peace of the slavish security, of the drugs, of death.

Ignored by man, history, too, cannot be but dead. Without Jesus Christ, it would have always been dead: Dead men, broken vessels, civilizations in ruins, forgotten times, Hamlet's sleep full of self-inflicted dreams. The entire "march of history" remains meaningless even if we admit Christ into it merely as one admits an additional link into a chain. There remains only one way of evisaging history as something alive: by accepting Christ as the one who has risen from the dead, has freed the dead Adam from the state of waiting *(hádēs)* and is with us today, in every single moment of our lives.

The Christian message alone has always preserved the unique value of each particular human experience. Through the words of its faithful interpreters it has repeatedly insisted that while history may consist of innumerable situations, of an infinite number of variations-conditions, it is not an uninterrupted disappearance but rather a final sum of all situations. "Not as followers of learned visions", the apostle Peter declared, "we have made you acquainted with the power and the final coming of our Lord Jesus Christ, but as direct witnesses of his greatness."[31] And speaking of the "new skies and the new earth",[32] Ireneus – himself a disciple of Papias the Phrygian who used to sit in Ephesus at the feet of John the Evangelist – had this to add in his *Adversus haereses*: "For it is exactly in the very same creation in which they toiled and were afflicted and were tried in every way by suffering, that they should receive the reward of their suffering; and that in the very same creation in which they were killed for the love of God they should revive again..."

Of Light and Hell

> God through himself receives the vision of darkness
> not otherwise seeing darkness except through light.
> Dionysius Areopagita, *De divinis nominibus*

> As nothingness is not, as it has only an appearance of being, we should say that it is made to be or rather that is is made not to be. A being must there be whose function is to make nothingness to be as a nothing and to support it with its being...
> Jean Paul Sartre, *L'Être et le néant*

> Lord, when at the end I shall grope for my way
> leaving this dark night
> in which my dreaming heart has hardened so,
> admit me into the clear day without end...
> Miguel de Unamuno, *El Cristo de Velázquez*

Among the worries of the modern and post-modern Christian theologians one seems to be prominent: They are afraid of "losing the world". As early as the last century, some Western bishops spoke frequently about the danger of "losing the industrial workers"; actually they had first lost the factory owners. More recently, John A. T. Robinson, bishop of the Church of England, based an entire book, *Honest to God*, on the fear of losing practically everybody around. It is being presumed that the less outspokenly Christian one becomes, the smaller will be the danger of "losing the world". But it all seems to be a sign of little faith. Did not Feuerbach already stress that a true atheist is someone to whom "love" means nothing? God never loses anyone who has kept the faintest trace of love in his heart. As to those who have turned into themselves, absolutely and exclusively, and denied love, it does not seem probable that they could be somehow indoctrinated to cherish love again.

Perhaps the theologians should worry more about the obstacles they themselves have been heaping in the way of creative love by adhering to words and thoughts which obscure the character of the Creative Act.

A veritable abyss divides man's participation in the Creative Act – a choice, a matter of one moment of decision – from all the thinking which operates with the falsely mythical concepts of "continuity", "development" or "evolution". The author or authors of the first part of the book of *Genesis*, with their artful division of the creative act into "six days" – plus milleniums to follow – seem to have been already contaminated by this kind of "story-writer's presentation", although not nearly as much as were some Evolutionists in the nineteenth century or as have been Teilhard and Altizer in our own days. Even if one states that a creative thought is a glimpse into eternity, many listeners, instructed by these theologians, immediately think of the Aristotelian concept of eternity as an "eternally regular movement", of Gemistos Pléthōn's confusion between "eternity" and "durability", of Giordano Bruno's similar confusion between the "intensive infinity of God" and the "extensive infinity of the universe", or of Henri Bergson's *durée*.

Within the framework of such thoughts even "fulfillment" means, more or less, a "motion from one point of continuity to another". But any interest in such a "motion" contradicts the words of the apostle Peter counselling the Christians "to gather up the passing time of their dwelling on this earth".[1] It may indeed be difficult to speak of the Creative Act to anyone deeply involved in the "causal-chains" of thinking. Nevertheless, we have to try to show that "fulfillment" does not consist of "continuation". We have to attract the observer's attention to the fact that "fulfillment" is a decision and a clash. And that leads us directly to the concept which so many theologians anxious not to lose the world would like to avoid – the concept of evil inherent in the passing time.

Evil, undoubtedly, is very real. In a preceding essay, while discussing the "ultimate renaissance" ideal, we refused to accept such formulations as that of a "shattered vase, to be gradually or eventually mended", "a defect in organization", "a mere distance from truth", or a "privation of good". We can regard none of these as sufficiently expressing the reality of evil. While we had to reject doctrines which, following Plato's *Phaedo*, brand our bodies and the earth as "that evil thing with which our souls are mixed" and while we insisted on the entirety of man's person, we nevertheless also admitted the fact that man himself may become really evil.[2]

It is indeed necessary also to reject thoughts which, hastily condemning all "Materialism", may, at the same time, lead to the identification of evil with all things visible. As Christians we should always remember that whatever we simply call "matter" – what we perceive through our senses – has been honored and sanctified through Jesus' life and suffering. Perhaps it would be of some advantage to regard "matter" as "an airfield strip on which messages can land much superior to those which matter itself may tell us".[3] And yet again we recognize that there may be real evil inherent in things visible – whenever, for instance, they involve decomposition and death.

A realistic view of man, we have maintained, should include his share in the Creative Act.

There is only one Creative Act of which we know. The meanings of things known to us are not isolated but interdependent. To speak of the Creative Act means to speak both of its origin and of its consummation. It is definitely not anything measurable in chronological units. And yet it is also a drama. Its explosion as well as its consummation stem from creative love. It is centered on the loving God as well as on man from whom love is expected. This we have to accept as the basic reality of our world. We have not proven it. There is no way of proving it – in the "geometrical" sense of the word "proof". We have simply to accept it as the only way to understanding the meaning of our life.

We try to understand all this as Athanasius understood it when he stressed that Christ since always is with the Father and since always acts – or at least as Duns Scotus saw things when he asserted that: "The Incarnation of Christ was not foreseen as a contingent event, but was seen by God directly as an end from eternity; so Christ, in his human nature, since he is nearer to the final purpose than other things, was ordained to lead them."[4] But, above all, if the Creative Act is to be understood as an act of love, it means, seen from man's point of view, that it is an opportunity for decision, for a choice. If the purpose of God's Creative Act is to give man the possibility to choose and thus to demonstrate his own love, then man must be flanked not only by a "Yes", but also by a "No" – otherwise he would be a mere robot, uncapable of love.

Is the possibility of saying "No" to be regarded as a mere possibility or is something else standing behind it?

The mythical visions of the exploding cosmos overflow with symbols and parables which, to a great extemt, depend on man's varying poetical talents. Some talk of Michael's battle with the Satan and symbolize the recession of Darkness before Light by speaking of Satan as Lucifer – *lucem ferens*, the one who merely reflects the Light but belongs to the realm of Darkness. Some speak of the Demiurg, a personified double line of creation in whose divided character both Michael and Satan seem to be integrated. Some other again, such as the Pahlavi works describing the ancient Mazdean traditions, distinguish between the complete time of God *(hastīli)* and the negative reality of Ahriman *(nestīli)*.[5] The Hebrew-Christian tradition, with its sharp distinction between Michael and Satan, points clearly to the view that all creation comes from God's hands. Other symbolisms, however, find it sometimes difficult to admit that even the illusory "shattered time" is a time of some kind and that it was not imposed on the creation "from outside". Thus to the followers of ancient and medieval Manicheism the "shattered time" seemed to have come from the hands of Satan rather than from those of God.

What is the relationship of Light and Darkness like? John the Evangelist says: "The Light shines in the Darkness and the Darkness has not overcome it." But he also remarks: "The whole world is in the power of the evil one."[6]

It is well known that the post-modern physicists regard matter as a "battlefield of electrical charges" and that they see the most significant distinction between a "particle" and its "antiparticle" within an atom as stemming from their "enmity"; they can "annihilate" one another. The same scientists would also tell us that the products that "carry away" – what a truly mythical description! – the energy resulting from such an annihilation are "new particles" known as mesons or pions... After all, no matter how hopefully and heroically even great physicists of the kind of Pierre Duhem may protest that "the belief in an order transcending physics is the sole justification" of their work in the laboratory,[7] they seem always to be only able to produce just another "possible conception of physical relations", just another set of "convenient conventions" as Henri Poincaré used to say.

The old myths have always known more. Their authors did not waste time by proclaiming that "from nothingness to being is an infinite distance which no power could ever have bridged."[8] Is the distance between Light and Darkness "finite" or "infinite"? Light is real and so is Darkness – while expressions such as "distance", "finite" and "infinite" are not to be taken seriously outside the realm of geometrical postulates. Light was always and everywhere the most popular and the most obvious symbol of life, of whatever aims at a purpose and is capable of exercising an influence.

Light was always the most widely used symbol of the Creator himself. Sun had become the most natural source of light known to man. "Sometimes", we are told by an outstanding Egyptologist, "the Creator created everything at once, sometimes in successive stages. One belief, however, was prevalent throughout the whole country (of Egypt): The "first occurrence" was the emergence of the order of the world from chaos, and this order was by no means secure and final. Its existence was threatened every time the sun went down."[9]

"The Calendar Stone", another prominent archeologist tells us, "embodies a finite statement of the infinity of the Aztec universe. In the center is the face of the Sun God, Tonatiuh, flanked by four cartouches which singly give the dates of the four previous ages of the world and together represent the date of our present era."[10] The Greek myths still overflowed with the same primeval lore. Orpheus, the famous Phanes, had been born in a blaze of light.[11] As relatively recent a work as Aristophanes' late fifth-century comedy *The Birds* speaks in gentle verses about the birth of Love With Golden, Gleaming Wings in the very center of the incipient universe. The Hebrew Creator, as is well known, "began" his work with Time and Light itself and only then proceeded to create the sun and the other celestial bodies.

Wherever Light lives, there is no Darkness. We use the verb "to live" in this connection as it always should be used – in the sense of radiating and affecting. Of course, it should not be forgotten that even in this most truthful sense the verb "to live" – as also the verbs "to light" or "to enlighten" – usually conveys to us an experience within the flowing time. Even when we say that a light illuminates or enlightens, we think of moments which are filed in our memory as a series. This, evidently, was the core of the difficulties experienced by the narrators of the primeval myths. They were anxious to describe an "act". But the symbols they had at their disposal were human symbols and therefore conducive to the description of an "activity". An "act" does not have passing time, while "activity" operates with illusory "continuity".

It might be useful, at this juncture, to recall Kierkegaard's assertion that nothing is impossible for God and to complete this assertion by saying that, therefore, anything coming from God's hands means a creative, loving act. But the primeval *mythopoios* had to convey this idea through a visual parable. He was eager to stress that the creative act happens *in illo tempore*, *i.e.*, in the complete time. He was equally eager to underline that it happens in the "center" rather than in the "beginning" of things. Thus the Hebrew word *re'shith*, used in the Mosaic report on creation, not only seems to have the same meaning as the Greek *arché*, but it is also completed by Isaiah's expression *aharith* which evidently describes the "complete" and "final" character of the creative act. Even the Phythagorean – possibly very old, pre-Pythagorean – word *diakósmēsis* suggested a far-reaching, thorough act, certainly not a process of any duration.

As often as he could, the *mythopoios* tried to convey the instantaneous character of the creative act to his listeners by describing it as a clash.

Having reached this particular topic, the myth concerning the primordial struggle between Light and Darkness, we have also reached the level where we have to step beyond the realm of the myths. Ours is not a study in the eagerness of the *mythopoioi* to express as distinctly as possible, yet in a narrative way, the origin of the universe.[12] We are here more concerned with the later ancient phase when man did not, as yet, underestimate myths[13] but had already become more concerned with their inner experience than with their dramatic plots. Thus the Greeks became increasingly anxious to learn more about the Darkness whose representatives, the Titans, had been called by the seventh-century poet Hesiod the "first divinities."[14] Thales, Anaximander, and the other early Greek scholars were still "hylozoists"; they accepted the primeval man's view that everything was alive. While only small fragments of their work have reached us, it seems evident that they all operated with the clash between the passive Darkness (Thales' "water", perhaps also partially Anaximander's *tò ápeiron*) and the generative Light *(to gónimon.)*[15] Anaximander's Creative Flame reappeared in the fifth-century work of Heraclitus who also stressed again the basic tension between the airy Light and the subterraneous Waters. Eventually, in Anaxagoras – even before the atomic theory was formulated – we find an identification of Light with the Supreme Mind, with Light's priority before the formless Darkness, and also with "seeds of light" as predecessors, not so much of Democritus' atoms or Plotinus emanations as of Plato's ideas.

Anaxagoras' thoughts were reflected in Aristotle, in spite of the Stagerite's preoccupation with "chains of material causes". The Living Light operating through energy *(enérgeia)* became to the great preacher of the "auxiliary-verb philosophy" the "shape" *(morfé)* of everything. On the other hand, he recognized the Darkness of the primeval traditions as "that which is shaped" *(hýlē)* and in which "energy" becomes a "force" *(dýnamis)*.[16] While "that which is real" does not, in Aristotle's view, necessarily mean "that which lives", it is important to realize that "whatever is shaped" *(hýlē)* may be real, but only as "something that does not live" *(mḗ ón)*. This "reality which does not live" thus replaced Anaximander's *tò ápeiron*. However, at the same time, it became "that against which or within which light becomes apparent" – as Light appears in Darkness. Darkness is thus envisaged as *tò hypokéimenon*, that which surrounds Light. Darkness, however real, does not live, does not affect.

Darkness is only brought to reality through Light. Its opposition to Light is real, but not alive. We might be tempted to ask "how long" does it remain real. But this truly "anthropomorphical" question lacks sense. Light itself is an explosion, not measurable by any units of passing time. Consequently the resistance of Darkness also escapes our "chronological endeavors". This, obviously, also formed an obstacle for the narrators of mythical cosmogonies. In some old texts, the Great Clash was seemingly placed at the "beginning" – but we should not forget that this "beginning" *(illud tempus)* was really the center of the complete time. In the Judeo-Christian tradition, the narrators speak of the Great Battle always in connection with the final consummation. In the *Old Testament* we do not find any mention of it before we reach Daniel's prophecy where the clash is clearly connected with the end of the passing time.[17] In the *New Testament*, either the clash is described as something happening within the passing time, or it is distinctly placed at that time's consummation.[18]

Most important of all, the tradition of the *Sacred Scriptures* as well as that of the Fathers of the Church both maintain that the creative act is entirely God's work. Whatever lives, lives through God's love and grace. In the first place, Jesus, the God-Who-Sacrifices-Himself, is to Paul "the radiance of his Father's splendor" and to Ireneus, the "giver of life and light". But as the entire universe is created for the purpose of Christ's sacrifice, the entire creative act constitutes, in the words of John of Damascus, "a rushing forth of light *(éxalma)*," or, as another Eastern Christian theologian, the eleventh century Simeon the Younger puts it, a return to an "uncreated Light without beginning and without matter".[19] That Simeon the Younger deemed it necessary to say "without matter", had an obvious reason: The obtrusive presence of Manicheism within the various contemporary schools of Christian thought. It is well known that the Iranian teaching which Mani helped to popularize in the third century after Christ had stemmed from the vision of a dual creation – partially God's, partially his Dark Opponent's. While the Christian Churches rejected the body of the Manicheist teaching, their theologians, above all in the West, did not remain unaffected by it. In the first place, the distinction between things "spiritual" and things "material" which, somehow, had become most popular among theologians, appears a rather problematic distinction – and certainly apt to serve as Manicheist tool. It had been absent from the Apostolic Fathers. Origen did not regard it as useful. The bishops assembled at Nicea in 325 preferred to speak of things "visible" and things "invisible".[20] They certainly were quite consistent in their decision: Even if Darkness is "realized" through the explosion of Light, it does not become "matter" in the sense of anything alive; things visible themselves are of Light. As late as the fifteenth century, Nicolas of Cusa regarded "matter" or "chaos" as that "which can happen" *(quod fieri potest)* and which is brought into existence through the Creative Act.

But the Christian East had to pass through the period of the iconoclastic frenzy which was of Manicheist provenience, in spite of its instigators delight in speaking so often of the Mosaic law. Manicheist tendencies were instrumental in the popularization of the "dove-in-the-cage" Platonic theory of soul and body, which replaced the older concept of "soul" as "life" and made the "spiritual soul" imprisoned in the "material body". Manicheism was behind the "celibacy fever" which overcame the Western Church around 1000 AD. And while as late as the middle of the twelfth century Domingo Gundisalvi, the Toledan scholar and indirect disciple of Ibn Sīnā, regarded God as source of all "forms", including the visible ones, to Thomas Aquinas, a century later, matter became something distinctly opposed to the Creator. Aquinas certainly admitted, in his general declarations, that even matter comes from God; nevertheless, to him, matter "individuates", divides, threatens the unity of the creative act.[21] From Aquinas we could again reach as far as Teilhard de Chardin; throughout his writings, "creation is an act of uniting", *i.e.*, the Creator merely impresses his will on a kind of "cosmic stuff".

A historian of the Christian tradition can also follow the influence of the Manicheist dualism along the various ways which theologians used in dealing with angels.

The Hebrew expressions of the *Old Testament* spoke of "messengers" *(māl'ak)*, "divine agents" *(elohim)*, "God's trustees" *(b'ne elohim, b'ne ēlim)*, "ministers" *(m'shartim)*, or "servants" *(abadim)*;[22] time and again the strange, hardly translatable names "cherubim" and "seraphim" were employed. Aristotle in his *Metaphysics* reserved the expressions *enérgeiai* for "such movements in which their tasks are inherent". In the Greek of Paul's epistles they became "forces" *(dynámeis)*, "with power entrusted" *(exousíai)*, "leaders" *(archái)*, "dominators" *(kyriótētes)*, "seats of power" *(thrónoi)*.[23] At that time and even later they were certainly envisaged as real and living creatures which penetrate the entire universe. Basil the Great speaks of their fiery nature and so does the sixth century African bishop Fulgentius.[24] Throughout the works of the Greek-writing Fathers the terms *enérgeia* and *dýnamis* were also employed without much distinction; they were used for those aspects of the creative act where one speaks of God himself as well as for those where one speaks of tasks entrusted to God's messengers. But nowhere is there any trace of excluding "God's messengers" from any part of the universe around us. From here the way leads directly to scientific concepts such as *impetus* of Nicolas d'Oresme or "energy" of Isaac Newton and the more recent generations of scientists.

It is only mostly in relatively recent books of theologians that, when angels are referred to, one finds an explicitly Manicheist attitude toward "matter" as something opposed to "spirit". Angels are presented as "spirits" whose activities in the "physical" world is restricted to "causal influencies upon corporeal beings". An encyclopedia recently published under the auspices of the Church of Rome goes as far as to castigate the Fathers of the Church for their attitude to "angelology" because it allegedly stemmed from a "lack of clear philosophical distinction between body and spirit".[25] In the meantime, many artists illustrating such doctrines – doctrines clearly opposed to the very essence of Christianity – moved toward effeminate (spiritual?) bodies provided with sugary faces and later even to over-fed infants resting on little clouds. But this, of course, should not be held against the artists; they were not guilty of betrayal (as the theologians certainly were) but only occasionally of a lack of good taste.

"According to the current views the sole basis of evil lies in the world of the senses or in animality or the earthly principle, since people do not contrast Heaven with Hell, as would be proper, but with Earth."

When Friedrich Schelling wrote these words, a century and a half ago, he was not speaking of the medieval Manicheists – and, of course, he could not have been speaking of Teilhard de Chardin. He was simply describing what in his days appeared as the prevalent tendency: to deny the origin of evil in the choice of those who are granted the capability to choose; to blame it, rather, on the "evil character of matter", on the "shattered vase which has to be mended", and soon also on some "slight imperfection in the arrangement of the evolutionary process."

Schelling had to remind his readers that "evil is not derived from finitude in itself, but from finitude which has been exalted to independent being."[26] Or again: "The mere consideration of the fact that man, the most perfect of all visible creatures, is alone capable of evil, shows that (evil) can by no means consist of insufficiency or deprivation; according to the Christian view, the Devil was not the most limited but rather the least limited of the (invisible) creatures."[27]

One essential difference seems to gape between the messengers of God and men: Suffering.

That man was made somehow "to the image of the Creator" is asserted by all the primeval traditions. It has been presumed, from the earliest times until our own days, that the words "to the image" mean merely man's capability to share, extremely slightly, the knowledge of the meaning of things.[28] There have always been Christian teachers, nevertheless, who suggested that it is also suffering which completes this image. "When I am close to the sword, I am close to God," says Ignatius, disciple of the apostles and bishop-martyr of Antioch, "and when I am surrounded by lions, I am surrounded by God."[29] Teresa of Avila in the sixteenth century and Ioan Kronstadtskij in the twentieth century expressed the same persuasion.

Choice, undoubtedly, belongs to both angels and men. In both cases the creature – because it is a creature and not an emanation – may be taken in by the illusion of its own independence, if it becomes interested exclusively in itself and rejects love. In both cases there is one, single choice taking place in the complete time. But the angel's choice does not involve the sorrows of passing time. It is the privilege of man, including the man Jesus, to integrate into their choice the sorrows of his terrestrial, chronological life as summed up in its entire value. Raphael, "bearing common deliverance to the suppliants of a single hour", is only a guardian-companion of an unexperienced boy. Gabriel conveys his tremendous message with a humble greeting.

But as to the One-Who-Reflects-the-Light, whose decisive choice is known to God as everybody else's choice, what can he do? What is his "struggle" like? What does it mean that he stands in God's presence and "accuses" men?

Nowhere, perhaps, are we more at a loss when asked to translate the dramatic narration into a language which would convey to us a shadow, at least, of the complete time. Aeschylus, the genial playwright of ancient Greece, when speaking of the suffering of someone who had thirsted for light, left his audience only with the dark vista of the "black depths of death":

> "Look for no ending to this agony
> until a god will freely suffer for you,
> will take on him your pain, and in your stead
> descend to where the sun is turned to darkness,
> the black depths of death."[30]

Perhaps we should remain with the poets who had always created myths. The theologians lack the words, the philosophers even the alphabet. The anguish of man has often been depicted in symbols involving the resurgent, rebellious waters of Darkness. Plato's *méga chásma* reappeared in the *Apocalypse* when the serpent sent a flood of water against the Woman who had been given the Great Eagle's wings.[31]

But someone who through his own choice is not alive and bears or rather only reflects light, may really not be able to affect anything. Darkness can only be real through the presence of Light. It can seduce where our own whims or intentions seduce us. It can accuse by the fact that the shadows of man's evil deeds move over its surface. Those shadows even seem to protect it:

> "Moi, je veux des hommes partout: autour de moi,
> au-dessus de moi et qu'ils me cachent le ciel..."[32]

In Dame Julian of Norwich – whom we have already quoted and who, beside being a great theologian was also a master of the poetical parable – the Angel of Resistance becomes a mere "ravine".

In all that was shown to Julian "in a moment where her understanding was led into the Lord",[33] when discussing the basic "existential category" of man, she abstained from using the expression "original sin", and even that of "death", and used rather a simple parable about a "fall into a ravine". The Lord's servant who had found himself in the ravine – "I understood that he was shewed for Adam... in the sight of God every man is one man, and one man is every man" – could not rise or help himself; "through the sore bruising that he had taken" he was "blinded in his reason and stunned in his mind"; he lay alone, "in a lonely, hard and grievous place". "And I beheld with deliberation to discover if I could perceive in him any fault; or whether the Lord would assign to him any kind of blame; and truly there was none seen..."

"His loving Lord full tenderly beholdeth him..." "Here an inward shewing of the Lord's meaning descended into my mind; in which I saw that it must needs be in accord with his great goodness and his own worship..." "In the servant (who, as I say, was shewed for Adam) I saw many diverse properties that could in no way be ascribed to the single Adam..." "In this parable the secrets of the whole revelation were yet much hid." "This man was hurt in his powers... stunned in his understanding ... but his will was preserved in God's sight; for his will I saw our Lord commend and approve..."

"Next I saw that only pain blameth and punisheth; but our courteous Lord comforteth and succoureth..." "The loving look that the Lord turneth upon his servant continually and especially in his falling, methought it might melt our hearts for love, and break them in two for joy..." "This fair looking shewed itself as a seemly mingling... One part was ruth and pity, the other joy and bliss." "The joy and the bliss was for the falling of his most dear Son who is equal with the Father..." "There was a treasure in the earth, which the Lord loveth...I saw in the Lord that he hath within himself endless life and all manner of goodness, save the treasure that was in the earth; and that, too, was grounded in the Lord, in marvellous deepness of endless love; but it was not all to his worship until his servant should have prepared it, and brought it before him, presenting it in himself; outside the Lord was naught but wilderness." "When Adam fell, God's son fell; because of the true oneing which was made in heaven, God's son could not be separated from Adam, while by Adam I understood every man..."

The Christian symbolical imagery is very clear when examined in its original sources. It is not so clear when examined in the poetry and the paintings or the Gothic and the Baroque periods. The concern with the struggle against evil, against "passing time", preoccupied the Christian mind to such an extent that a rather misleading and confusing change took place in the use of the symbol of light: The light of salvation appeared as the flames of punishment.

In the books of the *New Testament* the symbol of "the light which enlightens every man coming into this world" is used in a most clear and consistent way. It mean's God's presence. It means his grace and help. It means the freedom and the wisdom given by God. But the decision of love is required – from Christ in the first place and from any other man; the fetching of the treasure from the earth, the treasure of love which Julian of Norwich's servant had to present "in himself". Thus the frontier between Light and Darkness rises before our eyes. Behind this frontier there is "naught but wilderness", the "external darkness" or the "storm of darkness".[34] If this were a static vision, there would probably be no difficulties. It is, however, a most dynamic and realistic vision. It is the exact contrary of the vision cultivated by Voltaire's generation which called itself "Enlightened" and yet, while using thus the primordial symbolism of light, denied the reality of shadows, darkness and evil.

The dynamic vision depicts one single explosion, the self-manifestation of God in love. The bursting flames of this explosion are the flames not only of creation but also of consummation. They are the same flames which many archaic myths depict as consuming the entire cosmos in the *ekpýrōsis* or *ragnaroek*.[35] "Christ is as the purest fire," says Nicolas of Cusa, "inseparable from the light... He is that fire of life and knowledge which consumes all things... judging everything as if through an ordeal of material fire."[36] However, if in some of the archaic traditions this ultimate purpose of light might have assumed a terrifying aspect, it is not so in the *New Testament* – or, at least, it should not be so if the reader is careful enough to grasp the meaning of the words which he has before his eyes.

Already the prophetic books of the *Old Testament* had reached great clarity in this respect, in spite of the at times superficial interpretation of the Messianic change and in spite of the rather unspecified meaning of the expression *sheol* which the Hebrew authors used when speaking of man's survival. "Thy dead man shall life, my slain shall rise again," says Isaiah; "awake and give praise, ye that dwell in the dust; for thy dew is the dew of light and the land of the giants thou shalt pull down into ruin."[37] We have, in this text, the heart of the Hebraic vision. The dew which revives the dead is the "dew of light". Light's ultimate penetration of the entire cosmos – in the "vertical" sense, as Berdyaev would say, not in the horizontal sense of "passing time" – means the end of death. Through that same light the "giants", the Titans of the ancient Greek cosmology, the Angels of Darkness, will be "pulled down into ruin". Turning to the *New Testament*'s eschatological vision, we again hear the announcement of the victory of light, Isaiah's questions – "Which of you, sinners, can dwell with the devouring fire? Which of you shall dwell with the everlasting flames?"[38] – are again answered in a negative way. The victory of light means annihilation of darkness – a "complete destruction" *(ólethros aiōnios)*, to use apostle Paul's lapidary expression, the "lake of fire which is the second, final death" *(houtos ho thánatos ho deúterós estin hē límnē toū pyrós)*, as the *Apocalypse* puts it.[39]

With the choice accomplished, naturally, the frontier of darkness and darkness itself disappear. The choice made on Calvary as well as each man's choice constitute the disappearance of darkness and the victory of freedom. However, the truly mythical, almost archaic presentation of the Hebrew, Aramaic and Greek texts could hardly avoid presenting this victory in a most dramatic way – as the defeat of the "Beast of Darkness" and its followers, of all those who had rejected freedom and had given preference to the slavery of passing time. Christ himself spoke of the "weeping and gnashing of teeth".[40] As to the *Apocalypse*, its author dramatizes the issue by remarking that "the beast and any man who shall adore it" will be tormented with fire "in the sight of the holy angels and the Lamb".

This last mentioned text, together with some other dramatized observations of a similar kind, contributed to the rise of all those artistic conceptions representing the "torments of the damned" as one half of the spectacle, the bliss of the saints forming its other half. It was a most unhappy distortion. But if men of genius, Augustine, Gregory the Great, Dante or Michelangelo, were attracted by the idea, how could one blame the little narrators of Medieval legends and fairy tales in which devils with tridents kindle fires under large cauldrons overflowing with "damned souls"?[41]

To reach a truthful and sensible evaluation of the Christian vision, it is necessary, in the first place, to realize that the light and its flames are symbols of God, while man's terrestrial condition is symbolized by the "darkness in which the light shineth". It is perfectly consistent that the victory of light, the engulfing and the destruction of the darkness by the "lake of flames"[42] should take place in the sight *(enópion)* of the Lamb and his angels. It could hardly be otherwise, because God, the Lamb, is himself the fountainhead of these flames of illumination which destroy darkness.

Second, the books of the *New Testament* distinguish very carefully between the realm of the agonizing who are in need of purification and the realm of those who have definitely rejected the love of God. The first of these states or situations is called *hádēs* – an equivalent of the Hebrew *sheol*, as is evident from the *Septuaginta* translation. It quite evidently belongs to the realm of passing time. It is from *hádēs* that the rich man lifts his eyes up to Lazarus. It is *hádēs* which Christ visits after his crucifixion to announce his victory.[43] Together with the terrestrial death, this "situation" is eventually forced to give up its inmates. Then, again together with the terrestrial death, this realm is "cast into the lake of fire which is the second, the final death."[44]

On the other hand, *geénna*, the final fate of those who have definitely rejected love, who "sinned against the Holy Spirit", is quite evidently the equivalent of the ultimate disappearance of darkness. There is no heir to this realm of darkness, simply because there is no "after" which would follow its abolition. While warning men that they should not fear the comparatively insignificant damages they may suffer during their earthly pilgrimage, Jesus tells them that they should rather "fear him that can destroy both life and body in the *geénna*."[45] The verb which is used here – "to destroy", *apóllymi* or *apollýō* – does not mean anything else but utter annihilation. The apostle Paul speaks with equal clarity when teaching the Thessalonians about those who have rejected God and "suffer the punishment of eternal destruction from God's face".[46] In this case, not a verb, but a noun is used, *ho ólethros;* it also has only one, unequivocal meaning, "destruction" or "undoing".

This last mentioned text from Paul's epistles possesses two other interesting aspects. It speaks of the victorious light as "streaming from the Lord's face". Evidently, it was a symbolism current among Jesus' disciples – above all those who were present on the Mount Tabor or Paul who went through an extraordinary experience on his way to Damascus – and accessible to all who listened to them or read their messages. That the Lord's light hurts the darkness seems also apparent from the words uttered by the rich man in the story about Lazarus.[47] Second, the apostle's text employs, in connection with the noun "annihilation", the adjective *aiónion*. We have translated it by the English adjective "eternal". But is this really the adjective we should use?

The way in which the nuances of the rich Greek vocabulary – not to mention its Semitic predecessors – have been frequently treated in the text of the *New Testament* by translators, old and modern, is most regrettable. To so many of them, for instance, both *hádēs* and *geénna* mean just "hell". And yet the first means evidently a situation within the kingdom of the passing time, while the other is the final result of the creative act, behind which, as has been mentioned, there is no "after". The adjective *aiónios* has received even less attention. In the *New Testament* it always has the significance of something "final" and "conclusive". There is a "conclusive", "unchangeable" sin *(hamártēma aiónion)*.[48] There is also a "conclusive", "final" "flame of light" *(tò pỹr tò aiónion)*.[49] Occasionally, the noun *aiṓn* is used, or even a double plural of the same noun, *eis aiōnas aionōn*.[50] But the meaning of this noun is clearly and always that of a "closed, finished time". The use of "eternal" as the English equivalent of *aiónios* becomes thus more than dubious. "Eternal", in English, had always meant "lasting" or "durable" in the sense of a "passing, continous time". *Aiónios* means the exact opposite of "lasting" or "continuous"; it means the "complete now".

All in all, the eschatological doctrine of the *New Testament*, expressed in rich but consistent vocabulary, is quite clear in spite of the highly dramatic parables in which it is enclosed. The apostle Paul may speak of "just punishment" in connection with the final victory over darkness. This punishment, nevertheless, being of man's own choice, is a "conclusive destruction".[51] The *Apocalypse* may depict the "smoke" ascending from the Beast of Darkness, tormented by fire and deprived of any rest, day or night. But it quickly adds that the smoke ascends "into the conclusion of all the conclusions".[52] In another place, repeating the same vision, it says that the "fire descending from heaven" "devoured" *(katéfagen)* the Beast and the False Prophet and that not only the Beast and the Prophet, but also Satan himself was cast into the "lake of flames".[53] Two other texts of the same book bring the vision to its dramatic climax by stating that even human death and the *hádēs* are both cast into the same "lake of flames" and that this is their real end.[54]

After that comes only a postscript: "Whosoever was not found written in the book of life, is also cast into the lake of flames."[55] Such man is, by his own choice, not alive. What is being consumed by the light, is merely his shadow.

The tremendous *theoria*, the cosmic vision which accompanies the Christian message, is perhaps slightly more difficult to comprehend than the vision of the contemporary physicist concerning the "interior of the atom". But even those who may not be able to comprehend should try to understand.

It is not a timeless vision. Time, evidently, is something very real, even if it is all in a "now". Within that "now" is also the illumination before which the frontier of darkness recedes into the abyss – the frontier of decision and of the shattered, passing time. The decision, if it is a decision toward freedom, participates in the creative act. It takes place, basically, in the complete time. It also takes place on the Calvary. It takes place in each decisive moment of each individual human life. Through the frontier of darkness the ray of the human life is decomposed into the spectrum of critical moments. Thus, through a "distension of the mind", the illusion of a continuous line is brought forward, prolongable into the "past" and into the "future". In a similar way, the "now" of mankind is made to resemble a "distension of humanity" which we know as history.

Behind history – "behind" in the vertical or centrifugal, not the horizontal sense – there is the victory of light, the "second and final death" and the annihilation of the Beast of Darkness and of all those who have rejected creative love and "accepted the Beast's sign". Darkness will die in the flames of Light. Whoever remains alive, will know the complete time.

However, we are still within history. We live in shattered time, constrained to file our experiences along the illusory, "past to future" line. That the world around us in "unreasonably" silent, as Camus used to say, is a most evident reality. But is this silence not coming from a quarter to which we are addressing our questions by mistake?

Ever since the days of Voltaire and Condorcet we have been turning with our questions to the "future part" of the illusory line of pasing time. Even Berdyaev when he revolted, shortly before the Bolshevik upheaval, against the "Christian circles" of his native country, began to speak of a "true religious epoch of creativness which will realize another sphere of being."[56] He expected this to be accomplished "without any Holy Scripture", "in man and in humanity". He also discovered that the *Zohar* was the "one basic book which removed the fetters of limitation and subjection." Moreover on his way to this "liberation" man was expected by him to "pass through mechanization". Berdyaev thus became a temporary victim of the charms of the "ultimate renaissance" in a way slightly similar to which was later trod by Teilhard de Chardin.

But Berdyaev then already knew that "the New Jerusalem will appear catastrophically."[57] By 1926, he became "inclined to greater pessimism" and saw "no hope for the possibility of an immediate move into religious creativity"; he began to stress that "man is a creator not only in the name of God but in the name of the devil as well".[58] This, of course, was a rather misleading idea. The great thinker himself knew that "the creative act is an act of loving choice". There may be only reflecting or "aping" of the creative activity on Satan's side, but no real creation – as much as Voltaire's "freedom from" is only a caricature of the real freedom, the "freedom for".

The "kindling of fire out of freedom", which accomplishes the truly creative act, is conditioned by the humble embracement of love. In pride and selfishness one ignores freedom – no matter how much one may remain under the illusion of a feverish and thoroughgoing activity. But once decided for freedom, man has been promised God's own help, his grace. As Antonio Machado said, in his *Proverbios y cantares:* "Behind living and dreaming looms the most important: to awaken."

This world of ours always remains silent. After all, it consists of a mere fringe of light, of a frontier between light and darkness. Its silence should not concern us. God's silence is different. It is reflected in our own astonished silence.

At times it seems as if we were left mute and deaf. The experience of a mother who, having lost her sons in one calamity, faces, alone and hopeless, another catastrophe, or the experience of an old inmate of a concentration camp who, after a new "liberation" of his country had taken place, is led into another concentration camp – even such very existential experiences seem to have become meaningless to us. We may look, stunned for a moment, at the disfigured body of a dead child in the ruins of a bombarded city – also one of our own accomplishments – but then we would not understand anything and would rapidly return to our ambitious dreams. In such a mood we would, probably, not even listen to Dostoyevskij's assertion that the existence of Evil is a demonstration of the existence of God and that if the world consisted wholly and uniquely of goodness and righteousness – or should we say, of things normal? – the world itself would be God.

God's silence is a deafening silence. But it is also, obviously, a necessary silence. Were it not for God's silence, there would be no freedom. Without Christ's absolute loneliness on the Calvary, without his *Eli, Eli, lamma sabakhtani?*, there would be no salvation.

God's silence resembles an expectation. Father is expecting his son's return from the vain and empty future, from his illusory excursion into the time of dreams.

A British observer has visited twice, within the space of three years, the city of Prague under the Bolshevik domination. During his first visit, he found the Czech dramatists asking questions such as: How much of a man belongs to the all-powerful state, and how much to himself? Where do the demands of the state-enterprise begin to encroach intolerably on his selfhood? When the observer arrived for the second time, he noted the advent of another preoccupation. The heroes of the dramas were now forced to come to terms not merely with the dictate of the state-enteprise, but also with the most basic fact of death. One of the theatres even introduced, with considerable success, a Czech Baroque play entitled *The Passion and Death of Jesus Christ*.[59] The sequel of these changes is most illustrative. First comes the retreat from the social dreams. The modern, nineteenth-century visions of an endless and automatic progress have been found by the post-modern man to lead into an impass. One had to retreat within the boundaries of one's own life. But human life ends in death. And such is the preoccupation with the illusory future, that most questions are then centered on death. Death is called the "ultimate experience". And often, above all if it is a suicide, it is identified with the "ultimate assertion of man's independence", with the goal of the "ultimate renaissance".

And yet both the "historical future" and death are unimportant. Both of them are only imaginary entities, limitary concepts, standing behind the present moment, behind the all-important *kairós* which is with us right now. The fear of death is only a reversal of that foolish expectation of the fictitious epoch when man should no longer be bound by the "old morality"... *Ista vetus pietas aevo moritura futuro*...[60]

Once again, for the last time, we may return to the story of the Grand Inquisitor. Is it really true that people have laid all their freedom at his feet in exchange for a dream of false security? The central point of the story – of which Dostoyevskij is very much aware – is in the identification of security with a false image of freedom.

Above all since the gradual establishment of the state power, this false image of freedom has been with us. It has exercised an ever increasing impact on our thoughts and actions. Incapable of life and incapable of any ideas of his own, the Prince of the Fringe of Darkness has furnished men with a caricature of freedom. While real freedom cannot be rescinded from love toward God and through God toward other men and things, the caricature of freedom is equal to the selfish quest for security. "You will be like gods," says the Prince. "You will not be required to take anything else into consideration but yourself. Whatever you do, will be perfect."[61]

Historically, this suggestion has always been presented in some connection with the idea of an inquisitorial power – a power which will take care of men and provide them with the illusion of freedom and security. In Marsiglio of Padua's fourteenth-century program – conceived at the time when states began to replace kindgoms – the influential element *(valentior pars)* in the body politic was expected to assume this role. When, in the sixteenth century, Jean Bodin was drafting his doctrine of the "sovereign state", he conceived this state as situated above all laws *(legibus solutus)* but still taking good care of its subjects. In the doctrine about the "absolutely enlightened monarchs" or again in Robespierre's concept of the "general will incorporated in the leaders of the people", we would find further developments of this same idea. During the nineteenth century it began to assume a scientific, technocratic coloring. Augustyn Jakubisiak, analysing the thought of Henri Bergson – perhaps the most outstanding preacher of "progressive freedom" at the beginning of our century – described his role in these words: "Under the pretext of serving the cause of free will, Bergson's doctrine allies itself closely with a conception of progress very popular among our contemporaries, a conception which excludes personal God from history and presents man, preferably collective man, as the only efficient and final cause of his own evolution, declaring, at the same time, this evolution to be as illimited and undetermined as the future on which it essentially depends."[62]

This very creed has then been identified by the politicians with their own activity. Finally, a potentially decisive suggestion has been spread under the name of "pluralism". In a society commanded by the "leadership of progressive authorities" all moral judgements, according to this suggestion, should be accepted as having the same social value, *i.e.*, none of them should be accepted as representing the truth.

But the perfectly organized society of biologically and sociologically preconditioned men is opposed to the Kingdom of God.

The three invocations of Our Lord's prayer speak of a name, a kingdom, and a will. "Hallowed be Thy Name, Thy Kingdom come, Thy Will be done on earth as it is in heaven..." Together with the appeal which precedes them – "Our Father who art in Heaven" – these invocations alone form a *theoria*, a vision of the cosmos. Through the words they employ, they are deeply rooted in the archaic, mythical way of thinking. We have already noticed the significance of the expression "Name" – as opposed to the "Being" of the auxiliary-verb philosophers. The concept of the Kingdom has an equally great significance. If "Name" means the Godhead from whom, as from a fire, both light and heat proceed, then "Kingdom" belongs to the Son, and "Will" belongs to the Spirit who brings grace to the incipient hope. The "Kingdom", however, has a very historical meaning. It means the adherence of all those who have heard of Jesus to his person and to his joyful message. It is built on the knowledge that "the poor will always be with us" – that is, no matter how perfectly organized the human society might be, there will always be need for creative decisions, for deeds of love and charity.

This the Prince of this World does not admit. Even while playwrights and all the other thinking men are retreating, terrified, from the vision he has to offer, he persists. Every time he is accepted, a tragedy ensues and then despair. The despair which lurks between Camus' lines is undoubtedly the ultimate temptation. The frightening vision of the all-powerful world-state – or any kind of political entity in which the police state and the economic trusts might coalesce – seems to be here to stay. It is quite possible that George Orwell, in his novel *1984*, by adopting some of the features and colors which characterized the Nazi and the Soviet regimes, missed the true character of the "perfect society" of the future and that Hugh Benson, in his *Lord of the World*, written in the first years of our century, came much closer to it.

The methods of gaining influence and power, which the totalitarians have developed, seem already oldfashioned. Some much more progressive managers of men may replace them with methods less doctrinaire, more alluring, and efficacious. We may well think of an important medical invention, some drug which will cure men of many sicknesses, but also deprive them of their ability to give normal life to new generations. We may think of full automation, which will once and for all solve the problem of industrial workers, but also immensely strengthen the hold of the powerful on the leisure of their subjects. Or we may think of the alredy fast approaching possibility of provoking, artificially, the success of certain potential mutations – something a most progressive leader might well use to change human society into a bee-hive, a prolonged agony.

Of despair, we have recently heard a great deal above all from authors whose penetrating, analytical spirit is not easily taken in by outward appearances. Thus Bertrand de Jouvenel concluded his meditation *On Power* with the following words: "Do we know whether it is the destiny of societies to avoid the mortal errors which beset them? Or whether they are not led into them by the same dynamism which carried them to their prime? Whether their seasons of blossom and fruitfulness are not achieved at the cost of a destruction of the forms in which their strength was stored? After the firework display, the darkness of a formless mass, destined to despotism or anarchy."[63]

Despair is forced on us, of course, not by the failure but, rather, by the success of the state-managers who seem to have all the scientific knowledge on their side. Shatov, one of Dostoyevskij's persons, asks another one, Stavrogin: "Do you mean to tell me that if it were mathematically proved that truth is not in Christ you would adhere to him rather than to truth?" But perhaps the biological "truth" will now become more important than the mathematical one. Then the question might arise whether one should adhere to a perfectly harmonious, but choiceless agony, hardly to be distinguished from a perfect euthanasia, or to a struggle in which real love is still possible.

We have only Christ's own guarantee that there will be always, until the very end of history, some who will recall his words. They will remember the Son of Man and the times when he walked along the dusty roads of Galilee and spoke of the beauty of the lilies of the field. They will know that human hope does not lie in any future time but rather in the present moment, when man stands in front of his Creator as much as at any other time. They will know that time as well as history is brought into existence as a closed affair. The presence of God above history and his presence in history, on the Cross of Calvary, will give them the correct sense of time and of the human achievements in it. It will help them to place the value of the moment above that of the arrow of passing time. And the darker such moment will be, the greater love it may bring into existence – "for a witness unto all nations; and then shall the end come."[64]

Notes

NOTES TO "THE OLD AND THE NEW MYTHS"

1. The magisterial essay which Walther F. Otto wrote to preface his *Dionysus, Myth and Cult* (Indiana Univ. Press, 1965) is particularly worth of study in this respect. Simone Weil's meditations on the same topic, which she had prepared, shortly before her death, may be found in *Institutions pré-chrétiennes* (Paris, 1951). Vyacheslav Ivanov's classical *Dionys i pradionisichestvo* [Dionysus and Pre-dionysism], although difficult to obtain, still overflows with observations which should be explored.
2. Daniel Halévy, *Essai sur l'acceleration de l'histoire*, Paris, 1948.
3. Juan José López Ibor, *La aventura humana* (Madrid, 1964), p. 162. A postmodern philosopher (C. D. Broad, "Two Lectures on the Nature of Philosophy", in H. D. Lewis (ed.), *Clarity Is Not Enough* (London, 1963, p. 64), described the "causal doctrine" in the following words: "The physicist thinks of one system as acting on another when *energy* is *transferred* from the former to the latter or when the former *modifies* the direction of motion of some of its parts by fixed *constraints*." At least four expressions in this description are genuinely mythical. But then we know that the intellect can only reach – or "construct", "carry out" – the truth with the help of "words-pictures" or "words-parables". These represent the real key to man's consciousness, to his awareness of his own purposefulness within the "theoria", within the vision of the universe. As another contemporary British thinker, H. H. Price, remarks (ibid., p. 38), we tentatively replace any of such notions by a newer one in order to discover one which will illuminate us more comprehensively. – A Marxist thinker might say: "Man's perpetual task is in historical activity; hope which goes beyond that is essentially a mere myth and consolation, not a reality." He fails to recognize that the very concept of "reality" is truly a "mere myth".
4. Errol F. Harris, "Misleading Analyses", in H. D. Lewis (ed.) *Clarity Is Not Enough* (London, 1963, p. 211). – Werner Heisenberg (in *The Physicist's Concept of Nature*) states: "What is, and always has been, our mainspring, is faith... I believe that I may act; I act that I may understand."

5. Only a segment of Lev S. Vygotskij's work has so far been made accessible to the English readers: L. S. Vygotskij, *Thought and Language*. (transl. by E. Hafmann and G. Vakar, Cambridge, Mass., MIT Press, 1962).
6. An explanation of the Creator's will to let himself be "visibly know" had been written already in the fourteenth century by Gregory Palamas, bishop of Thessalonica, against Barlaam of Cathinara (*cf*. Jean Meyendorff, *St. Grégoire Palamas*, Paris, 1959). Nevertheless it is interesting, rather sadly interesting, to observe a penetrating sixteenth-century thinker, fray Luis de Granada, struggling in his Dominican monastery with the superstitious, equally cumbrous and abstruse, Aristotelian and Thomistic nomenclature and then refusing to content himself with the notion of the "first cause" in which the expression "first" no longer means the central foutainhead of everything, the only and absolute Cause, but merely the first point of a line. Fray Luis' deep taste for the beauty of nature as well as the structure of his own thought (his ideas, for instance, concerning the teleology of creatures) carried him toward regarding the visible beings, with the help of both bodily and intellectual sight, as mirrors in which the prefections and attributes of the Creator are now and directly reflected (*cf.* Pedro Lain Entralgo, *La antropologia en la obra de fray Luis de Granada*, Madrid, 1946, pp. 63–64). It is God's life which is thus being reflected in the visible beings. – As to the primeval man, his concept of "life" was, evidently, incomparably more powerful and all-penetrating than the futile Aristotelian exercises in the conjugation of the auxiliary verb "to be". See, for instance, Placide Tempels, *La Philosophie bantoue* (Paris, 1949) or Alexis Kagame, *La Philosophie bantu-rwandaise* (Bruxelles, 1956).
7. Among works devoted to the study of the primeval thought, as reflected in the concepts, expressions and traditions of the still extant primitives, that of the Dutch scholar Placide Tempels, *La Philosophie bantoue* (Paris, 1949), deserves particular attention. While trying desperately to fit the results of his investigation into an Aristotelian framework (talking constantly, for instance, about Bantou "ontology"), Tempels, nevertheless, reveals a great deal of truth about his subject. Here are a few quotations: "In every Bantou dialect one easily discovers words and locutions employed as symbols of a force which is not exclusively physical, but totally human; they symbolize the force of our complete being, of our entire life; they express the integrity of being" (p. 30). "While trying to free themselves from metaphors, the Bantou speak of God as the Powerful One who possesses the force in himself and who is also the progenitor of the force of all creature" (p. 31). "The entire intellectual striving of the Bantou is directed toward the power of life; the fundamental notion in their conception of being is the concept of the vital force" (p. 33). "We, the Wester-

ners, envisage force as an attribute of being and we have elaborated a notion of being freed from the notion of force; but the primitives did not interpret the reality in this way; their notion of being is essentially dynamic... being is a force" (pp. 34–35). "In the created force *(ens contingens)* the Bantou sees a causal action which emanates from the very nature of the created force and influences the other forces" (p. 40). – Jean Capart, a prominent Egyptologist, while commenting on Tempels' book and admitting that he had found in the ancient African thought the key to many aspects of the Egyptian civilization, writes: "It is only the concept of life which gives the Egyptian religion its entire value and frees it from parasitic additions" (*Ibid*. p. 25).

8. More about this topic may be found in the last essay of this book.
9. José Camón Aznar has written a profound analysis of the ancient concentration on the real time as reflected in art. "The Egyptians", he states, "have created the most stable forms, totally exempt from time and the vicissitudes of history... The mass of the pyramid is centered on the tomb where the means are exhibited which the "double" of man needs to exist eternally... The time of the dead, the chthonic time, the subterranean time, less transparent and slower than the geological time, governs this world without stars and without hope. It is a lethal time, the future of which bears the mask of death, ruled by an eternal calm, without the possibility of consumption... The horror of space which characterizes the Egyptian architecture is also the principal element of the architectural atructure... The longing for an eternal life has been materialized in these monuments; at the same time, however, concrete and terrestrial forms have been brought over into this existence without end" (*El tiempo en el arte*, Madrid, 1958, pp. 20–27). It should be noted that, in this relationship, the "time of the dead" means the time of those who had accomplished their mission, potentially creative mission, in the "passing time", but who are alive in the "full time" because their own meaning has never been restricted merely to the realm of "passing time".
10. *II Thessal.*, 2 : 11.
11. Denis de Rougemont, *La Part du diable* (Neuchâtel, 1943, chapt. 23).
12. A wealthy American who, during the 1960's, had his views broadcast on radiostations, prophecied that the second coming of Christ will take place in a very short time. But what, according to him, will then be the first task of the "new man"? To "build clean, rapid and comfortable means of transportation..."
13. Edmund Wilson, *Piece of My Mind* (New York, 1958).

Notes to "Time as History's Background"

1. Efforts aiming at the establishment of historical chronology as a critical discipline led to a special branch of literature. Saligero's book *De emendatione temporum* (1583) was followed by a collective work of the eightteenth century Benedictine monks (*L'Art de vérifier les dates*, 1770) and by many more recently published works, such as A. E. Stamp, *Methods of chronology* (London, 1933), Jean Delorme, *Chronologie des civilisations* (Paris, 1949) or Frederick E. Zeuner, *Dating the Past: An Introduction to Geochronology* (4th rev. ed., London, 1958). For a criticism of the "Carbon 14" method see H. E. Suess, "Secular Variations", *Journal of Geographical Research*, Dec. 1, 1965.
2. The abstract quality of the idea of time can hardly be done away with by introducing other equally a more abstruse concepts such as "das Urständige", suggested by Werner Gent (*Das Problem der Zeit*, Frankfurt a. M., 1934). A realistic description of the basic issue is offered by Errol E. Harris. "If we are to rule that an event which takes time is made up of events which take none, we must assume either that there is a lapse between the timeless events, or that there is not. If there is no lapse, then it takes no time to pass from one timeless event to the next and it will be impossible to understand how events which take time can be constituted. If, on the other hand, there is a lapse between timeless events, that lapse will itself be made up of events which take no time. So we should have infinite regress and should still fail to "picture" the way in which timeless events could add up to make those which filled some duration". (See "Misleading analyses" in H. D. Lewis (ed.), *Clarity is Not Enough*, London, 1963, p. 210).
3. This seems quite an old idea. *Cf.* Paul Mus, *La Notion du temps reversible dans la mythologie boudhique* (Melun, 1939).
4. *Cf.* Ananda K. Coomoraswamy, *Time and Eternity* (Ascona, 1947, pp. 57–58).
5. Plato, *Timaeus*, 41 e. It should be noted that the Greek word for "number", *arithmós*, is the opposite of the word for "rhythm", *rithmós*, and that both are derived from *rein*, "to flow". *Cf.* Simone Weil's penetrating remark: "Le rythme ne se définit pas par la régularité, mais par les arrêts."
6. See, for instance, Harold F. Blum, *Time's Arrow and Evolution* (Princeton, 1951) and Hans Reichenbach, *The Direction of Time* (Univ. of California Press, 1956). A sensible exposé of the entire issue may be found in E. Huant, *Connaissance du temps* (Paris, 1950). G. F. Whitrow's *The Natural Philosophy of Time* (London, 1961) is concerned with mathematical theories of time. J. T. Fraser (ed.), *The Voices of Time* (New York, 1966) is a voluminous symposium on the problem of time, written by some scholars but also by some completely unquali-

fied contributors – such as the Jesuit author of the article on the idea of time in the *Bible*, who did not take the least care to learn something even about the vocabulary which the biblical authors use when speaking of the different kinds of time. – Beside the voluminous and most penetrating works of Piaget, Paul Fraisse's *La Psychologie du temps* (2nd. ed., Paris, 1967) is a most useful introduction into the ways in which the human mind perceives the various time-values. – The present author, to his regrets, has not been able to gain access either to the writings of J. M. E. McTaggart, concerned with the reality of time, or to those which Dimitrij V. Boldyrev published in Kharbin in 1935 and allegedly mainly concerned with the dependence of an object's reality on its distance in time and space.

7. *Cf.* Adolf Portmann, *Biologische Fragmente* and, above all, *Probleme des Lebens – eine Einführung in die Biologie* (Basel, 1949).
8. The ancient Chinese vocabulary did not speak of "causality", but rather of "coincidences". A similar concept has been introduced by the famous Swiss psychologist Carl G. Jung. Speaking of the parapsychological experiments conducted by J. S. Rhine in Duke University, Jung expressed the opinion that such experiments had demonstrated the possibility of "eliminating causality". "Although," he declared, "meaningful coincidences are infinitely various in their phenomenology, as causal events they nevertheless form an element that is part of the scientific picture of the world." He then suggested that the word "sychronicity" should be used to designate "the parallelism of time and meaning between psychic and psychophysical events which scientific knowledge so far has been unable to reduce to a common principle". *Cf.* C. G. Jung, "On Sychronicity", in *Man in Time*, (Eranos Yearbook, New York, 1957, p. 210 *et seq.*). See also M. L. von Franz, "Time and Synchronicity in Analytic Psychology", in J. T. Fraser (ed.), *The Voices of Time* (New York, 1966, p. 218 *et seq.*). – It is known, mainly since Einstein's days, that in case of great velocities, coincidence depends on the observer's motions in relationship to the observed object as well an on their distance apart.
9. Ananda K. Coomoroswamy, *Time and Eternity* (Ascona, 1947, p. 105). The quotation from Plutarch is from *Moralia*, 392 D.
10. Hans Reichenbach, *The Direction of Time* (Univ. of California Press, 1956), p. 264 *et seq. Cf.* also E. Stueckelberg, "La Notion de temps", in *Disquisitiones mathematicae et physicae*, Bucuresti, 1942.
11. There seems to be a certain similarity between these mathematical endeavors and the efforts of a "yogi" who tries to escape from a normal passing time into a "slower time" through the regulation of breathing. *Cf.* Coomoraswamy, *op. cit.*, p. 47: "... in yoga practice, of which the purpose is involutionary,

we find a contemplation of time, directed toward the immediate realization of ever greater duration and pursued until the whole of time can be experienced now." – *Cf.* also Alex Wayman, "No Time, Great Time and Prophane Time in Buddhism", in J. M. Kitagawa and Ch. H. Long (eds.), *Myths and Symbols* (Univ. of Chicago Press, 1969, p. 51): "No Time means the revelation of reality everywhere, always. Man may or may not intuit the dazzling ultimate. It is other than Great Time when nature predicts by omens and man obeys. It is other than Profane Time when man predicts by reason and nature obeys."

12. Berdyaev's views concerning history are contained mostly in two of his books, *The Meaning of History* (a new edition of G. Reavey's translation, Cleveland, 1962) and *The Beginning and the End* (a new edition of R. M. French's translation, New York, 1957). I am quoting from the Russian originals of these two works. Alexei A. Kozlov's main work, *One's Own World*, appeared in 1888.

13. If I use the expression "evidently" while speaking of our lack of capability to grasp the entire creation at once, I do so in perfect awareness of the fact that some "progressive" Christian theologians do not regard the "fall of man" – which is just another word for that same lack of capability – as evident. The connection between the belief in automatic progress and the refusal to see things as they are has been established quite some time ago. – Prayer, on the other hand, can be, in a sense, envisaged as a means by which we can defend ourselves against the consequences of the "fall". I should like to quote, in this context, from Simone Weil's *Attente de Dieu* (Paris, 1950, pp. 40–41): "Parfois les premiers mots déjà arrachent ma pensée à mon corps et la transportant en un lieu hors de l'espace d'où il n'y a ni perspective ni point de vue. L'espace s'ouvre. L'infinité de l'espace ordinaire de la perception est remplacée par une infinité à la deuxième ou quelquefois troisième puissance. En même temps cette infinité d'infinité s'emplit de part en part de silence, un silence qui n'est pas une absence de son, qui est l'objet d'une sensation positive, plus positive que celle d'un son."

14. Augustyn Jakubisiak, *Essai sur les limites de l'espace et du temps* (Paris, 1927, p. 123). C. H. Hinton's *What Is the Fourth Dimension?* (London, 1887) which develops a theory somewhat similar to that of Jakubisiak, is known to the present author only from reviews. But J. W. Dunne's and G. J. Whitrow's criticism of that work (see Whitrow's *The Natural Philosophy of Time*, p. 308) seems hardly justifiable. In the first place, the "transfer of attention" is not "continual". Second, the "transfer of attention" does not produce time – it only grasps it as "passing time". Whitrow's book seems rich in partial observations and uncorrect judgements. – Some interesting conclusions might result from a comparison between Jakubisiak's understanding of time and the concep-

tions of A. A. Kozlov (see note 12 above). Kozlov described space as a subjective representation of the order of our communications with other intellects, primarily with the Creator (*cf.* N. O. Losskij, *History of Russian Philosophy*, London, 1952, p. 159). – Again, considering the central importance of the logical principle of contradiction in Jakubisiak's thought, it should be interesting to compare his work with that of the Neo-Kantian teacher Ivan I. Lapshin who first in Petersburg and later in Prague expounded his doctrine according to which the applicability of the above mentioned principle depends on the spatial coexistence or synthesis. Lapshin's *Laws of Thought and Forms of Knowledge (Vsyelenskoe chuvstvo)* were published in 1906. Stéphane Lupasco (see, for instance, his *La Tragédie de l'énergie*, Tournai, 1970) approaches the same problems from a completely new view, based on contemporary research.

15. Hans Reichenbach, *The Direction of Time* (Univ. of California Press, 1956).
16. Benjamin Lee Whorf, *Language, Thought and Reality* (Harvard Un. Press, 1956).
17. *Cf.* Richard B. Onians, *The Origin of European Thought* (Cambridge Univ. Press, 1954, p. 411 *et seq.*).
18. Mircea Eliade, *The Myth of the Eternal Return* (New York, 1954, p. 27 *et seq.*).
19. Alexis Kagame, *La Philosophie bantu-rwandaise*, Bruxelles, 1956. There really seems hardly a possibility open for those speaking Bantu-Ruanda to conceive existence in any other way than as a distinctly individualized movement. Localization alone is insufficient to express the difference between two events or even between two entities.
20. William Chase Greene, *Moira: Fate, Good and Evil in Greek Thought* (Harvard Univ. Press, 1944) and the above mentioned book of R. B. Onians (see note 17) represent an excellent introduction to this vocabulary. For a thoroughgoing analysis of the ancient Greek ideas concerning time it is advisable to go to José Camón Aznar. In his masterful book, *El tiempo en el arte* (Madrid, 1958), he studies in detail the primeval mythical thought as reflected in Homer, Hesiod, Empedocles, Pythagoras and Parmenides, the "conciliation of the absolute and the temporal" and the circle as an "expression of the eternal immobility". The reader is immediately reminded of Jakubisiak. "Nature has a spatial and permanent character; eventually this character is the only element which defeats time; time in Greece is a property of the space; however, it swallows man..." (p. 38). Concerning the "pessimism" of Heraclitus, Camón has this to say: "An essential, harmonious symphony of all things does exist. But the human ear is unable to perceive it. There is no melody, simply because there is no receptive organ. Man can only contemplate the turbulent and irrational succession of events; their transitional character and their certain death are the

only norms which he can derive from such observation" (p. 41). About the works of Phidias: "These statues appear free of all humanity as well as of any historical moment. Their serene quality originates from the fact that the river of time does not touch them" (p. 43). About the Dionisiac time in Plato: "... that eternity does not have the significance of living in an unchanging situation; rather it is a perpetual creative activity which becomes manifest in phenomenons."

21. A more detailed discussion of the concept of the "golden time" remains outside the scope of this essay. However, the opportunity should not be bypassed to mention the excellent study, "Chronological Primitivism in Greek and Roman Mythology", in Arthur B. Lovejoy and George Boas, *Primitivism and Related Ideas in Antiquity* (Baltimore, 1935). – Aristotle's words are quoted from *De coelo*, B 1, in F. M. Cornford's translation. It should be noted that Aristotle's definition of infinity was not "that beyond which there is nothing", but rather "that beyond anything extant" (*Phys.*, IV, 206 b, 33).

22. See Mircea Eliade, "Time and Eternity in Indian Thought", in *Man and Time* (Eranos Yearbook, New York, 1957, p. 186).

23. Thorleif Boman studied this vocabulary in his essays on the Hebrew thought, *Das hebräische Denken* (2nd. ed., Göttingen, 1954; also available in an English translation, *Hebrew Thought Compared With Greek*, Philadelphia, 1960). However, his picture of the ancient Greek as standing and reflecting, while a Hebrew "reaches his zenith in ceaseless movement" is perhaps a bit onesided. The Hebrew possessed a very clear awareness of the fact that all passing time and all physical movement do not even reach toward God. "For he is my protector and I shall be moved no more" (*Psalm* 61 : 3).

24. *Cf.* H. S. Nyberg, "Questions de cosmogonie et cosmologie mazdéennes" in *Journal asiatique* (Paris, 1929, CCXIV, 2). In the Chinese vocabulary, *chiu* means obviously "complete time" and *shih* the "critical moment", while there seems to be no particular concept for "passing time" – unless one would use the word *yun* which also means "spontaneous circulation", or the expression *sù sai*, which means "primarily human life" as contrasted with immortality. – It might be mentioned at this juncture that the Chinese vocabulary has always devoted much attention to the concept of 'duration' (if, of couse, we are right in using this originally Latin expression in translating some of the Chinese words). Thus *shih gaen* refers to a "finite duration" as distinguished from an infinite or unmeasured duration; the rather complex expression *mo hun din gee shih gaen* refers only to an "indefinite duration" and *kwong yum gee korr whou* implies a "certain lapse of duration". There are also: *kae hun* which refers to a "definite portion of duration" whether past, present or future; *shih hun* denotes

a "certain period of duration" required to accomplish something; *guy shih fae* means a "duration measurable", for instance, by the movements of the sun; *yumgee pā gē*, finally, is a "rhythmical duration" which can be arranged in the way the musical composer arranges his tones between successive bars. Finally, bypassing the expressions used by chroniclers and historians to denote epochs of the past, one should mention two expressions, *shih yaedt* and *say kae*, which both may mean a solemn occasion or decisive moment, such as the hour of death. If we add that the Chinese expression for the "universe", *yu-chiu*, means literally "space-time", we have, at least, offered a few, but certainly not exhaustive illustrations from a very ancient and conservative language in which the mutual interdependence of space and time was always one of the basic conceptions. (The author is obliged for these remarks to his former student, Dr Joseph Yee).
25. See the penetrating analysis of the concepts *arché* and *ápeiron* in F. M. Cornford's *Principium Sapientiae* (p. 171 *et seq*.). – Another succinct description of the "time of God" may be found in José Camón Aznar's book, *El ser en el espiritu* (Madrid, 1959, p. 19 *et seq.*).
26. *Phys.*, 4, book 10, chapt. 14, 219 b: *arithmós kinéseos katà to próteron kài hýsteron*.

Notes to "Time and the Unity of the Person"

1. *Genesis*, 2 : 7.
2. *Qu'rān*, 96, 1–2. The absence of any "body-soul" dualism from Semitic traditions is stressed by Georges Pidoux, *L'Homme dans l'Ancient Testament* (Neuchâtel, 1953).
3. *I Cor.*,: *spéiretai sõma psychikón, egéiretai sõma pneumatikón*. The apostle's words were ignored as early as the second century by Origen who, under the impact of the Platonic "soul-and-body" vision, preached only a kind of a "spiritual resurrection" of man.
4. As Bruno Snell states (*The Discovery of the Mind*, Harvard Univ. Press, 1953) Homer also used other symbolical words of a similar nature: *thymós* as the center of emotions and *noũs* as the seat of thoughts.
5. *Cf.* W. K. C. Guthrie, *In the Beginning* (Cornell Univ. Press, 1957, pp. 59–60), W. C. Greene, *Moira* (New York, 1963, p. 340) and – for Orphism – W. K. C. Guthrie, *Orpheus and Greek Religion* (rev. ed., New York, 1966, pp. 156–157).
6. François Masai, *Pléthon et le platonisme de Mistra* (Paris, 1956, p. 266).
7. *Matth.*, 22 : 32: *ouk éstin ho theós nekrõn alla zontõn*.

8. Pius XII, *Humani generis*. An ever deeper confusion characterizes Robert North's, SJ, *Teilhard and the Creation of the Soul* (Milwaukee, 1967) where it is stated (p. 261) that Teilhard "cannot be thought heretical as long as he maintains that the human soul owes its being to God and is *immortal*". It is surprising indeed to notice how deep a root the Platonic vision concerning the "immortal soul" has taken among the basically pro-Aristotelian Western Christians. To Aristotle himself, as is well known, *psýchē* meant approximately the same "life-principle" which it also meant to the authors of the *New Testament*. It simply did not exist without a body and it is most succinctly described as the "actuality of a body which is potentially endowed with life" (*De anima*, 412 a 16). If it is endowed with an intellect, this endowment exists only as long as some thinking is actually done (*ibid.*, 429 a 18).
9. *Ecclesiastica Xaveriana* (1964, XIV, pp. 133–137).
10. O. Decroly, *Études de psychogenèse* (Paris, 1932); Jean Piaget, *Le Développement de la notion de temps chez l'enfant* (Paris, 1946); Alfred Adler, *Understanding Human Nature* (New York, 1929); Gordon Allport, *Becoming, Basic Considerations for a Psychology of Personality* (Yale Univ. Press, 1955) and *Pattern and Growth in Personality* (New York, 1961). Adequate attention should also be devoted to the investigations of Wilder Penfield and his associates, above all to their capability to produce, by mechanical means, a sudden and astonishing "presence" of a detailed past in the human memory.
11. M. Cole and I. Maltzman (eds.), *Contemporary Soviet Psychology* (New York, 1969, pp. 121–162). Vygotskij's *Collected Psychological Investigations* have been published in Russian in 1956 by the Moscow Academy of Pedagogics.
12. *De Trinitate*, IX, 3, 3. *Cf.* also "flesh and blood have not revealed this to you but my Father in heaven" (*Matt.*, 16 : 17).
13. W. C. Greene, *Moira* (New York, 1963, p. 194).
14. *De An.*, II, 5. In one respect Aristotle came closer to the Christian view than Plato: *mímēsis* (derived from *mnaein*, "to direct one's mind to an object") meant to him a real participation in the creative act, not merely an imitation of an eternal idea.
15. W. F. Lynch, *Christ and Apollo* (New York, 1960, p. 35).
16. *Summa Theologica*, pars I, quaest. 84, art. 1. – The 1917 edition of the "Canon Law" of the Church of Rome, canons 589 and 1366, order the students of theology to follow Aquinas and the teachers "to hold his principles inviolately". One would wish that some "canon law" could transform a restricted intelligence into an instrument of understanding and knowledge.
17. *Proverbs*, 8, 22–31.
18. *Philebus*, 30 b. At times Plato seems to prefer the primeval mythical symbol

of the Demiurg – *ho áristos tōn aitiōn* (*Timaeus,* 29 a-d) – to denote the Creator's Wisdom. But even the twelfth-century Provençal-Jevish treatise *Bahir (Brightness)*, one of the very early works generally grouped under the title of the *Cabala*, still states specifically that Shekinah means God's union with his own Wisdom.
19. It should be noted that the awe-inspiring name of the Creator in the *Old Testament* was "The One Who Gives Life", certainly not "I Am Who Am".
20. Vyacheslav Ivanov, *Freedom and the Tragic Life, A Study in Dostoyevskij* (New York, 1960, p. 113).
21. Speaking of the judges of the dying, te ancient Egyptian ruler Gheti admonishes his son Merikara: "Do not trust in length of years, for they [the judges] look upon a life's span as but an hour; when man remains after death, his deeds are heaped beside him; what is there is there for all eternity" (Pierre Montet, *Eternal Egypt*, New York, 1968, p. 218).
22. G. L. Vaillant, *Aztecs of Mexico* (New York, 1966, p. 179).
23. P. Geyl, *Napoleon – For and Against* (Yale Univ. Press, 1949).

NOTES TO "OF HOPE AND ANGUISH"

1. English translations are available of most of Teilhard's writings, particularly of his two most important books, *The Phenomenon of Man* (New York, 1959) and *The Divine Milieu* (New York, 1960). My quotations are from the French texts.
2. Blaise Pascal, *Pensées*, no. 347.
3. *Cf.*, for instance, Gregory of Nyssa, *Contra Eunomium* (2, p. 368): *akolouthían kai archèn doũnai pásē tẽ anthropínē fýsei tēs ek nekrõn anastáseōs.* – A similar argument will be found in Francis Bonaventura's *Itinerary of the Mind to God* (5, 8): "The absolute life is without duration and always present so that it embraces and penetrates all distances in the escaping time, as if it were both their center and their circumference, at once least and most complicated; thus within all things and without them an intelligible sphere exists whose center is everywhere and circumference nowhere". – José Camón Aznar (*El tiempo en el arte*, Madrid, 1958, p. 82 *et seq*.) shows that, with the spread of the Christian kerygma, "time overpowers space, makes itself independent from it and settles down at the bottom of the mind as generator of both anxiety and hope". Or again: "God is not a victim of time according to the manner of the gods of Greek mythology; on the contrary, he expresses himself and acts through the temporal process". – It should be noted, nevertheless, that this comparison concerns the Christian thought as contrasted rather with the ancient

Greek preoccupation with the cosmos than with the primeval and ancient attitudes in general. Also, while aware of the completness of time in God, the Christians had still to go, each one of them in his personal time and their Church in history, through the unavoidably human experience of passing time which cannot become independent from the concept of space.

4. Perhaps it should also be stressed again that "the Greek philosophers who speculated so busily about the physis of existence did not use the word "cause", *aitía*, in the pre-Socratic period, except with the human association of moral responsibility" (W. C. Greene, *Moira: Fate, Good and Evil in Greek Thought*, chapt. IX. 1).

5. All the three popularizing abstracts of post-modern science, which S. Toulmin and J. Goodfield have recently published, *The Architecture of Matter*, *The Fabric of Heavens* and *The Discovery of Time*, are written in this spirit. It is rather amusing to see it flourishing even in the works of a much advertised present-day economist, John K. Galbraith. In his *The New Industrial State* (Boston, 1967), the final, the *point omega* social entity has been baptized "technostructure"; it comfortably swallows both the Newtons and the non-Newtons. – And yet, oddly enough, the Evolutionists, with all their easy-going ubiquitousness, have never found the time to answer Boris N. Chicherin, a rather independent Russian scientist who, in his *Experiment in Animal Classification* (Moscow, 1892), spoke against the conception of the higher organisms as springing from the lower ones by means of the struggle of life. He argued that the lower organisms were more fertile, less demanding and therefore better adapted to environment. According to him the growing complexity of organisms was not due to the struggle for survival, but arose in spite of it. He also envisaged chance as useless for that struggle and unable to create the systematic unity of a new organ (*cf.* N. O. Losskij, *History of Russian Philosophy*, London, 1952, p. 134 *et seq.*).

6. Giambattista Vico's *La scienza nuova* is available in a revised English translation, *The New Science of G. Vico* (New York, 1961).

7. These eighteenth century developments have been studied by Christopher Dawson in *Progress and Religion* (new ed., New York, 1938) as well as by Kingsley Martin in the eleventh chapter of his *French Liberal Thought in the Eighteenth Century* (3rd rev. ed., London, 1962).

8. The influence of Thomistic scholasticism is particularly evident in this sentence. Man's intellect is no longer regarded as free to chose – to love or to act selfishly. Man becomes a robot. Evil has no reality.

9. It is sad indeed to see so many translations of the *New Testament*, often published with the approval of the various Church authorities, in which absolutely

no attention is paid to the immensely important nuances in the meaning of the ancient Greek expressions *kairós, chrónos, archḗ, plérōma, aiōn, télos,* etc. – An even lesser amount of attention is paid by modern and post-modern theologians to other Greek words employed by the Eastern Fathers of the Church – such as the Stoic *tropé* which in Gregory of Nyssa replaced *chrónos* and induced him to characterize the Creator as *átreptos.*

10. Nicolas of Cusa, *The Vision of God,* chapt. 11 (available in E. G. Salter's English translation, New York, 1960).–The Hebrew word *re'shith,* used in the Mosaic myth of creation, not only seems to have the same meaning as the Greek *archḗ,* but is also completed by Isaiah's expression *aharith (Isa,* 44 : 6 and 48 : 12) which evidently describes the instantaneous, complete and final character of the creative act. – Cusanus defined the escaping time as an "arranged presence" *(praesentia ordinata); cf. De docta ignorantia* (III, 26); To him, the entire creative act is coming from beyond time (...*sic est mundus aeternus, quia est ab aeternitate et non a tempore; Ludus globi,* I, 212). Elsewhere he says: *Cum in tempore intueor, omnia in successione explicari comprehendo (De venatione sapientiae,* III, 300). – It might be interesting to compare mutually the various statements of the *New Testament* where the expression *archḗ* is used: *Matt.,* 19 : 48; *Luke,* 1 : 2; 12 : 11; 20 : 20; *John,* 8 : 25; *II. Thess.,* 2 : 13; *Jude,* 6. – Gregory of Nyssa frequently identifies *archḗ* with *exousía (mían archēn, mian tōn pantōn exousían).* To Aristotle, of course, *archḗ* meant the initiative behind an infinite process – but not always a linear process – beyond which a retrospective or comprehensive look is unable to reach.

11. *Eccles,* 18 : 1 and 17 : 2. – Fray Luis de Granada, the sixteenth century Spanish mystic and theologian, not only accepted the basic idea of instantaneous creation, but also endeavored to explain why Moses had to have recourse to the division into six days: "... our understanding proved unable to grasp such and enormous thing as is this universe... and becase of that the Prophet had to divide it into many parts" *(Introducción del símbolo de la fé,* I, 38). Even he, curiously enough, failed to notice that the *Genesis* speaks of the first three "days" ("afternoons" and "mornings") *before* coming to the creation of the sun and the moon.

12. *II Cor.,* 4:16.

13. The Hebrew word *dór* (in plural *dórót*) meant he same as *ólám, i.e.,* the complete time. – J. Duchesne – Guillemin, in *Ormuzd et Ahriman* (Paris, 1953, p. 123), sees in the *Avesta* a distinction between a *temps sans limites* and a *temps à la longue domination.*

14. In his *Sein und Zeit* and elsewhere.

15. Time in its passing, escaping form is always a construction of pure mind. We

are able to represent a story or a process not only because our mind has registered a certain number of situations, but primarily because we endow this registration with a kinetic interpretation. Jean Piaget (*Le Développement de la notion de temps chez l'enfant*, Paris, 1946) has observed that the child at first constructs the relationship between situations in an intuitive way, without, as yet, reaching any such interpretation which would require the concept of "reversibility". He also was able to study the close relationship between the increasing coordination of movements and the appearance of the "past" and the "future" files of the child's memory. Distance and velocity emerge first in the child's thoughts; the concept of flowing time is only gradually derived from them through correlation of co-displacements. Frequent anticipations and reconstructions have an essential share in this derivation.

16. The outstanding East-European thinker of our days, Semyon L. Frank, has devoted to these matters the second chapter of his magisterial book, *Nyepostizhimoe* [The Unfathomable], published in Paris in 1939. As a contrast to his views, one may recall the teaching of Martin Heidegger, according to whom "anxiety" originates in the fact that all "future" is irrevocably engulfed by the "past".

17. Virgil's *Fourth Eclogue* and the *Apocalypse* share the honor of being the most frequent targets of scholars anxious to obliterate the literature of prophecy. See, for instance, Jérôme Carcopino's *Virgil et le mystère de la quatrième eclogue* (Paris, 1943). What should it really mean to the readers of the *Eclogue* that a boy was born in 40 BC to a Roman officer, Gaius Asinius Pollio, and that Virgil honored the father with his poem? What was the consul's boy supposed to have in common with the great things which the *Eclogue* announces? Was he really expected by Virgil to reintroduce the "golden generation", the "last age" of the Sibylline prophecy, "Apollo's age"? Notice also that "fullness of time" meant to Virgil the *archḗ* or the *plérōma* and not any point on an imaginary line or a phase of any process.

18. At times, Augustine went even further in his not very consistent or meaningful analysis by speaking of *predestination* as of "a preparation for the granting of grace". *Cf.*, for instance, *De praedestinatione sanctorum*, 19.

19. Augustine, *De civitate Dei*, 4,9: *Qui omnes rerum causas praescivit, profecto de eis causis etiam nostras voluntates ignorare non potuit.* – In *Ephes.*, 1:4-5, the timelessness of the *"en autō"* is most important.

20. *I Cor.*, 4:5. – *Cf.* also *Eph.*, 5:13.

21. C. S. Lewis, *Of Other Worlds* (London, 1966), in the essay "On Stories".

22. Thomas Aquinas, *Compendium theologiae*, I, 3. It should be stressed again that at least one of the really outstanding representatives of the thirteenth century

Western Christian thought, Francis Bonaventura, enthusiastically combatted the Aristotelian concepts and defended the identification of the creation of the universe with that of the passing time.
23. Daniel Halévy, *Essai sur l'acceleration de l'histoire* (Paris, 1948)
24. *II Pet.*, 3:7 and 10.
25. *Matt.*, 24:22, which predicts the tribulations preceding the end of history, speaks of the "maiming" *(kolobóō)* of those days as necessary "for the sake of the elect". Could this mean "acceleration"?
26. *1 Cor.*, 7:29: *ho kairós synestalménos estín.* – It is indeed refreshing to find, in contrast to the many books written by "Christian Aristotelians", the work of a scholar well versed in ancient literature and capable of grasping the Christian message: John Jones, *On Aristotle and Greek Tragedy* (Oxford, 1962, p. 60:) "Even Christians have believed, and not during the early centuries only, that they were in the Upper Room "again" with their Lord each time they took the bread and wine; and they have been untroubled with questions of then and now and eternity, with the superstructure of sacramental theology, which a lineal and inexorably progressive notion of time calls forth".
27. *Cf.* H. S. Nyberg, "Questions de cosmogonie et cosmologie mazdéennes", in *Journal asiatique* (Paris, 1929, CCXIV, 2).
28. *Cf.* Louis Massignon, "Time in Islamic Thought", in *Man and Time* (Eranos Yearbook, New York, 1957).
29. *Cf.* W. Ivanov, *A Guide to Ismaili Literature* (London, 1933).
30. This quotation comes from D. A. Lowrie's translation of Berdyaev's *The Meaning of the Creative Act* (New York, 1962, p. 63).
31. *Ibid.* (p. 93).
32. *John*, 4:35. See also the above mentioned (p. 29) *Gospel of St Thomas*.
33. *II Pet.*, 3: 8–9. An example of Schweitzer's and Teilhard's influence is evident in the late Tomas Merton's last book, *Conjectures of a Guilty Bystander* (New York, 1966). Merton calls the belief in the Satan, so frequently manifested by Jesus himself, a "paranoid obsession with one presumed source of evil" (p. 62). He asks whether – while "the Parousia seems indefinitely delayed" – "we should not rather attempt to change God's plan, and forget the whole business", "ask God to let us build the Kingdom in our own way", "a kingdom consistent with what we have begun", "at once a sacred enclave in the world and also politically in collaboration with the world" (p. 108). He then continues: "Suggested emendation in the Lord's prayer: take out *Thy kingdom come* and substitute *Give us time*. But then what? What are we going to do with time? Make deductions from past history, devise a system – a Christian system–and put it to work? Or rather consider the systems devised by others and baptize them,

making them suddenly Christian, and discovering in them the unexpected Kingdom?" (p. 109) – Reading Merton's thoughts one is forcibly reminded of a clairvoyant paragraph in Paul Claudel's *Introduction à l'Apocalypse* (Paris, 1946, p. 16): "The antithetic, red woman, opposed to the other one crying aloud in the sun, the woman who drinks the blood of the martyrs from a golden cup – I see in her the image of a degenerated Christianity. We should not seek the explication of the number of the Beast, 666, in any game with the letters from which the names of Nero, Napoleon or Hitler are composed. Six is the number of the days in which creation reached as far as man – before the seventh day was added, the day of the Lord. It is the number of humanism, of the pagan perfection, brought from the order of hundreds to that of tens and of units..." – Merton speaks of "systems devised by others". He couldn't have meant anything else than the totalitarian systems, the "technostructures", of our days. It should therefore be also noted that some theologians, following the example of Deissmann's *Licht vom Osten*, accept the reading of "666" as *kãisar theós*, in plain English "deified state". *Cf.* Heinrich Schlier, *Principalities and Powers in the New Testament* (New York, 1961, p. 89).

34. Viktor Weizsäcker, in his critical treatise on euthanasy, had to formulate and also answer the question "Is an incurably mentally sick man still a man?" ("Euthanasie und Menschenversuche", in *Psyche*, Heidelberg, 1947).

35. *I Cor.*, 15:51–52. – John Henry Newman belonged to those relatively recent Christian scholars who were troubled by the silence of the *Scriptures* concerning "the long interval which separates Christ's first and second coming" and during which "millions of faithful souls are waiting it out". Failing to recognize that he had become a victim of the non-Christian, Platonic myth of the "soul-dove in the body-cage" as well as of a lack of knowledge of the *New Testament's* original vocabulary, he reached the conclusion that a "development of doctrine" had become imperative, *i.e.* the belief in a "Purgatory as the explanation of the Intermediate State" (*An Essay on the Development of the Christian Doctrine*, 16th impression, London, 1920, pp. 62–63).

36. *Apoc.*, 10:6. "*Chrónos*", in spite of O. Cullmann's suggestion, never means "delay" Cf. *Apoc.*, 22:20, or John of Damascus, *De fide orthodoxa*, 2,1.

Notes to "Man in the Exploding Time"

1. Walter Lippman, *The New Imperative* (New York, 1935, pp. 47–48).
2. The growth of Lin Yutang's thought may be studied in his *With Love and Irony*

(New York, 1934), *The Importance of Living* (New York, 1937) and *Between Tears and Laughter* (New York, 1943).
3. Emanuel Mounier, *Be Not Afraid* (New York, 1962). In sharp contrast to Mounier, Sergei N. Bulgakov had been very much aware of the real trend of events as early as 1910 when he published his *Apocalyptics and Socialism*.
4. P. W. Bridgman, *The Way Things Are* (Harvard Univ. Press, 1959, pp. 262–263).
5. Christopher Dawson, *The Crisis of Western Education* (New York, 1961, p. 104).
6. Semyon L. Frank, *Realnost i chelovyek* (Paris, 1956, p. 284).
7. *Cf.* Nicolai A. Berdyaev's autobiographical work, *Dream and Reality*, translated into English by Katherina Lampert (London, 1950).
8. Mircea Eliade, "Time and Eternity in Indian Thought", in *Man and Time*, (Eranos Yearbook, New York, 1957, p. 199).
9. Something truly pathetic characterizes the strenuous and yet always failing endeavors of the Evolutionists to respect both "continuity" and "difference". Teilhard de Chardin, for instance, to whom even creation is a "continuous procedure", reminds the readers of his *Phenomenon of Man* that: "Nothing is so delicate and fugitive by its very nature as is a beginning... In every domain when anything really new begins to germinate around us, we cannot distinguish it... Where, even after the shortest lapse of time, are the first autos, planes or movies?" And what did Teilhard mean by "anything really new"?
10. Aristotle, *De anima*, 406–17; Plotin, *Enneads*, 5, IV. 4,1: *áchronos pāsa he noēsis*. *Cf.* also Augustine's *Confessions*, 10, 11: "...*per ipsam animam meam ascendam ad illum.*" – It might be noted that the Aristotelian doctrine, perhaps owing to the inconsistency of the thinker himself, perhaps to that of his disciples whose notes constitute our only source of his doctrine, seems to hesitate whether or not to accept the Platonic concept of *kósmos noētós*. While in several places Aristotle asserts that concepts are "derived" from perceptions (whatever the verb "to derive" may mean) and that the mind is a mere "developed perfection" *(entelechéia)* of the body, in at least one of his works we find the surprising – or, at least, not very clear – remark that the understanding *(noũs)* really enters man's mind "from outside" *(thýrathen eisiénai)* *(De gen. an.*, II, 36, 736 b).
11. Quoted from the chapter on Islamic art in José Camón Aznar's *El tiempo en el arte* (Madrid, 1958).
12. The two quotations are from Geofrey L. Bickersteth's translation (Harvard Univ. Press, 1965). The original texts:
Paradise, 13, 10–13: "*la bocca di quel corno
che si comincia in punto de lo stelo
a cui la prima rota va ditorno*"

Paradise, 17, 16–18: *"cosí vedi le cose contingenti*
anzi che sieno in sè, mirando el punto
a cui tutti li tempi son presenti."
13. Damascius, *Commentary to Parmenides;* Augustine, *Confessions,* XI. 11.
14. *Eccles.* 7:25.
15. Pindar, *Dirges,* 131: *aiõnos éidoulon léipetai*
16. *John,* 4:23.–*II Cor.*, 6:2: *idoũ, nýn kairós euprósdektos; idou, nýn hēméra sōterías.*
17. Arnold J. Toynbee, *An Historian's Approach to Religion* (London, 1956).
18. Giovanni Papini, *The Devil* (New York, 1954).
19. *Cf.* also Victor White, *God and the Unconscious* (London, 1952).
20. Ernst Bloch, *Das Prinzip Hoffnung* (Frankfurt a. M., 1959).
21. Agustyn Jakubisiak, *L'Essai sur les limites de l'espace et du temps* (Paris, 1927); *La Pensée et le libre arbitre* (Paris, 1936); *Vers la causalité individuelle* (Paris, 1947). His name does not even figure in the Encyclopédie Larousse.
22. Jakubisiak, *L'Essai sur les limites,* pp. 135 and 23. – It may be of interest to compare these thoughts with those expressed by José Camón Aznar in his book *El ser en el espiritu* (Madrid, 1959, p. 21 *et seq.*), above all with his notion of "alteridad": "In the theocentric time, it may be said, the otherness (alteridad) is the law of the beings; each being is different; but also, in as far as beings participate in the knowledge of God, they feel themselves interrelated as integral parts of the harmonious divine order". A similar view has been expressed by Simone Weil in her *Cahiers:* "*L'existence est du temps, la valeur de l'eternité; comment n'y aurait il pas déchirement?*"
23. *Cf.*, *eg.*, Benson Mates, *Elementary Logic* (Oxford Univ. Press, 1965, p. 144).
24. Jakubisiak, *L'Essai sur les limites* (p. 149). Jakubisiak was probably not acquainted with the writings of Martin Heidegger. There exists, nevertheless, some affinity between their thoughts. Heidegger recognizes the "spacial" nature of the universe, but in his vision the space is dominated by meanings rather than by geometrical rules; the "milieu" of every thing emanates from its meaning. Ideas appear as exteriorization of man's preoccupation with his own life. And his life is always, at each given moment, directed toward something (an observation which also comes close to Berdyaev's conception of man's participation in the creative act).
25. Semyon L. Frank, *Nyepostizhimoe* [The Unfathomable] (Paris, 1939). Frank's thought may be studied also in his earlier works, *Predmyet znania* (1915; a French translation appeared in 1937 under the title *La Connaissance et l'être*) and *Dusha chelovyeka* (1917). His conclusive work, *Realnost i chelovyek,* was finished in 1949, a short time before his death, and published in Paris in 1956.

26. Semyon L. Frank, *Nyepostizhimoe*, p. 322.
27. Semyon L. Frank, *Realnost i chelovyek*, p. 160.
28. Ibid., p. 202.
29. *Neypostizhimoe*, p. 68. Studying Frank, one is reminded, at times, of Samuel Alexander's conception of the universe resting on the three notions of "space-time" (stemming from our attitude toward it or its parts) and "emergence" (which includes the "dawning" of truth on man's mind).
30. Miguel de Unamuno, *Vida de don Quijote y Sancho*, cap. 58.
31. Thomas Merton, *Conjectures of a Guilty Bystander* (Garden City, NY, 1966, pp. 300-302).
32. *Ibid.*, pp. 315-316.–"The seventh chapter of St Anselm's *De casu diaboli*," says Merton, "raises a rather modern question: Our creativity, that is to say the creative power of our liberty in the world, is resolved perhaps into the choice to be nondestructive and to freely cooperate in creation. Creation itself is beyond our power. If we accept creation, if we are open to the mysterious creative power of God's will (even when it appears to us to pose a threat), we concur in creation. We do not have the power to create, but we have the seeming power to destroy, by reason of our capacity for the refusal of creative and positive power from God. Actually the power to destroy, like the apparent power to sin, is no power at all. It is a metaphysical illusion, though destruction itself can be very objective and real. More truly creative is the free consent by which we really participate in the dynamism of the world created by the love of God. – But our power to destroy, like our power to sin, seems to us more of a power because it seems to be more unique, more personal, more autonomous. It seems to be uniquely ours. Especially when we cannot really believe in our consent and our freedom, we fall back on this illusory power. We destroy in order to affirm our freedom and our "reality". The more we doubt our freedom and our identity, the more we are impelled to destroy. – St Anselm, accepting this negitivity in man, even says that to refrain from destruction is to participate in creation. We "make" something when we are capable of unmaking it and do not do so. This, of course, is not our only way of making things, but it is important to remember this rather humble estimate of our power in this age of destructive power and violence. – Problem: the difficulty of realizing that our power of consent is real and creative, when it vanishes into the creative background of God's will..."
33. Miguel de Unamuno, *Del sentimiento trágico de la vida*, cap. VIII.
34. Pedro Laín Entralgo, *La espera y la esperanza* (Madrid, 1957, pp. 471, 484, 493, 558). – While Laín Entralgo does not show any intention of developing his penetrating thought into a philisophical "system", we may well ask ourselves

what would have been the fate of, for example, the High Medieval thought' had Aquinas and Duns Scotus abandoned their naive squabbles about the "priority" of "understanding" and "volition" and replaced these words by the term "expectation" *(espera)*, meaning both a "question concerning the meaning" and "one's attitude to the meaning". Spinoza later inclined toward a similar nomenclature. After all, much depends on the vocabulary of the inherited mythical traditions. Is human "understanding" really anything more than "asking and expecting"? Thomas Merton admits frankly: "The best I can do is to look for some of the questions" (*Conjectures of a Guilty Bystander*, Garden City, NY, 1966, p. 38).

35. Juan José López Ibor, *La angustia vital* (Madrid, 1950); quotations from pp. 17, 115 and 125–127; *La aventura humana* (Madrid, 1965); quotations from pp. 7, 25, 67, 71, 75 and 141.
36. Nikolai A. Berdyaev, *The Meaning of the Creative Act* (transl. by D. A. Lowrie, new ed., New York, 1962, p. 46).
37. *Ibid.*, p. 135. See also Berdyaev, *The Beginning and the End*, cap. III, part 2 which begins: "Ontological philosophy is not a philosophy of freedom". *Ibid.*, p. 158: "It is possible to take the view that there is more in potency than in act, more in movement than in immovability, and that there are greater riches in freedom than in being." From here we may again go as far back into the past as the primeval wisdom. Thus the Bantu tribes distinguish between the "nganga" (the man who loves creation) and the "kulowa" (the man who is an enemy of creation).
38. *Ibid.*, p. 137. – *Cf.* also *Ibid.*, p. 139: "Freedom is not consciously accepted necessity, as the German idealists taught; necessity is an evil, sub-conscious freedom, a freedom not illuminated by the Logos."
39. *Ibid.*, p. 139.
40. Nikolai Berdyaev, *Opyt eschatologicheskoj metafysiky* (Paris, 1952; transl. by R. M. French: *The Beginning and the End*, New York, 1957, pp. 155 and 170).
41. *Ibid.*, p. 141.
42. "Felix culpa quae tantum et talem meruit habere Redemptorem." – *Cf.* Bernhard W. Anderson's *Creation versus Chaos* (New York, 1967, p. 123 *et seq.*, and p. 141) which discusses in detail Deutero-Isaiah's conception of the creative act as including, from the very beginning, all God's saving actions.
43. Berdyaev, *The Beginning and the End*, p. 248. – *Cf.*, by contrast, Thomas Merton's analysis of Anselm's *Cur Deus Homo* and *Proslogion*. "Christ could justly have used his power... but he preferred to save man by a renunciation of power" (*Conjectures of a Guilty Bystander*, p. 312). If the coming of Christ can be described as the sanctification of the human, passing time, evil can be

characterized as counter-time. The illusory, from-the-past-into-the-future concept of time actually expresses the only hope of the Angel of Darkness. – See also Camón Aznar's discussion of Augustine's view of this topic in *El tiempo en el arte*, p. 97.
44. Semyon L. Frank, *Nyepostizhimoe*, p. 308.
45. All the force of this symbolism is centered in Christ's own words: "I came to throw fire on this earth... *pŷr élthon baleĩn epì tèn gèn, kài tì thélō ei édē anérfthē*..." (Luc., 12:49). – Thomas Aquinas also seemed attracted by its majesty, but evidently remained at a loss as what to do with it; see *Summa theologica*, I, 67, 2–3. – An outstanding American scholar, Bernhard W. Anderson, devoted, in his *Creation versus Chaos*, much penetrating attention to the primeval symbols of sees and waters, or again to that of the "bottomless deep" *(tzulah)*, as a version of the imagery by which man tried to "name" the outer darkness – the very contrast of the explosion of light which is God's creative act. – It may also be noted that, in the Hebrew-Christian tradition, the role of the one who merely reflects the light, Lucifer, is a part of the creative explosion from its very center (*I John*, 3:8) and that Lucifer "stands on the sea" (*Apoc.*, 12:18) – the sea still being the same primordial image of the formless "outer darkness". When the apostle John speaks of the resurrection, of the "new sky" and the "new earth" he remarks that the "sea no longer exists" (*kai hē thálassa ouk éstin éti*, *Apoc.* 21:1). Here again, evidently, the "sea" should he interpreted as a symbol of the "void". – Gregory of Nyssa used frequently, as late as the fourth century, two other Greek words, *methórion* and *homíchlē*, both in the sense of the "frontier of darkness". – One may also recall John Milton's beautiful line:"... since God is light and never but in unapproached light dwelt from eternity... bright effluence of bright essence increate."
46. See Henri Corbin, "Cyclical Time in Mazdaism and Izmailism", in *Man and Time* (Eranos Yearbook, New York, 1957, pp. 119–134), and Richard Reitzenstein, *Das iranische Erlösungsmysterium* (Bonn, 1921, p. 172 *et seq.*). – In the Homeric mythology the divine light does not throw any shadows. See some more detailed observations on this in Camón Aznar's *El tiempo en el arte* (p. 29 *et seq.*).
47. Masaharu Anesaki, *History of Japanese Religion* (Rutland-Tokyo, 1963, p. 24 *et seq.*).
48. See William R. Inge, *The Philosophy of Plotinus* (London, new ed., 1948), and M. de Bandillac, *La Sagesse de Plotin* (Paris, 1952).
49. Nikolai A. Berdyaev, *The Meaning of History*, p. 41. – One may also recall Jean Guitton's sentence: "*Une chute ne se difinit pas, elle se raconte*", or again G. V. Florovskij's words: "Evil is a void of nothingness, but, paradoxically,

a real void" ("The Idea of Creation", in *The Eastern Churches Quarterly*, 1949, p. 77).
50. Empedocles, quoted in Simplicius, *Phys.*, 158.
51. Karl Jaspers, *Der philosophische Glaube* (München, 1948, p. 58).
52. Berdyaev, *The Meaning of the Creative Act*, p. 140. Berdyaev here evidently takes up A. S. Khomyakov's view that God is freedom for "all pure beings", law for the "unregenerated man" and necessity for the Satan (see N. O. Losskij, *History of Russian Philosophy*, London, 1952, p. 35).
53. Augustine, *De civitate Dei*, V. 9: "*Qui omnes rerum causas praescivit, profecto in eis causis etiam nostras voluntates ignorare non potuit quas nostrum operum causas esse praescivit.*" – This may be regarded as an answer to the rapid sequel of questions which Simone Weil put down in her *Cahiers*: "*Le tissu du monde, c'est le temps, et qu'est-ce que le temps hors de ma pensée ? Que seraient le present et l'avenir sans moi qui le pense ? Et s'ils ne sont rien, l'univers n'est rien, car que' est-ce qu'être un seul instant ? Comment ne serais-je pas dès lors associé à la création ? Mais il faut que je pense le temps comme un co-créateur...*"
54. Jean Guitton, *Le Temps et l'éternité chez Plotin et saint Augustin* (Paris, 1959, p. 372).
55. Friedrich Schelling, *Of Human Freedom* (transl. by James Gutmann, Chicago, 1963; all quotations are taken from this translation).
56. *Ibid.*, p. 364.
57. Jean Plagnieux, *St Grégoire de Nysse théologien* (Paris, 1951, p. 400).
58. Frederick J. Streng, in an excellent treatise on Emptiness (*Emptiness, A Study in Religious Meaning* (Nashville, 1967, p. 38), states: "Becoming and knowledge are coextensive. The English word "realize" captures the two elements in the sense that man can be said to "realize certain possibilities."
59. Herbert Butterfield in *The Origins of Modern Science* (rev. ed., New York, 1965, pp. 137 and 169) notices how Newton "was prepared to believe that gravity represented a living being that pervaded the whole of space" or again how his Cartesian contemporaries derided the now generally accepted concept of "an influence which could operate between bodies that did not touch one another". – *Cf.* also Pierre Duhem, *Aim and Structure of Physical Theory* New York, 1962, p. 47). – An interesting view was held by the fifteenth century Byzantine Humanist Gemistos Pléthon to whom "angels" meant mythical deities or Platonic ideas as well as Hebrew or Christian messengers of the Creator.
60. Post-modern theologians, mostly still imprisoned in the Aristotelian "categories" of thinking, experience continuous difficulties in this field. *Cf.* Karl Rahner's *Theological Investigations* (London, 1961, I, pp, 347 – 382).–It is, of

course, regrettable that the not very sensible interpretation of the "fall" still predominates in so many catechisms and devotional works of Christian authors.

61. I am talking here about the much publicized *New Catechism* of the Dutch bishops of the Church of Rome (English transl., New York, 1967). It states on p. 263: "...the authentic enlightenment is to be sought not in the beginning but in the course of things and their culmination." "Hence the beginning is less important to us than it was in earlier days." It states again on p. 269: "We need not imagine that man once existed in a state of paradisiac perfection and immortality... We really know nothing about the actual beginnings..." As a contrast to this new species of "know-nothingism" it should be noticed that this same book (p. 418) strictly demands that "taxes should be paid in the way the State expects". A "Christian" message, indeed.

62. Paul Ricœur (*The Symbolism of Evil*, New York, 1967, p. 333) attracts our attention to the Pauline concept of the "flesh" and the "body" as designating "not a substantial reality" but an "existential category." – But we may as well go back to the fifteenth century Nicolas de Cusa and read in his *Sermons* (no. 36): "With God, Adam does not precede Christ and Christ does not precede Adam. If you consider all the creatures at the same time as they stand before God's face, the orderly unity becomes evident, which is grasped by our intellect within the category of plurality; only in that way is Christ the Beginning and the Head." – Two quotations from Schelling's *On Human Freedom* seem appropriate here: "In original creation man is an undetermined entity–which may be mythologically presented as a condition antecedent to this life, a state of innocence and of initial bliss. He alone can determine himself. But this determination cannot occur in time. It occurs outside of time altogether and hence it coincides with the first creation even though as an act differentiated from it. Man, even though born in time, is nonetheless a creature of creation's beginning – the centrum. The act which determines man's life in time does not itself belong in time but in eternity (p. 385)".–"The greatest obstacle to the doctrine of freedom has ever been the relation of the assumed accidental nature of human conduct to the unity of the world-whole as previously planned in Divine reason... The authors of the doctrine of predestination... did not seek this determination in the whole eternal act contemporaneous with creation, but in an absolute, i.e. wholy unfounded decision of God... Thus they destroyed the root of freedom... As man acts here so he has acted since eternity and already in the beginning of creation... (p. 387)".

63. Bernard of Clairvaux has this idea evidently from the so much neglected text of the apostle Paul in *I Cor.*, 7:14: *hegíastai gàr ho anḗr ho ápistos en tē̃ gynaikí, kài hēgíastai hē gýnē hē ápistos en tō̃ adelfō̃, epèi ára tà tékna hymṓn akathartá*

estin, nỹn dè hágia estin. – Always faithful to the devise *"la charité parfaite est le fruit du désir"*, expressed in his *Commentary on the Canticle of Canticles*, Bernard did not consider the mutuality of men in any way interrupted by death; to the widow-countess Ida de Nevers he wrote: *"Donnez vous garde de nuire à vous-même ici bas et à votre mari là où il est."*

64. It has always been one of the tenets of the Christian creed – stated already in *Luke*, 1:28: *chaĩre kecharitōménē* – that Mary, Jesus' mother, was full of God's grace from the very first *kairós* of her life, so that, while she bore all her suffering, she remained without the blemish of sin. Regrettably, while she could have remained satisfied with the beautiful Latin expression *immaculata*, the Church of Rome, imprisoned in the Aristotelian "chains-of-causes" vocabulary, chose to speak of a "conception". That Church's theologians now have to explain that "Mary's parents conceived her in the same way that the rest of mankind was conceived" (see Louis Bouyer, *Le Trône de la sagesse*, Paris, 1960, chapt. 7; the Eastern Christian view is stated in Sergei N. Bulgakov's *The Wisdom of God*, p. 174).
65. *I Cor.*, 15:20: *aparchḗ tōn kekoimēménōn.*
66. This and the subsequent statements come from the excellent essay on Zen in Nancy W. Rose, *Three Ways of Asian Wisdom* (New York, 1966).

Notes to "The Death of History?"

1. *Peri psychḗs kai anastáseōs ho lógos*, Migne, Patr. Gr., vol. 46.
2. One may wonder what would be Darwin's reaction to some of the new uses of the word "creation". Theodosius Dobzhansky (*Heredity and the Nature of Man*, New York, 1964) stresses that "creation is a process, not an act" because "it continues now, before our eyes and is accessible to scientific study". Many modern scientists have felt bound, sooner or later, to accept the purely fictitious concept of the "continuously flowing time". Their predictions – and predictions is what technology requires from them – presuppose repeated verifications and these, in their turn, postulate the category of "flowing time". Moreover, one may ask whether the very concept of "determination" is not identical with that of *entelechy:* something meaningful can be achieved only if there is an intention to achieve it. If the answer is positive, there is simply no place for any "chance" in a "determinist" system. – In this way, paradoxically, many scientists operate on a level which Lucien Lévy–Bruhl falsely denotes as "primitive", describing the basic idea of this level as a "time extending indefinitely in imagination, something like a straight line, always homogeneous by

Notes to pages 141–157   213

nature, upon which events fall into position, a line on which foresight can arrange them in a unilineal and irreversible series and on which they must of necessity occur one after the other" (*Primitive Mentality*, Boston, 1966, p. 123).

3. *De anima*, 412 b 17.
4. In a review published anonymously in the *Spectator*, 24th March 1860.
5. *Cf.* Julian Huxley discussing C. H. Waddington's views in *Evolution: the Modern Synthesis*, 2nd ed., 1963.
6. Bertrand Russell, *Mysticism and Logic* (New York, 1957, p. 45).
7. Herbert Spencer, *Social Statistics*, p. 79.
8. Chapt. VI, "Organs of Extreme Perfection and Complication".
9. *Origin of Species*, chapt. IV.
10. L. T. Hogben, *Genetic Principles in Medicine and Social Science* (London, 1931).
11. See "Criticisms on the *Origin of Species*", reprinted in the second volume of his *Collected Essays*.
12. G. W. Leibniz, *Nouveaux essais sur l'entendement humain* (1765).
13. *Summa contra gent.*, 4, 79. Truth, of course, is not destroyed by flowing time. But that only means that the human intellect, while partially reaching a truth, reaches something which does not change with the passing of time. It does not mean that the intellect itself, the functioning of our mind, cannot be interrupted or stopped by changing situations. No way leads from "knowing" to "immortality."
14. In sharp contrast to this fashion of thinking, Piaget has concluded that "before we can establish the existence of a causal relationship by experiment, we must first correlate our measurements and this involves appealing to our memory or to reconstructions characteristic of psychological time (*The Child's Conception of Time*, London, 1969, p. 278)".
15. P. B. Medawar, while reviewing *The Phenomenon of Man* in *Mind*, 1961, vol. LXX, pp. 99 *et seq.* Equally negative is the judgement pronounced above Teilhard by Stéphane Lupasco (*La Tragédie de l'énergie*, Tournai, 1970, p. 76).
16. *Luke*, 12:56 and 23:43.
17. *The Joyful Wisdom*, chap. V.
18. Thomas J. J. Altizer, *The Descent into Hell* (Philadelphia, 1970, p. 161).
19. *Ibid.*, p. 123.
20. *Octogesima adveniens*, dated 14th May, 1971, was published to commemorate the eightieth anniversary of *Rerum novarum*, an encyclical of Leo XIII, concerned with social morality and economico-social problems.
21. The positive aspects of the encyclical may be found above all in chapters 9, 10, 31, 38, 39 and 44.
22. *Octogesima adveniens*, chapts. 4 and 5. Pope Paul VI evidently derives the

biblical support for the idea of "progress" from the frequent parables concerning only and exlusively a man who sows the grain or cultivates his estate. See his allocution of 7th of July, 1971.
23. *Ibid.*, chapts. 7 and 9. The reader, however, is left in sheer uncertainty as to whether Paul VI realizes at all what he means by "nature". In par. 16 and elsewhere, for instance, discriminations of all kinds are enumerated – safe the one which has always been most patent : nature's refusal to endow men with equal gifts. In a fully industrialized society nature's discrimination – the difference between the few who understand a highly ramified science and technology or parts of it and the many who do not – comes more to the foreground than anywhere else.
24. *Ibid.*, chapt. 15.
25. *Ibid.*, chapt. 45.
26. *Ibid.*, chapt. 47.
27. *I Cor.*, 10:4
28. Thomas J. J. Altizer, *The Descent into Hell* (Philadelphia, 1970, pp. 52 and 85).
29. *Ibid.*, p. 107. Paul's text: *I Cor.*, 15:28.
30. *Ibid.*, p. 191.
31. *I Pet.*, 1:16.
32. *Ibid.*, 3: 13.

Notes to "Of Light and Hell"

1. *I Pet.*, 1:17: *ton tēs paroikías hymõn chrónon anastráfēte*... The inability – or unwillingness – of the translators to render the full meaning of this exact counsel sadly illustrates the contemporary attitude toward the *Scripture*. Not only is *chrónos* once again translated as mere "time" (instead of "passing time"), but the verb *anastréfein* which really means "to gather up" or to "roll back" is usually rendered as "to converse" or even "to conduct oneself".
2. Paul Ricœur (*The Symbolism of Evil*, New York, 1967, pp. 334–335) sketches well the gradual surrender of the Christian scholars to the Hellenic and Hellenistic inheritance: "Adam's fall will no longer be different from the fall of the souls in Plato's *Phaedrus*... Platonizing Christianity adopts the opposition between contemplation and concupiscence... Everything leads the Christian experience of sin from pride toward concupiscence... Christianity will tend toward the identification of evil and the body... Among the motives of that transformation we ought to give a special place to the experience of death or, rather, of dying..."

3. Luis Cencillo, *Hyle* (Madrid, 1958, p. XIII).
4. Duns Scotus, *Opus oxoniense*, III, dist. 19.
5. See Henri Corbin, "Cyclical Time in Mazdaism", in *Man and Time*, (Eranos Yearbook, New York, 1957, p. 116). In one sector of the Zoroastrian inheritance, Ormuzd, the angel of light, precedes the face of the Creator, to "help him to manifest himself". It would exceed the scope of this study, if we wanted to discuss those creatures of God, about whom all the ancient traditions knew something and whom the Christian message calls "angels". Whoever visited the cathedral of Reims, known as "the cathedral of the angels", has realized how much attention was paid to them as late as the High Middle Ages. They certainly have never been conceived by Christians as mere symbols. Rather the concept of "force," so dear to all scientists, above all since Isaac Newton's times, is a derivation of the archaic and Christian concept of the angel. Should we identify the energies of the Creator, about whom the Eastern Fathers of the Church used to write, with the "messengers" or "angels" or "deities" or "gods" of the primordial and ancient man? The apostle Paul himself (*II Thess.*, 2:11–12), while speaking of God as sending Satan to present man with the choice between "justice" and the "approval of injustice", calls him, the Angel-Whose–Darkness-Reflects-Light, an "energy of illusion" *(enérgeia plánēs)*. In *Heb.*, 1:7, he quotes *Ps.* 103 (4): *"ho poiōn toùs angélous autoũ pneúmata, kài toùs leitourgoùs autoũ pyrós flóga"* (with a remarkable carelessnes, many modern translators render here *pneúmata* as "winds"). – *"Anges, dieux dans Platon..."*, Simone Weil has remarked, *"au cours du même instant éternel ils sont portés à l'être, et, par amour, cessent d'être"* (*Cahiers*, III, p. 25). – Sergei N. Bulgakov, in his *Jacob's Ladder* (Paris, 1929), expressed a similar opinion concerning the identity between Plato's ideas and the angels, the created bearers of the Eternal Wisdom – in particular guardian angels of men, Churches, cities, but also animals and elements.
6. *John*, 1:5: *kài tó fõs en tẽ skotía fáinei, kài hē skotía autò ou katélaben.* – *I John*, 5:19: *ho kósmos hólos en tõ ponerõ kẽitai.* – *Cf.* also *II Cor.*, 11:14. But perhaps the author of the *Fourth Gospel* intended to say what Philolaos seems to have meant when he spoke of the "unlimited" quality of light and the "quasi-limiting" quality of darkness: *hē fýsis en tõ kósmō hyrmochthē ex apéiron te kài perainóntōn kai hólos ho kósmos kài tà en autō pánta.* – *Cf.* also *Eph.*, 5:13: *pãn gàr tò faneroúmenon fõs estin*
7. Pierre Duhem, *The Aim and Structure of Physical Theory* (P. P. Wiener's translation, New York, 1962, appendix, p. 335). In contrast to Duhem the hypothesis built up gradually by Stéphane Lupasco und summed up above all in his *La Tragédie de l'énergie* (Tournai, 1970) makes the concept of this uni-

verse as a *limit* or *frontier* of the creative explosion astonishingly real from the scientific point of view. His *principe d'antagonisme* appears very close to the Christian *theoria* as well as to the theme of the struggle between Eros and Anteros, dear to the sculptors of Ancient Greece. Lupasco's sole disadvantage seems to be in his attitude toward the principles of the "classical" logic. *(Cette logique n'est que le passage à la limite, mais une limite impossible...)* Human expressions, generally speaking, are here to exempt our concepts from change; yet they are also capable of characterizing change itself. Lupasco's own system of logic certainly does not contradict the claims of "classical" logic; it only develops its tools a few steps further (see his *Essai d'une nouvelle théorie de la connaissance*). – Another recently published work, *Science et nescience* by Manuel de Diéguez (Paris, 1970) develops a vision which also agrees with the concept of the creation as an explosion – the same concept the acceptation of which has already been facilitated so much by Arthur Eddington's views concerning the expansion of the closed universe. Perhaps a few quotations will suffice to give the reader an impression of the vision embraced by de Diéguez. "*Einstein se servait du temps-énergie, en croyant que c'était du temps, et Bergson opposait à ce temps-énergie un temps intérieur qu'il croyait seul véritable, sans s'apercevoir que l'homme est lui-même en mouvement... La cosmologie de l'énergie doit permettre de montrer la généalogie du temps, en tant que leurre enfanté par le mouvement que je suis et par les mouvements qui m'environnent* (p. 335). *Le temps construit sur le mouvement-étalon, et le mouvement ramené à l'énergie q'est à son tour la matière elle-même* (p. 336). *Le temps, à suivre la course de la lumière, s'est revelé n'être lui-même que la dépense d'énergie d'un corps en mouvement, arbitrairement choisi comme étalon du temps...* (p. 339). *L'appel au temps est justement la chute originelle; la chute dans le mouvement de la matière...* (p. 351).

8. Such assertion seems to have been sympathetic to many scholars educated in the traditions of the Greek philosophy. It was most emphatically proclaimed by an outstandic Sephardic thinker from Bordeaux, David Gradis, in his *Dissertation sur l'origine du monde*, published in 1797.
9. Pierre Montet, *Eternal Egypt* (transl. by Dorren Weightman, New York, 1968, p. 188).
10. G. C. Vaillant, *Aztecs of Mexico* (New York, 1966, p. 170).
11. W. K. C. Guthrie, *Orpheus and Greek Religion* (New York, 1966, p. 96): "The derivation of the name from *fáinō* is universal in ancient authorities. He is called Phanes because he first shone forth – appeared in a blaze of light – or alternatively because he makes visible, gives light to, the rest of creation. He is sometimes called light itself, or by a slight and very natural transference is

identified with the sun, though this fusion was probably not made in the Rhapsodic account of the Creation, which seems to have been remarkably consistent, and according to which, of course, Phanes existed before the sun, which was first created by him..."

12. The narrators were not so sure whether Light was "born" from Darkness or Darkness from the explosion of Light. As recently as the time when the parables used in the fourteenth book of the *Illiad* were composed, Night and the Dark Waters could still be envisaged as the "superior power", while in the *Genesis* the Creator and the "formless, dark void" were seen "together" and the "Tusked Cosmic God" of the oldest American pre-Columbian tradition known to us had to battle, "from the beginning", with a fishy-watery adversary (*cf.* E. P. Lanning, *Peru Before the Incas*, New York, 1967, p. 126) – in a way resembling the basic plot of the now lost *Titanomachia*, attributed to Eumelos of Corinth or Arkinos of Miletus.

13. Aristotle himself, it seems, was after all not as much of a "rationalist" as most of his students' notes depict him. In one place he is said to have stated: "Man who finds himself perplexed and puzzled is aware of his ignorance; because of that it can be asserted, in a sense, that whoever is devoted to the myths acts as a a true lover of wisdom – because myths contain things admirable" (*Metaphys.*, 982a).

14. Hesiod's expression *próteroi theói* clearly uses the word *theós* in the sense of a force, not in that of the Cosmic God. Titles such as *chthónioi* or *hypotartárioi* implied their symbolical distance from the sun. – Walter F. Otto in his classical work *The Homeric Gods* stresses the rebellious and "wicked" connotation of the name Titan. – Cf. also *Apoc.*, 12:7–9, where the Satan is called directly a "serpent of the primal age". Something of this nomenclature remained in Gregory of Nyssa's careful classification of angels as *hyperkósmioi* in contrast to the other creatures, classified as *enkósmioi*.

15. It is rather touching to observe the desperate efforts of some postmodern historians, such as F. M. Cornford and W. K. C. Guthrie, to excuse the "lack of capability" of these early Greek scholars to emancipate themselves from the "unconscious" subservience to "pre-existing mythological solutions" and to reach a "purely scientific scheme". Have Newton, Pasteur or Niels Bohr ever reach this fictitious "purely scientific level"?

16. Aristotle's decisive text is to be found in *Metaphys.*, 1045: *ei d'estín, hósper légomen, tò mèn hýlē, tò dè morfḗ, kái tó mèn dynámei, tò dè enérgeia, oúketi aporía dóxeien àn éinai tò zētóumenon.* – One of the not altogether useless subtleties of the "ontological" thought is the differentiation between *mḗ ón* (what is real, but does not live, *e.g.*, vacuum) and *oúk ón* (what does not live and

cannot even be real, *e.g.*, a quadrilateral circle). As to the difference between *enérgeia* and *dýnamis*, it seems that *enérgeia* was, to Aristotle, a true aspect of the creative act, while *dýnamis* meant to him something connected with the pseudo-mythical concept of "continuity" and with the succession of events in the passing time. Xenophon used the term *dýnamis* when speaking of the fertility of the earth. During later times, both *dýnamis* – in the case of the Hebrew scholar Philo – and *enérgeia* – in the writings of the Eastern Fathers of the Church – were used again to denote the messengers of God. Gregory of Nyssa used both words indiscriminately to describe manifestations which "make God accessible without destroying his inaccessibility". At the beginning of the fifth century, Cyril of Alexandria spoke of the entire creation as "the task of energy". In the early fourteenth century, Gregory Palamas compared the participable testimonies of God's presence, known as energies, to the rays of the sun. Eventually, since Newton's times, "energy" has become a mythical-scientific term, while by "dynamics" one means today the realm of "motion-producing energies". – Very recently, the Jesuit Pierre Teilhard de Chardin, following the nineteenth century Russian scholar Fyodorov, has repeatedly used the concept of "activation of human energy", in which the Creator is hardly involved. It may also be interesting to notice that some twenty years before the posthumous publication of Teilhard's works, the English novelist and poet Charles Williams had already described Teilhard's influence in his *Shadows of Ecstasy*.

17. *Daniel*, 12:1. – One of the more distressing examples of the naiveté of postmodern theologians in this field may be found in Hubert Richard's *What the Spirit Says to the Churches* (London – New York, 1967), p. 95, where the readers are warned "not to be too quick" in identifying Michael's apocalyptical struggle with "the fall of the wicked angels which we place at the beginning of history". Father Richard had spent fifteen years as Professor of Scripture in a seminary of the Church of Rome. – Nevertheless, the lack of reverence and the carelessness manifested by Western theologians toward the scriptural conception of time is not of recent origin. The very text of the Nicean creed which speaks of the *parousía* in a present tense (*erchómenon krĩnai zõntas kài nekróus* in Greek, *graduščago suditi živych i měrtvych* in Old Slavic) was wilfully transplanted by the Latins into a distant future *(et iterum venturus est)*. While the canon of the liturgy of Basil the Great "remembers" the second coming of Christ as an accomplished event, there is no trace of this most essential tenet of faith in the Roman liturgy. And yet no distances of the shattered, flowing time are involved here, but only this present moment or the very next one. "Little, little remains and he who comes *(ho erchómenos)* arrives and does not delay" (*Hebr.*, 10:37). – In this context John S. Mbiti's admirable *New Testa-

ment Eschatology in an African Background (Oxford Univ. Press, 1971) may show us what happens when a well-meaning African theologian, trained in the scholastic conception of time, realizes the jarring disagreement between his own people's ancient and sound traditions and the Aristotelian and scholastic concepts. The Akamba people in Kenya, speaking the Kikamba language, differentiate between the present *(mituki)* and the indefinite past *(tene)* into which the present disappears in our daily experience. In perfect agreement with the determinist minded scientist's thought their vocabulary refuses to consider "future" as anything real. Mbiti, instead of welcoming this astonishing harmony between this people's ancient tradition and the Christian message seems to be troubled by what he calls the "radically different character of the Christian eschatology" which, he thinks, does not fit into the notions of the traditional African thought. No such disparity exists. On the contrary, the "traditional notions" of the Kikamba language seem much more ready to accept the Christian message than is any European mode of thought corrupted by scholasticism. There is certainly a profound "newness" in Christ and in his teaching, but this "newness" has absolutely nothing to do with any illusory "future" or with any "waiting for the Parousia". The present *kairós* is really that what counts. When Paul speaks of the "entire creature groaning up to now" (*Rom.*, 8:22, *áchri toũ nỹn*), there is no reason why we should not accept his words in their literal sense. Professor Mbiti himself is certainly on the right track when he speaks of the Resurrection as paralysing and neutralising the future dimension of the flowing time as well as negating and reversing its past dimension (p. 168).

18. *II Pet.*, 2:4. "Angels who have sinned are bound with ropes of darkness in which they have to await their sentence." – Cf. *Jude*, 6; *Matt.*, 25:41 and, above all, *Apoc.*, 12:7–9 where, in the only biblical report concerning archangel Michael's victory, the Spirit of Darkness is called "the serpent of the primal age" – an interesting reminder not only of the Greek Titans, but possibly also of the huge animals with whom the primeval man might have warred and who thus to him became visual symbols of Evil.

19. These thoughts are beautifully echoed in Friedrich Schelling's already quoted essay. "All birth is a birth out of darkness into light; the seed must be burried into earth and die in darkness in order that the lovelier creature of light should arise and unfold itself in the rays of the sun" (p. 360). Schelling's thoughts seem the more valuable because they originated in the Romantic climate whose poets constantly operated with the Platonic "soul-dove-body-cage" theory and, as a consequence, frequently made the Creator responsible for the "cruel universe" and, following the fashion established by Byron and de Vigny,

expressed deep sympathy for the rebellious Satan. The voluminous study devoted to this topic by Max Milner *(Le Diable dans la littérature française: de Cazotte à Baudelaire,* Paris, 1960) might be followed by parallel studies devoted to many other literatures of the early nineteenth century. – In sharp contrast to these relatively recent attempts to glorify the Spirit of Resistance it may be noted that even a not very sophisticated early Christian author, Theophilus – who according to Eusebius had become bishop of Antioch in 169 AD – while calling Satan a *drákōn*, derives this name from his "having fled from God" *(dià tò apodedrakénai apò tõu theoũ).* The primeval awareness of the dark nothingness fleeing away from the Creative Light was still very accessible to early Christians.

20. *pistéuomen eis héna theón... pántōn horatōn te kài aorátōn poiētén...*
21. *Summa Theol.*, quaest. 14, art. 11.
22. *Ps.*, 8 : 6; 28 : 1; 88 : 7; *Job*, 1 : 6; 2 : 1; *Ps.*, 102 : 21; *Job*, 4 : 18.
23. The usual Latin translations of these Pauline terms are: *virtutes, potestates, principatus, dominationes, throni.*
24. Basil, *Spir.*, 38 : *ousía autōn...pýr*; Fulgentius, *Trin.*, 9: *corpus igneum.* And yet Fulgentius adds that angels who had chosen selfish pride have only *corpus aereum.*
25. *The New Catholic Encyclopaedia* (New York, 1967) in articles on "Angelology" and "Angels". It was for exactly the same distinction that the thirteenth century Holy Inquisition burned the Albigensian Manicheists on the stake.
26. Friedrich Schelling, *On Human Freedom* (transl. by James Gutman, Chicago, 1936, pp. 370–371).
27. *Ibid.*, p. 368.
28. More about this in the present author's book *Early History and Christ*, (New York, 1969).
29. Ignatius of Antioch, "Epistle to the Smyrnaeans", quoted from Maxwell Staniforth (transl.), *Early Christian Writings*, Baltimore, 1968, p. 120.
30. *Prometheus Bound*, 1026–29. But Aeschylus' Prometheus hated men.
31. *Apoc.*, 12 : 15–16. – Schelling said: "Following the eternal act of selfrevelation, the world as we now behold it, is all rule, order and form; but the unruly lies ever in the depths as though it might again break through, and order and form nowhere appear to have been original, but it seems as though what had been initially unruly had been brought to order" (*op. cit.*, p. 359). He also spoke of some "striving back": "We can presumably explain in this way, too, the Platonic dictum that evil is derived 'from primal nature'. For all evil strives back toward chaos..." (p. 374). Or again: "At last there results the crisis in the 'turba gentium' which overflow the foundations of the ancient world as once

the waters of the beginning again covered the creations of primeval time..." (p. 380).
32. Goetz in Jean Paul Sartre's *Le Diable et le bon Dieu*, onzième tableau.
33. Quoted, as above, from chapt. 51 of *The Revelations of Divine Love* (new ed. by James Walsh, New York, 1961).
34. *Matt.*, 25 : 30: *tò skótos to exóteron.* – *Jude*, 1 : 13:: *ho zófos toũ skótous*. This conception has been revived, in a rather clumsy way, by some twentieth-century existentialists in their descriptions of the passing time as "a way toward death and annihilation" and of the earthly life as a "time-issue".
35. A. Olrik, *Ragnaroek* (Berlin, 1922).
36. Nicolas of Cusa, *De docta ignorantia*, III, 9. It should also be noted that, according to apostle Paul, when the end arrives, Christ will "surrender the kingdom to God the Father... that God may be all in all" (*I Cor.*, 15 : 24–28). Elsewhere (*Col.*, 1 : 18), Paul calls Christ *prōtótokos ek tõn nekrõn*, whose ultimate task is to *apokatallázai tà pánta*. *Heb.*, 12 : 29 also proclaims God a "consuming fire".
37. *Isa.*, 26 : 19. See also *Isa.*, 30 : 27–28 and *Mal.*, 3 : 19.
38. *Isa.*, 33 : 14.
39. *II Thess.*, 1 : 9; *Apoc.*, 20 : 13–14 and 21 : 18. – It was a "fire from heaven" which destroyed Sodoma (*Luke*, 17 : 29). Also to Clement of Alexandria fire was primarily a divine tool whenever he spoke of its symbolism in his *Stromata*. As to Origen, he constantly kept in mind the text *kài gàr ho theòs hymõn pýr katanalískon* (*Heb.*, 12 : 29; *Deut.*, 4.: 24; 9 : 3; *Isa.*, 33 : 14). – *Cf.* Camón Aznar's commentary on the illustrations adorning the apocalyptical literature of the epoch preceding the year 1000 AD. "It is the apocalyptic time which dominates these forms, crusted and, at the same time, resembling flames. No temporal process, but rather an explosion is noticeable in these images, It is, above all, in the manuscripts of the *Commentaries on the Apocalypse*, composed by the monk Beato of Liebana (in the Asturian Mountains), that these visionary figures appear, with their eyes deflected through the sudden and already eternal lightning. They are simple figures, but of flaming colors, dressed in pleated attires whose curves resemble those of the petals of flowers" (José Camón Aznar, *El tiempo en el arte*, Madrid, 1958, p. 90). – It might also be interesting to mention, in this connection, Ibn Sina's commentary to the 113th sura of the *Quoran* (in a translation published by Henri Corbin in his *Histoire de la philosophie islamique* (Paris, 1964, p. 23): "*Je prends refuge auprès de Celui qui fait éclater la tenèbre du non-être par la lumière de l'être et qui est le principe primordial...*" Or again a quotation from the *Cahiers* (III, p. 86) of Simone Weil: "*Un anéantissement qui est lumière, c'est la vie éternelle...*

L'enfer est une flamme qui brûle l'âme. Le paradis aussi. C'est la même flamme. Mais selon l'orientation de l'âme cette seule et universelle flamme consitue le mal infini ou le bien infini, le feu de l'enfer ou celui du Saint Esprit."

40. *Matt.*, 13 : 42. Notice that the Greek text uses a present time: *ekẽi éstai ho klauthmós kài ho brygmós tõn odóntõn.* – A similar timeless attitude is evident in *Jude*, 1 : 13: *hõis ho zófos tou skótous eis aiõna tetérētai.*

41. *Cf.* Berdyaev's vehement reaction to this allegory in *The Beginning and the End*, p. 235–6.

42. *He límnē tõu pyrós...*, sometimes, *e.g.*, *Matt.*, 13 : 42, also called "the furnace of fire". We are certainly reminded here of Heraclitus: "Fire, having come upon them, will judge and seize upon all things" (*Fragm.*, 66). It is, however, questionable whether the verb "to torment" – which figures so frequently in our translations of the *New Testament* – really represents the original idea. The Greek verb *basanizō*, used, for instance, in *Matt.* 8 : 29, certainly means "try" or "examine". If it was ever employed to signify torture, then only in a very secondary way. – The post-modern teologian, above all, seems hardly able to understand what he reads in the *Scriptures*. Thus the *New Catechism* of the Dutch bishops of the Church of Rome, which we have already quoted, hastily tells the readers (p. 480 of the English translation) that they "need not take as literate descriptions the terrifying words" about "darkness, gnashing of teeth, fire". What a pity Our Lord did not have a couple of Dutch bishops at hand as publicity agents to warn him that he might "lose the world" with such nasty vocabulary. To be "thrown into the outer darkness" means, of course, quite obviously, to be indentified with this darkness precisely when it is overpowered by light and ceases to function. *I Tim.*, 6 : 16, states clearly that "immortality belongs to Jesus Christ alone" in his "dwelling in unapproachable light". From that follows not only that there are no "naturally immortal souls", but also that the Spirit of Darkness who Merely-Reflects-the-Light disappears completely with the Darkness with which his own choice identifies him. Men who choose similarly disappear with him because he "ruins not only their body but also their life (*psýchēn*)" (*Matt.*, 10 : 28). Precisely because Darkness means man's "death condition", the disappearance of Darkness is the "second and final death", *i.e.*, death of death. Why should anyone be terrified by the "gnashing of teeth" of the dying Shadows of Death? How incomparably different from any post-modern Dutch bishops was Ignatius, bishop of Antioch, who, in 107 AD, during Traian's reign, was being brought in chains to Rome for execution and profited from his last opportunity to write: "Now that which had been perfected in the Divine counsels began its work; and all creation was thrown into a ferment over this plan for the utter destruction of death" (transl.

by Maxwell Staniforth, *Early Christian Writings*, Baltimore, 1968, p. 81). – On the other hand, it is perhaps understandable that many, Christians as well as non-Christians, taking for granted the monopoly of the "passing time" and identifying it with "eternity", reached visions in which Nothingness surpassed and engulfed the Creator. "*Le sentiment,*" writes the young Flaubert, "*ou plutôt l'idée du Néant dépasse l'idée de Dieu... Le Non-Être enferme en soi l'Être*" (quoted from M. Milner, *Le Diable dans la littérature française*, Paris, 1960, t. II, p. 232).

43. *Luke*, 16 : 23: *en tõ hádē epáras toùs ofthalmoùs autõu.* – It is most regrettable that so many Christians are led even today, while worshipping, to recite that Christ "descended into hell" – a faulty translation stemming merely from the laziness of theologians who have never learned their Greek.

44. *Apoc.*, 20 : 13–14 and again 21 : 8: *kài ho thánatos kài ho hádēs édōkan tòus nekròus tòus en autõis... kài ho thánatos kài ho hádēs eblēthēsan eis tèn límnēn tõu pyrós; hóutos ho thánatos ho déuterós estin, hē límnē tõu pyrós.*

45. *Matt.*, 10 : 28: *fobéisthe dè mãllon tòn dynámenon kài psychèn kai sõma apólesai en geénnē.*

46. *II Thess.*, 1 : 9: *hóitines díkēn tísousin ólethron aiōnion apò prosōpou tõu kyríou.*

47. *Luke*, 16 : 24: "I am tormented in this flame" *(odynõmai en tẽ flogí táutē).* Let us, however, notice again that this takes place in the *hádēs*, in the agony of waiting, not in the *geénna*.

48. *Mark*, 3 : 29.

49. *Matt.*, 25 : 41. The irresistibility of this flame is sometimes stressed by another adjective, "unquenchable", *ásbestos; cf. Mark*, 9 : 42 and *Luke*, 3 : 17.

50. *Apoc.*, 14 : 10–11 or 20 : 9–10. In *Ephes.*, 1 : 23, Christ is *plérōma*.

51. *II Thess.*, 1 : 9: *ólethros aiōnion.* The conclusivness of this final result of the creative act is also evident from quotations such as: *I Cor.*, 15 : 26: *éschatos echthrós katargẽitai ho thánatos; Apoc.*, 21 : 1: *kài hē thálassa ouk éstin eti*, and 22 : 5: *kài nýx ouk éstai éti; II Thess.*, 2 : 8: *kài tóte apokalyfthésetai ho ánomos, hón ho kýrios Iesõus anelẽi tõ pnéumati tõu stómatos autoũ kài katargései tẽ epifanéia tẽs parousías autõu.* There appears a certain, although not altogether consistent tendency in the *New Testament's* vocabulary to distinguish between the illuminating nature of the *fõs* and the annihilating nature of the *pyr*.

52. *Apoc.*, 14 : 10–11.

53. *Apoc.*, 20 : 9–10.

54. *Apoc.*, 20 : 13–14 and 21 : 8.

55. *kài éi tis ouch heuréthē en tõ bíblō tẽs zōẽs gegraménnos, éblēthē eis tèn límnēn tõu pyrós.* – In the early sixth century, when a belated and not very refined polemic against Origen's intellectual heritage broke out, started by the Roman

bishop Vigilius and the profligate Byzantine emperor Justinian, an anathema was declared against those who would assert that the Prince of Evil will find his end "within passing time" (*ei ti légei... próskairon ẽinai tẽn tõn daimónõn... kólasin, kài télos katá tina chrónon autẽn héxein...*). *Cf.* Diekam, *Die origenischen Streitigkeiten* (Münster, 1899). But this has nothing to do with the "second death", in which even passing time, *chrónos*, itself perishes. – Giovanni Papini reminds us that Jerome – who, in his youth, used to study and admire Origen – declared in his commentary on Paul's letter to the Ephesians, that, at the moment of the general restoration at the end of this world, everybody would return to what he originally had been and even the apostate angel would again become what he used to be (Giovanni Papini, *Il diavolo*, Firenze, 1954, p. 343). Much depends here on the meaning of the expression "originally" which is only valid within the framework of the passing time. Gregory of Nyssa speaks very distinctly on this subject when he uses the words: *tẽn pròs tò ex archẽs apokatástasin* (*Apologia in Hexaemeron*, 113 A). Thinking of the glorified resurrected man we may well imagine that he would return to the best sum of all the decisive moments of his terrestrial existence and not appear as he was, for instance, during his last sickness only. But man, in God's creative act, has a much more glorious destiny than the angels. For the angels only one, truly original, but also absolutely unique and singular decision is contained in the Creative Act. They can be only what this original and final decision makes them through their own will. We may well mention, in this context, the words of the apocryphal *Acts of Andrew:* "Blessed is our generation. We are not thrown down, for we have been recognized by the light. We do not belong to the passing time, which would dissolve us... We belong to the light which has expelled the darkness..." (quoted from Paul Tillich, *A History of Christian Thought*, New York, 1968, p. 36). – In Thomas Aquinas, whose dependence on the Aristotelian subordination of thought to the rules of the Greek syntax did not always stop him from attempts to reach the root of things, we find the interesting statement that Evil, were it "something integral", would automatically destroy itself *(malum, si esset integrum, destrueret seipsum)*. Integral or not and while certainly very real within the framework of the passing time, Evil gives up its life in a definite way through its own real meaning. True enough, the authors of the primeval myths, always centered on the act of creation, experienced, as has been mentioned, some difficulties with the images of Darkness, Chaos or Nothingness. Similar difficulties evidently troubled the mind of the abbé de Lamennais during the later, embittered part of his life when, in 1843, he wrote the curious pamphlet entitled *Amschaspands et Darvands*. He preached in it an eventual purification and repentance of the "spirits of evil". Both Ernest

Renan, faithful to the conceptions expressed in his *L'Avenir de la science*, and Pierre Joseph Proudhon were inclined to grant Darkness a participating, perhaps a revolutionary role in the "creative evolution". So did the abbé Alphonse-Louis Constant who published some of his works under the curious pseudonym of Eliphas Lévi. Among our contemporaries, José Camón Aznar decided to follow the path of those who had made Nothingness the "cradle" of the Creator. He describes the primordial darkness – which, to him, is also a "death without end" and "nothingness which cannot be annihilated" – as the *materia prima* of creatures. And yet, once again, much depends on what vocabulary we choose. Achilles may catch up with the tortoise or again he may not. Thus to ask whether a "nothingness" "is" or "is not" or whether it could be "annihilated" rather than "destroyed" does not seem to have much sense. We can only fall back on expressions practically as old as history. The contrasting concepts of "life" and "death" may tell us a great deal. But perhaps the other two contrasting concepts, those of "light" and "darkness" are the most advantageous ones. The symbolism of "light" is the most archetypal and also the most penetrating *theoria* – *i.e.* not a "closed form of vision" or a "paralysing factor in the scientist's work" as Karl Jaspers seems to think, but both a tentative and far reaching theory. When, for instance, scientists decide to regard the "classical laws" of physics as "simply a limiting form assumed by the formulae of the quanta theory whenever the number of particles is very large", such a decision is truly a mere tentacle of the always dynamic and always elastic theoretical action without which man's intellect would not be able to reach anywhere. The symbolism of "light" is, naturally, also the most visual of all theories. The Christian ikons, about whose significance we have learned much new from Yevzhenij N. Trubeckoj and from Professor Kondakov, have often represented Wisdom, God's Wisdom, the *Shekinah* of the *Old Testament*, through the symbolism of light. Their painters did so in an effort to bring the limitless Wisdom to man's awareness, to represent, before his eyes, the "complete time" of the Creative Act by which Wisdom is manifested. The dark, blue-black starry sky, which in the ikons often forms the background, symbolizes the "outer darkness", the Non-Life. Into it, the Loving Wisdom of Life bursts out, hypostasized by the Logos, the Son of God. Into the same darkness, through the Logos, the Fiery Light flames out. The stars in the darkness symbolize the fringe of this Light, the fringe born by Lucifer, the "energy of illusion". This is also the fringe where man decides, through the sum of all his moments of decision, which way to turn his face, whether into Nothingness or toward the Fountainhead of Light. The love of God's Son, the "Son of Man", manifests itself here. Human love may originate here. The Divine Wisdom itself is also symbolized in many ikons by a Woman whose roseate face usually stands out like dawn against the background of the night. A Woman – because birth has been, since primordial times and everywhere, the most frequently used symbol for the Creative Act. In the Great Mother, the Cybeles, the Demeter, the Isis and so many other primeval and ancient symbols the birth-giving Wisdom has found its temporary names. The fertile earth – the Mother Earth – grants us an insight into the same Creative Act in numberless radiations, photogenetic or photosynthetic processes, formations of cells and births of plants and animals. As Aeschylus exclaimed: "Earth, the one form of many names *(gãia pollõn onomátōn morfé mía)*". Finally the Wisdom is a real, human Woman; in Mary, mother of the Logos and the Son of Man, the supratemporal Wisdom found its most humble, unselfish "maid of God". It might also be noted – and perhaps in a not too speculative way – that the *New Testament* vocabulary seems to distinguish between the "world" (given to the already condemned "Prince of the World") and the "earth" (which, according to apostle Peter's second epistle will be renovated). The "fertile earth", in this vision, seems thus to extend beyond the boundaries of the "shattered time". If man can capture or release or transform life or light – producing or employing energy, producing organic structures in laboratories, and soon perhaps regulating the photosynthetic processes – he can only do so because Life and Light offer themselves to us in a Loving Action, in numberless "energies". Sacrifice is "from the beginning" included in the Creative Act. But, above all, Life grants freedom to man by granting him his creative knowing. Light brings with it the appearance of the cognizable, while darkness remains the best symbol of the "utter invisibility of each to the other", to use an expression of Pavel A. Florenskij.

56. Berdyaev, *The Meaning of the Creative Act* (pp. 97 and 101).
57. *Ibid.*, p. 272.
58. See the preface to the German edition of *The Meaning of the Creative Act*. In this context, Simone Weil's insistence (*Cahiers*, II, p. 347) that *"le travail n'est pas une imitation de la création, mais de la passion"* seems to acquire a most profound meaning. It should be considered that the Creative Act, manifesting God's love, includes also sacrifice as its basic manifestation. Of this, every painful effort in man's life seems to mirror a part. We certainly should not speak of work as "punishment". Whenever man gives up suffering in exchange for security, for a dream anchored in the illusory "future", he may still remain within the act of creation, but he no longer returns God's love.
59. The observer's report was published in the magazine *The New Yorker*.
60. Ovidius, *Heroides*, IV, 131.
61. Notice the similarity between the Satanic and the Aristotelian and Thomistic

concept of the Godhead as a perfect and "perfectly self-contained being". In contrast to this, Simone Weil says: "*Il ne peut pas y avoir des êtres pensants plus séparés que le Père et le Fils au moment ou le Fils pousse le cri éternel: Mon Dieu, pourquoi m'as tu abandonné? Ce moment est la perfection incompréhensible de l'amour. C'est l'amour qui passe toute connaissance*" (*Intuitions préchrétiennes*, Paris, 1951, p. 131). – Sergei N. Bulgakov might still have used the "ontological" vocabulary when he said that "God posits non-being together with being as its limit, its accompaniment or shadow" (*Unfading Light*, Moscow, 1917, p. 184). But in his vision we also find the cosmos, the "outburst" of Wisdom, as an immage of the self-immolating God. The subatomic particles offer their energy for use, the light of the sun offers food to the cells of the plants, the plants offer themselves to the animals, and the animals to other animals and to man. (See Bulgakov's *Agnyec bozhij – Du Verbe incarné*, Paris, 1933–34.) The "auxiliary verb philosophers" and the "ontologists" are, naturally, little capable of grasping God as Life, Life Loving and Life Illuminating. Conceiving him as an "absolute being" – without saying "being what"– they conclude that God is so "perfect" that he has no need for man or for the world. To that, only one remark is necessary: "being Love" is incomparably more than "being absolutely". God's Wisdom, Sophia, which includes in herself the opportunity granted to man to manifest his love, also includes the knowledge of man's free decisions. In that sense Sergei N. Bulgakov could declare that "Sophia is love and loves in return, and through this reciprocal love she receives all, is all" (*The Unfading Light*, p. 212). All men and all their creative decisions thus participate in the Wisdom. They form the mystical body of one man who is Adam in his pride but who is also Christ in his supreme self-immolation. Vladimir Solovyov (*Lectures on God-Manhood*, chapt. 7) paid much attention to this manifestation of both Wisdom and the Second Divine Person. He seems to go as far as to regard the multiplicity of individual human persons a purposeful aspect of Wisdom. The possibility of the "felix culpa" was granted with the view of the infinite variety of love it would engendre. As Yevzhenij N. Trubeckoj has pointed out (*Solovyov's World Conception*, II, p. 250 et seq.), it is not the common purposefulness *(ousía)* of all men, but rather the individual roles played by the individual men who, through their choice, establish themselves in Life or submerge themselves into the receding and finally burned up Darkness. Solovyov's own verses (in N. O. Losskij's translation) may be quoted here:

> But till the midnight hour with fearless foot
> I travel to the goal of my desires:
> Where on the summit, beneath a strange star,

Along the sacred roof will gleam afar
The line of victory fires...

Remembering Solovyov's vision of the Wisdom in the Egyptian desert ("all that was, and is, and ever shall be... the boundless was within its form enclosed") we may place side by side with it another vision of *tò ápeiron* enclosed by Light, this time described by Simone Weil – who had probably never read Solovyov – in her *Cahiers* (II, 259–60):

"*Concevant le rapport du temps indéfini au Père dont tous les événements qui se produisent, quels qu'ils soient, constituent la volonté, on pense la totalité du temps sous l'aspect du passé. Concevant le rapport du temps indéfini au Verbe, ordonnateur, qui répend sur toutes choses la lumière de la beauté et de l'immortalité, on pense la totalité du temps sous l'aspect du présent. Concevant le rapport du temps indéfini à l'Esprit, qui coupe les racines plongées dans le temps, qui descend dans les âmes pour les sauver et les transplanter, les enraciner dans l'éternité, les mettre dans la plenitude de la perfection, on pense la totalité du temps illuminé d'espérance, sous l'aspect de l'avenir.* Elthátō basiléia... *Trois aspects de l'eternité vue à travers le temps. La création. Tout déjà accompli par un acte de la volonté de Dieu. La de-création. Le terme du temps. L'immortalité dans la plénitude de présent.*"

62. Jakubisiak, *L'Essai sur les limites*, p. 191.
63. Bertrand de Jouvenel, *On Power* (New York, 1949). *Cf.* also Thomas S. Molnar, *Bernanos: His Political Thought and Prophecy* (New York, 1960). The *New Testament* concentrates on these matters in *II Thess.*, 2.
64. *Matt.*, 24 : 14.

Index

ABŪ HĀTIM RAZĪ
leaving the passing time 95
ACTON, JOHN
prize of all history 72; collections of historical writings 160
ADAM
author of names 25; Adam-Everyman 135–6
ADAMS, HENRY
acceptation of false myths XVII
ADLER, ALFRED
creative self 57
AESCHYLUS
essence of tragedy 66; black depths of death 175
ALBERT THE GREAT
mutability of organisms 77
ALCMEON
uniting beginning with end 99
ALEXANDER, SAMUEL
three elements-notions 33
ALLPORT, GORDON
functional autonomy 57
ALTIZER, THOMAS J. J.
abolishment of polarities and divisions 151; modern form of theology 152; attracted by the "necessary stream" 152; accepts the "full movement of history" 156; fascinated by a descent into totality 160; "immanence" and the "downward movement" 162

AMIEL, HENRI
on time 2
ANASTASIUS II
life-giving soul 53
ANAXAGORAS
on intelligence 15; light and supreme mind 171; "seeds of light" reflected in Aristotle 171
ANAXIMANDER
primordial shapelessness 48, 49; as reflected in Aristotle's "potential reality" 171; generative light 170
AQUINAS, THOMAS
accidental, substantial 18; body and soul 53; views of Plato's ideas 63; causal stream of nature 73; attracted by the "necessary stream" 152; "ridiculous" character of an infinite series 91; Creator as an overpowering center 125–6; matter as opposed to the Creator 173; basic defect of matter 81; evil as privation of good 147; cognition as adequation 143
ARCHITAS OF TARENTO
time as numerical expression of movement 33
ARISTOPHANES
birth of love 169
ARISTOTLE
popularity in the twelfth century 22; auxiliary-verb philosophy 77, 55, 63, 115; categories 64; essential, acci-

dental 17, 18, 19, 64; being vs. life 62, 126; knowledge from perception 25, 62; memory 57; concept of necessity 37; concept of cause 11, 73, 143; one cause of one only 133; matter and form 133; matter, form and Hopi language 46; Creator as absolute entity 125–6; Creator as primum movens 126; creation 87; harmonious nature 148; forms as reflecting Anaxagoras' "seeds of light" 171; "potential reality" as replacing Anaximander's "primordial shapelessness" 171; meaning of "energies" 173; body and soul 53; perfect and imperfect motion 48; time as numerical expression of movement 33, 50; time as circular movement 33; eternity 36; identity between time and universe 40; undivisible now 98

ARYAN INDIA
philosophy of the Self 5; separable soul 52; time continuity 35; circles of complete time 92; living in the passing time 108

ATHANASIUS
Aristotelian causality 11

AUGUSTINE AURELIUS
time as mind's distention 2, 31, 84, 111; memory and time 117; mind gathering knowledge 60; seminal reasons 74, 131; emergence of the City of God 132; predestination 90; torments of the damned 179

BACON, FRANCIS
knowledge as power 24, 158

BANTU-RUANDA
concepts of time and place 47; myth of creation 4, 5; death as an exterior agent 127

BARTH, KARL
Christ's loneliness 71; view of Satan 129

BASIL THE GREAT
fiery nature of angels 173

BENSON, HUGH
vision of the final society 186

BENTHAM, JEREMY
rule of greatest happiness 10

BERDYAEV, ALEXANDER N.
early views of history 96, 182; Böhme and the *Kabbala* 95; attitude to Frank's philosophy 124–5; obituary of Shestov 67; significance of the past 41; entropy 43; catastrophic character of the "world process" 130, 182; creative work as renouncement of the passing time 124; freedom as conflict 124; freedom as cosmic condition 131; God powerless to conquer by power 127

BERGSON, HENRI
influence on the pre-1914 generation XIII; criticism by Jakubisiak 185; modern myths 20; *élan vital* surpassing intelligence XIII–XVI, 56; duration (*durée*) 47, 166

BERKELEY, GEORGE
being and perception 62

BERNARD OF CLAIRVAUX
salvation of the dead-born 136

BLAKE, WILLIAM
God as the Eternal Body of Man 154; death of the Old God Urizen 156

BLOCH, ERNST
  principle of hope 112
BODIN, JEAN
  sovereignty of the state 184
BOETHIUS
  inseparability of body and soul 54
BÖHME, JACOB
  Berdyaev's view 95
BOHR, NIELS
  causality as mental category 88
BONAVENTURA, FRANCIS
  opposed to Aristotelianism 18, 73; concept of creation 126; light and fire symbolism 129
BONHOEFFER, DIETRICH
  being of man 54; being in un-truth 134
BOSSUET, JACQUES
  history as work of Providence 77
BRIDGEMAN, P. W.
  views of Christian ethics 105–6
BRUNO, GIORDANO
  space and time 55; "intensive" and "extensive" infinity 166
BUBER, MARTIN
  views of Christ 3; human suffering 21; unredeemability of man 96
BUDDHA
  intellectual suicide 3; sphere of influence 23; nature as stasis and destruction 35; Great Self as Great Zero 138; continuous chain of causes 150
BUFFON, GEORGES
  evolutionist doctrine 77; developing and changing patterns 154
BULTMANN, RUDOLF
  future resurrection 161
BURCKHARDT, JACOB
  influence on Berdyaev 96

BUTLER, SAMUEL
  robots 19

CALVARY
  location on the frontier of decision 132, 181; absolute loneliness 183
CALVIN, JEAN
  predestination 93
CAMÓN AZNAR, JOSÉ
  Islamic concept of time 110
CAMUS, ALBERT
  the world's unreasonable silence 99
CARLYLE, THOMAS
  degeneration of historiography XVI
CASTANEDA, CARLOS
  the Yaqui concept of power and death 71
CHESTERTON, GILBERT KEITH
  evidence of evil 127
COMENIUS, JAN AMOS
  opposed to Aristotelion causality 73
COMTE, AUGUSTE
  cult of humanity 78
CONDORCET, MARIE-JEAN
  doctrine of progress 36, 37, 77, 182
CUVIER, GEORGES
  advances in the complexity of life 144

DAMASCIUS
  idea as pause in the passing time 111
DANIEL
  end of time 171
DANTE ALIGHIERI
  gate of hell 14, 112, 135, 137; love as mind's union with object 60; astrology 83; fountainhead of time 110; torments of the damned 179
DARWIN, CHARLES
  speculation and observation XVII;

discussed by Wilbeforce 140; his critics and causality 143; ignored by scientists 159; creation 141; Creator and parasites 73; being as a tree 76, 81; better future 80; man and animals 141–2; positive and negative variations 79; laws of nature 142; stream of continuous time 143; changing relationship to the stream of time 145, 148; meaning of "origin" 146; concept of species 148; uniqueness of variations-conditions 149; usefulness of the perfectionist postulates 155

DAWSON, CHRISTOPHER
post-modern education 107

DECROLY, OVIDE
child's temporal conceptions 58

DE JOUVENEL, BERTRAND
destiny of society 186

DEMOCRITUS
body and soul 52; atoms derived from Anaxagoras' "seeds of light" 171

DENNIS THE AREOPAGITE
see: Dionysius

DE ROUGEMONT, DENIS
ascending march of man 25

DESCARTES, RENÉ
inert matter 16, 22; person's identity 63–4; attachment to Aristotelian ontology 115; attracted by the "necessary stream" 152

DE VRIES, HUGO
random variations 18

DEWEY, JOHN
Dawson's criticism of 107

DIONYSIUS AREOPAGITA
theological vocabulary 20; God's vision of darkness 165

DIRAC, PAUL
relativity of cosmic laws 34

DOSTOYEVSKIJ, FYODOR M.
Stavrogin's "dead things" 15; "vault of mirrors" 67; divinization of society 69; the Grand Inquisitor story 99–100, 184; Raskolnikov's delirium 137; Ivan Karamazov's future society 138; the terrible new freedom of Kirillov 161; evil as demonstration of God 183; Shatov's proof of truth 187

DUHEM, PIERRE
an order transcending physics 168

DUNS SCOTT
God's thinking "with respect to himself" 126; incarnation not a contingent event 167

ECKHART, JOHANNES
"undivided but also in the outbreak" 98

EDDINGTON, ARTHUR
entropy as arrow of time 37

EINSTEIN, ALBERT
efforts to save causality 12

EL GRECO
symbolism of lilies 53

ELIADE, MIRCEA
man's ahistoricity 47

ELIOT, T. S.
consciousness and time 51

EMMANUEL, PIERRE
lineal time 31

EMPEDOCLES
love 15; evolution 77

EPICURUS
accidental swerving of atoms 17;

philosophy intended to secure happiness 49
EUCLIDES
system of geometry 33
EURIPIDES
essence of tragedy 66

FEUERBACH, LUDWIG
definition of atheism 165
FRANCIS OF ASSISI
anti-Aristotelian thought 126
FRANK, SEMYON L.
attaining the unreacheable 116; reality which grows 117; freedom of evil acts 126
FREUD, SIGMUND
unity of man 55; forces within mind 57; death as man's goal 65
FULGENTIUS
angels 173
FYODOROV, NIKOLAI F.
"increase of love" doctrine 23, 79, 92, 96

GEYL, PIETER
fickle art of the historian 69
GOEDEL, KURT
models of universe 34
GOETHE, JOHANN W.
moment and aeons xi
GONSETH, FERDINAND
integration of person 57
GOODFIELD, J.
Newton and fools 76
GRAY, ASA
correspondence with Darwin on "adaptation to purpose" 146
GREEN, JULIEN
being and becoming xi, 67

GREGORY THE GREAT
torments of the damned 179
GREGORY XIII
calendar reform 32
GREGORY OF NYSSA
growth of the Christian message 73; Christ as Cosmic Adam 79; man's mind after death 141
GROSSETESTE, ROBERT
opposition to Aristotelianism 18, 73; light similes 129
GUITTON, JEAN
emergence of the City of God, 132
GUNDISALVI, DOMINGO
Creator as source of forms, 173

HALÉVY, DANIEL
acceleration of history 6
AL-HASAIN IBN MANSUR HALLĀJ
moments of decision 94–5
HEGEL, GEORG W.
divinization of society 69, 132; objective mind 78; creation 161
HEIDEGGER, MARTIN
myths 2; Hitler 3; being and nothing 18; thought and dwelling 85
HEISENBERG, WERNER
causality 38; principle of indeterminancy 60; idealists and phenomenologists 60
HERACLITUS
fire symbolism 24, 74–5; adherence to mythical wisdom 49
HILBERT, DAVID
mathematical concepts as postulates 6
HOMER
psýche as breath 52
HUGO, VICTOR
theory of art 28

HUXLEY, JULIAN
    man as victim, man armed with a moral purpose 147
HUXLEY, THOMAS
    ultimate perfection 23, 74; better future 80; taking the issue into one's hands 140; loss of faith in evolution 145, 147; chances of survival 146

IBN SĪNĀ
    influence on Gundisalvi 173
IGNATIUS OF ANTIOCH
    suffering as God's vicinity 175
IÑIGO DE LOYOLA
    tortures of hell 160
IRENEUS OF LYON
    resurrection in the very same creation 163–4; Jesus as giver of life and light 172
ISAIAH
    completeness of the creative act 170; "dwelling with the devouring fire" 178
ISRAELI, ISAAC
    adequation of intellect and object 60
IVANOV, VYACHESLAV
    Dostoyevskij's "vault of mirrors" 67

JAKUBISIAK, AUGUSTYN
    successive vs. simultaneous 45; interpretation of the Christian message 113–4; criticism of Bergson 185
JASPERS, KARL
    grasping a decision 131
JESUS
    medieval attitudes to XVI; resurrection and demythologization 2; in existentialist philosophy 3; in Martin Buber 3; answer to the problem of suffering 5; parables and myths 6; participation in history 22; "some who will still stand around" 29, 159; "evolutive Jesus" of Teilhard 94; "imminent harvest" 97; "flesh and blood did not reveal it to thee" 113; promise of resurrection 148, 152; scrutinization of the present moment 152; loss of the *psýche* 159, 179–180; universe as a struggle 163; "weeping and gnashing of teeth" 179; descent into *hádes* 179
JOHN, APOSTLE
    Antichrist 82; "hour arrived and is now" 111; symbolism of light 129, 168
JOHN OF DAMASCUS
    Jesus as a rushing forth of light 172
JUAN DE LA CRUZ
    no mysticism through human efforts 95
JULIAN OF NORWICH
    original sin 135; Adam-Everyman 135–6; the Angel of Resistance as a "ravine" 176
JUNG, CARL GUSTAV
    self-actualization 57; completeness of a person's life 66; Satan as aspect of the Creator 112

KANT, IMMANUEL
    soul's immortality as a "necessary postulate" 149
KELLER, HELEN
    breaking through isolation 134
KIERKEGAARD, SÖREN
    general salvation 154; unwilling Hegelian 161; nothing impossible for God 170

Kozlov, Alexei A.
   God's timeless knowledge 41
K'ung Fu-tsu (Confucius)
   barrier of ceremonies 3; sphere of influence 23
Kronstadskij, Ioan
   suffering 175

Lactantius
   universal conflagration 93
Laín Entralgo, Pedro
   credulity essential to human existence 121; project as form of expectation 121
Lamarck, Jean-Baptiste
   evolutionary concepts 16, 101, 142–3; tendency to perfection 144; universe as a stream 154–5
La Place, Pierre
   evolutionist doctrine 77; God as a superfluous hypothesis 126
Leibniz, Wilhelm G.
   perfecting principle 16, 45; time as a pattern of relations 33; immortality of soul 148
Lenin, V. I.
   mediator between man and the imaginary 15
Lessing, Gotthold E.
   immortality of soul 149
Lewis, C. S.
   myths 6; timeless and dimensionless purgatory 67; net of successive moments 91
Libby, Willard F.
   carbon fourteen method 32
Lin Yutang
   man's importance in the Creator's eyes 100

Lippman, Walter
   liberty as achievement of organized society 100
López Ibor, Juan José
   charisma acquired by words 8; the Saturnal character of utopias 99; intentionality of perception 121–2; vital anxiety 122–3
Lothar's cross in Aix-la-Chapelle 129
Lucretius
   God as accepted despair 160
Luria, A. R.
   unity of thought and speech 59
Luther, Martin
   prayers for dead 93
Lysenko, Trofim D.
   evolutionary concepts 16

Mach, Ernst
   time as a variable and causality 11
Machado, Antonio
   dreaming and awakening 182
Malraux, André
   religion as basis of civilization 1
Mani
   influence on Christian thought 172
Marcel, Gabriel
   on Teilhard's views 71–2
Marsiglio of Padua
   the influential element in society 184
Marx, Karl
   humanism 28; purposeful production and purposeless society 45
Massignon, Louis
   Islamic concept of time 110
Matthew, evangelist
   on Peter's misunderstanding 3
Maxwell, James Clark
   concept of universe 33

MERTON, THOMAS
   evaluation of the historical time 119; views of Anselm 120; man's power of consent 120
MICHELANGELO
   torments of the damned 179
MILTON, JOHN
   living soul, dead body 52
MOLIÈRE
   criticism of abstract concepts 8
MONET, CLAUDE
   repeated portrayals 66
MONOD, JACQUES
   directing efforts towards objectivity 140
MONTESQUIEU, CHARLES
   perfecting the stream of time 144
MOSES
   burning bush symbolism 24, 129; center or beginning 170
MÖSSBAUER, RUDOLF
   the M. effect 34
MOUNIER, EMMANUEL
   mass-production and ethics 102
MUHAMMAD IBN ZAKARIYA RAZI
   leaving the passing time 95
MURRAY, JOHN COURTNEY
   Church brought abreast of man's progress 25

NEWMAN, JOHN HENRY
   development of doctrine 73
NEWTON, ISAAC
   first rule of reasoning 11; concept of energy 25, 56, 173; dynamics 33; independent space and time 55; matter and force 133
NICOLAS D'ORESME
   concept of impetus 173

NICOLAS OF CUSA
   Aristotelian causality 73; clock as image of eternity 82; grasping the unreachable 116; matter as that which can happen 172; Christ as the purest fire 178
NIETZSCHE, FRIEDRICH
   eternal recurrence XVI; the superman 76; science as pain-bringer 139; concept of purpose 146; dead God or dead history 161

OCAMPO, JOSÉ F.
   soul and nature of man 54
ORIGEN
   spiritual vs. material 172
ORPHEUS
   Plato's interpretation of the myth 68
ORTEGA Y GASSET, JOSÉ
   man as a drama XVI
ORWELL, GOERGE
   vision of "perfect" society 186
OWEN, RICHARD
   quoted by Darwin 141

PALEY, WILLIAM
   evil not an object of creation 147
PAPIAS THE PHRYGIAN
   teacher of Ireneus 163
PAPINI, GIOVANNI
   understanding for Fyodorov 92; sympathy with Satan 112
PARMENIDES
   refusal of symbolical contradictions 49; continuity of beings 55; not-being cannot be 115
PASCAL, BLAISE
   geometrical proposition as sentiment 8; incapacity of proof, idea of truth

13; *esprit géometrique, esprit de finesse* 16; man vs. universe 73; Aristotelian causality 73; "Fire" testimony 129; expecting to be 139

PASTEUR, LOUIS
  ridiculed by scientists 16

PAUL, APOSTLE
  angels as flames 24; names of angels 173; spirit of darkness as energy of illusion 24–5; curtain of mystery 50; psychical and spiritualized body 52; short moment of decision 82; no mysticism through human efforts 95; "we shall not all sleep" 97–8; "now is the day of salvation" 111; Jesus as radiance 172; "complete destruction" 178, 180–1

PAUL VI
  Octogesima adveniens 157–160; *Populorum progressio* 157.

PAVLOV, IVAN P.
  second signal system 9, 59, 60, 117; independence of the psychic phenomenon 101

PENFIELD, WILDER
  agony and dreams 67

PERRAULT, CHARLES
  similarity of generations 77

PETER, APOSTLE
  attitude to Jesus' suffering 3, 158; universal conflagration 93; "the Lord delayeth not" 97; final coming of Jesus 163

PHILOLAOS
  matter as limit of appearances 9

PIAGET, JEAN
  time as coordination of motions 58

PICASSO, PABLO
  time-comprehensive paintings 62

PINDAR
  reflex of the complete time 111

PIUS IX
  Syllabus 157

PIUS XII
  pre-existing matter and soul 54

PLANCK, MAX
  causality 38

PLATO
  existence and becoming 1; philosophy and myths 49; man's mind 60; knowledge, recollection, experience 44, 62; all-times embracing mind 63; persons in the cave 50; ideas 64, 109, 171; complete universe 50; separable soul 52, 140, 148–9, 166; shattered time 73; Creator as an absolute entity 125; disparity between *Phaedon* and *Timaeus* 131; interpretation of the Orpheus myth 68; man's fall 134; *méga chásma* and the *Apocalypse* 175

PLÉTHON, GEMISTOS
  causality 11; immortal soul 53; involuntary character of selfish acts 126; eternity and durability 166

PLOTIN
  thought free of passing time 109; passing time identical with evil 130; man's fall 134; emanations 171

PLUTARCH
  disappearance of men 39–40

POINCARÉ, HENRI
  convenience of physical concepts 168

PORTMANN, ADOLF
  man as an incomplete creature 38

PYTHAGORAS
  operative nomenclature 61; *diakósmēsis* 170

RANKE, LEOPOLD
  historian's duty 69
REMBRANDT VAN RIJN
  aspects of the human face 66
RENAN, ERNEST
  morality of the gorilla 73
ROBESPIERRE, MAXIMILIEN
  soul's immortality as a law 149
ROBINSON, J. A. T.
  fear of losing the world 165
ROUSSEAU, JEAN JACQUES
  man's innate goodness 126, 132; general will 26; getting rid of selfish elements 104–5; God a superfluous hypothesis 126; applicability of democracy 159
RUSSELL, BERTRAND
  logical constructions substituted for inferred entities 9

SARTRE, JEAN PAUL
  being to support nothingness 165; darkness as protectrice 176
SATAN
  belief in and demythologization 2; Papini's sympathy with 112; C. G. Jung's view 112; denying creation 113; immortality 125; presence in the original sin 128; Karl Barth's view 129; Persian, Japanese symbols of 129–30; reality and immortality 130; fall 131; battle with Michael 168; as "ravine" in Julian of Norwich 176; cast into the lake of flames 181; aping of creativity 182; caricature of freedom 184
SCHELLING, FRIEDRICH
  action and speculation 62; between yes and no 131; man's person as relation to God 132; basis of evil 174
SCHOPENHAUER, ARTHUR
  struggling will as history's essence XVI
SCHWEITZER, ALBERT
  belated parousia 93–4, 97, 151
SENECA
  joy vs. strife 158
SHAKESPEARE, WILLIAM
  ignoring love and evil, 112
SHAW, GEORGE BERNARD
  modern myths 20–21; creation of the new God 156; God as a built-up life force 160
SHESTOV, LYOV
  impossibility to "unlive" 67; divinization of society 69
Shinto tradition
  symbols of creation and evil 129–130
SIMEON THE YOUNGER
  Jesus as Uncreated Light 172
SKINNER, B. F.
  subjects of experiments 139
SOCRATES
  decision to die 3; sphere of influence 23
SOLOVYOV, VLADIMIR
  Fyodorovian inclinations 79; on evolution 117
SOPHOCLES
  essence of tragedy 66; time as destructor 75
SOUSTELLE, JACQUES
  Aztec views of agony 68
SPENCER, HERBERT
  survival of fittest 79, 145; nature as a grand design 142; cognition as adjustment of relations 143–4; es-

tablishment of the greatest perfection 145; ultimate development of the ideal man 154, 161

SUAREZ, FRANCISCO
existence as time 72

SULLIVAN, J. W. N.
distinction between space and time 108

TEILHARD DE CHARDIN, PIERRE
"increase of love" doctrine 23; march of man 25; humanism 28; falsely mythical conclusions 71; disbelief in the finiteness of the world 71–2; meaning of suffering 72, 78–80; identity of existence with time 72; universe subject to hominization 73; matter as "matrix" of the spirit 74, 76, 78; spontaneities swarming to freedom 75; future political system 79; God as the Wholy Other 92; belated parousia 93–4, 97; ant-hill or world-state 96; mankind as a modality of the biosphere 101; evil as insufficient organization 127; direction of convergence 143; divinization of the continuous stream 150; point omega 156; orthogenesis 160

TERESA OF ÁVILA
no mysticism through human efforts 95; suffering 175

TERTULLIAN
view of Plato's ideas 63

THALES
symbols of cosmic order 86, 170

THOMAS AQUINAS
see Aquinas

THURBER, JAMES
ontological vocabulary 129

TOULMIN, S
Newton and fools 76

TOYNBEE, ARNOLD J.
refusal to distinguish between symbol and reality 100

TURGOT, ANNE-ROBERT
automatic progress 77

UNAMUNO, MIGUEL DE
time and space 31; unity of man 55; intrahistory 57; truth makes live 118; anguish 119–120; hardening heart 165

VASARI, GIORGIO
historical classification XVI; *rinascita* in Berdyaev's view 96

VICO, GIAMBATTISTA
humanity creating itself 77; new science 78

VIRGIL
fulness of time 89

VOLTAIRE
enlightenment as symbol 8; illusions of the future 182

VYGOTSKIJ, LYOV S.
animal cries and language 9; word-meaning 9; unity of thought and speech 59; independence of the psychic phenomenon 101

WALLACE, A. R.
correspondence with Darwin XVII

WEIL, SIMONE
Plato's ontology 21; void and time 38; time, cave and the future XI, 83; cross, symbol of space 51; indispensability of suffering 91; Satan as infinity 91

WEISS, JOHANNES
    eschatological scandal 151–2
WELLS, H. G.
    concept of progress 36–7; history's absent terrestrial goal 161
WHORF, BENJAMIN L.
    Hopi language 46–7
WILBEFORCE, SAMUEL
    discussing Darwinism 140

WILLIAMS, CHARLES
    important moments of life 51; man's agony 67–8
WILSON, EDMUND
    bathrooms and cathedrals 28

Zoroastrian tradition
    Ormuzd (luminous creation) and Ahriman (darkness) 129